STUDIES IN INTELLECTUAL HISTORY
AND THE HISTORY OF PHILOSOPHY
General editors: M. A. Stewart and David Fate Norton

This is a monograph series whose purpose is to foster improved standards of historical and textual scholarship in the History of Philosophy and directly related disciplines. Priority is given to studies which significantly advance our understanding of past thinkers through the careful examination and interpretation of original sources, whether printed or manuscript. Major works and movements in philosophy often reflect interests and concerns characteristic of a particular age and upbringing, and seemingly timeless concepts may vary with the changing background of knowledge and belief which different writers assume in their readers. It is the general editors' assumption that a sensitivity to context not only does not detract from the philosophical interest or rigor of a commentary but is actually essential to it. They wish to encourage studies which present a broad view of a subject's contemporary context, and which make an informative use of philosophical, theological, political, scientific, literary, or other collateral materials, as appropriate to the particular case.

Arnauld and the Cartesian philosophy of ideas

Steven M. Nadler

Arnauld and the Cartesian philosophy of ideas

Princeton University Press
Princeton, New Jersey

Published by Princeton University Press,
41 William Street, Princeton, New Jersey 08540

Library of Congress Cataloging-in-Publication Data

Nadler, Steven.
  Arnauld and the Cartesian philosophy of ideas / Steven M. Nadler.
  p. cm. — (Studies in intellectual history and the history of
philosophy)
  Bibliography: p.
  Includes index.
  ISBN 0-691-07340-6
  1. Arnauld, Antoine, 1612-1694.   I. Title.   II. Series.
B1824.A854N33 1989b
194—dc19   88-22922

Printed in Great Britain

Contents

Preface   vii
References and abbreviations   viii

I   *Introduction*   1

II   *Arnauld and Cartesian philosophy*   14
    1 Life and religious works   15
    2 Jansenism and Cartesianism   18
    3 Cartesian method   34
    4 Cartesian metaphysics: substance/modification   40
    5 Cartesian metaphysics: mind/body dualism   44
    6 Conclusion   59

III   *Ideas and perception in Malebranche*   60
    7 Ideas and sensations in perception   60
    8 Malebranche's representationalism   72

IV   *Arnauld's critique of Malebranche*   79
    9 History of the debate   79
    10 Malebranche and the object theory of ideas   80
    11 The Arnauld–Malebranche debate: what is at issue?   81
    12 Arnauld's critique of Malebranche's representationalism   88

V   *Arnauld's direct realism*   101
    13 Misinterpretations of Arnauld   101
    14 Arnauld's direct realism   107
    15 Descartes' theory of ideas   126
    16 Issues and problems   130

VI   *Intentionality and Arnauld's representationalism*   143
    17 Intentionality   143

18 Objective being in Suarez and Descartes   147
19 Arnauld's account of the intentionality of perception   165

Appendix: The theological debate   179
Bibliography   185
Index   192

Preface

This study of Arnauld and his contribution to the seventeenth-century way of ideas is intended to fill in an egregious gap in scholarship on the history of early modern philosophy. It is only rarely that one sees references to Arnauld, and these are usually to the Port-Royal Logic or his objections to Descartes' *Meditations*, the two writings on which his fame in the Anglo-American philosophical world mainly rests. And until now there has been no full length study of Arnauld's original philosophical contributions, and only very few articles, in any language. Recently, however, Cartesian scholars have begun to read seriously *Des vraies et des fausses idées*, both as a document in one of the most important episodes in early modern philosophy and as a valuable piece of philosophical inquiry in its own right. It is hoped that this book sheds some light both on Arnauld and on the problems and issues which inspired him, that it reestablishes his reputation as a central figure in the history of modern philosophy, and rekindles interest in a truly fascinating and important thinker.

I want to express my gratitude to Hidé Ishiguro, Charles Parsons, James J. Walsh, Scott Davis, Gita May, Daniel Garber, and Robert C. Sleigh, Jr for reading and commenting on the manuscript or various chapters.

I especially want to thank Charles Larmore (Department of Philosophy, Columbia University) for all the time and effort he gave to reading, commenting on, and rereading the manuscript while it was in its dissertation stages; and Richard A. Watson (Department of Philosophy, Washington University), also for reading an earlier draft, and for the inspiration and encouragement he has given me ever since I was an undergraduate.

For permission to use previously published material I am grateful to Oxford University Press (*Descartes: Philosophical Letters*, trans. and ed. Anthony Kenny, 1970) and Cambridge University Press (*The Philosophical Writings of Descartes*, trans. John Cottingham, Robert Stoothoff and Dugald Murdoch, 1985).

I am also very grateful to M. A. Stewart, the editor of *Studies in Intellectual History*, for his advice and encouragement, and to the readers for Manchester University Press and Princeton University Press for their helpful suggestions.

Finally, I dedicate this book to my wife, Jane, the direct and immediate object of all my thoughts.

References and abbreviations

Works by Arnauld

Logique	*La Logique, ou l'art de penser* (1662).
Examen	*Examen d'un écrit qui a pour titre: Traité de l'essence du corps & de l'union de l'Ame avec le corps, contre la philosophie de M. Descartes* (1680).
VFI	*Des vraies et des fausses idées* (1683).
Défense	*Défense de M. Arnauld, contre la réponse au livre des vraies et des fausses idées* (1684).
Reflexions	*Réflexions philosophiques et théologiques sur le nouveau système de la nature et de la grace* (1685).
Dissertation	*Dissertation sur le prétendu bonheur des plaisirs des sens* (1687).

All references to Arnauld are to the *Oeuvres de Messire Antoine Arnauld* (43 vols., Paris: Sigismond D'Arnay, 1775), by volume: page number. The edition of VFI contained therein (vol. 38) is that of Nicolas Schouten (Cologne, 1683). References to VFI are given by page number only. All translations of Arnauld are my own, unless otherwise noted.

Works by Descartes

AT	*Oeuvres de Descartes*, Charles Adam and Paul Tannery, eds., 11 vols. (Paris: J. Vrin, 1974–83).
CSM	*The Philosophical Writings of Descartes*, John Cottingham, Robert Stoothoff and Dugald Murdoch, trans., 2 vols. (Cambridge: Cambridge University Press, 1985).
Kenny	*Descartes: Philosophical Letters*, Anthony Kenny, trans. and ed. (Oxford: Oxford University Press, 1970).

Works by Malebranche

OC	*Oeuvres Complètes de Malebranche*, André Robinet, ed., 20 vols. (Paris: J. Vrin, 2nd ed., 1972–84).
Recherche	*De la recherche de la vérité* (6th ed., 1712).

LO   *The Search after Truth*, Thomas M. Lennon and Paul J. Olscamp, trans. (Columbus: Ohio State University Press, 1980).

Réponse   *Réponse de l'auteur De la Recherche de la Vérité au livre de M. Arnauld, des vrayes et des fausses Idées* (1684).

TL   *Trois lettres de l'auteur De la Recherche de la Vérité, Touchant La Défense de M. Arnauld Contre La Réponse au Livre des Vrayes et fausses Idées* (1685).

RLA   *Réponse du Pere Malebranche Prêtre de l'Oratoire, A la Troisième Lettre de M. Arnauld Docteur de Sorbonne, touchant les Idées et les Plaisirs* (1699).

Except for the *Recherche*, where I follow the Lennon/Olscamp translation, all translations of Malebranche are my own unless otherwise noted.

General note. Where no English translation is cited, all other translations of French or Latin sources are my own.

For Jane

I

Introduction

Understanding the thought of the seventeenth century involves studying not only those individuals whom we, today, have chosen as its luminaries, such as Descartes, Hobbes, Leibniz, Spinoza and Newton, but also those who were considered by these to be their colleagues in the search for philosophical and scientific truth. We ought, in other words, to extend the scope of our historico-philosophical attention to include men such as Marin Mersenne, Pierre Gassendi, Pierre-Sylvain Régis, Jacques Rohault, Pierre Bayle, and, not the least, Antoine Arnauld.

Arnauld has been neglected and misunderstood by historians of early modern philosophy. One reason for this may be that he was, first and foremost, a theologian. Most of his life was spent in deep religious controversy. He was not primarily concerned with purely "philosophical" questions, much less with elaborating a complete and coherent philosophical system. Nevertheless, Arnauld was an important, even central, figure in the intellectual life of the seventeenth century. His opinion on both philosophical and theological matters was earnestly sought by Descartes, Leibniz and others who had a profound respect for his philosophical acumen and for the logical rigor of his mind. He was not, however, merely a testing-ground for the thought of others. He was, in fact, an original thinker who, while enthusiastically adopting elements from the Augustinian and Cartesian systems, sought to employ these in the resolution of certain seemingly interminable questions in theology and philosophy.

Although Arnauld saw himself, in many respects, as faithful to the thought of Descartes, he was not an uncritical disciple. His objections to the *Meditations*, in fact, presented Descartes with some of the most difficult and (from our point of view) lasting problems with which he would have to deal. For example, it was Arnauld who raised the issue of the circularity of Descartes' proofs for the existence of God: how could the principle of the truth of our clear and distinct ideas play a role in the proof of God's existence if his existence is needed to validate that principle in the first place? Yet Arnauld raised his objections not with the hope of foiling Descartes' project, but rather with the aim of moving it towards greater consistency and success. He also sought to correct what he saw as misreadings of Descartes, and to defend Cartesianism against attacks from the Church, from the state, and from within philosophy itself. He did this while offering his own Cartesian solutions to problems which he felt Descartes did not deal with adequately (for example, body–mind interaction).

Arnauld's most important contribution to philosophy lies in his analysis of perception and his role in the polemic over ideas and knowledge that took place in the seventeenth century. In *Des vraies et des fausses idées* (1683), Arnauld offers a sophisticated direct realist theory of perception and an analysis of the intentionality of mental acts, in response to the doctrine of ideas and indirect perception presented by Nicolas Malebranche in *De la recherche de la vérité* (1712). The purpose of VFI was to undermine the philosophical foundations of a theology which Arnauld found unacceptable. The theological issues (grace, divine volition, providence) were taken up in a later work, *Réflexions philosophiques et théologiques* (1685). For the next decade, until Arnauld's death in 1694, these two men engaged in a public debate that attracted the attention of intellectual circles throughout Europe. Sides were taken in articles, reviews and letters in the foremost journals of the day, and the issues were debated by others as hotly as they were by the primary combatants themselves. Such celebrated thinkers as Leibniz, Bayle and Locke all had something to say not only on the matter at hand, but also on the debate itself. Although, as time went on, the discussion between Arnauld and Malebranche became filled more with personal rancor than with philosophical or theological analysis, it remains, nonetheless, one of the most interesting episodes in seventeenth-century intellectual history. Furthermore, it is an indispensable source for understanding some of the central philosophical issues of that period.

One of the pressing questions of seventeenth-century philosophy concerns the way in which the mind connects with the world to produce knowledge. On the one hand, there are external objects:

independent of the knower, yet (as experience informs us) knowable. On the other hand, there is the knower, who is a part of the world of objects (living within that world), but also outside of it, confronting it as something distinct from himself which he seeks to apprehend. How does it come about that the knower knows, cognizes, understands or perceives that world? How do mind and world meet? Or, to put the question in seventeenth-century terms, how is the world "rendered present to" the mind? The question, of course, is not new to the seventeenth century – Aristotle asked it; so did many medieval thinkers. By the time the seventeenth century comes along, however, a new kind of answer to this epistemological question appears.

In the Aristotelian and Scholastic picture, particularly in its Thomistic version, the mind knows the world because, in a sense, the world travels to the mind (though not in the fanciful manner in which Epicureans believed). Every material object is a composition of both matter and form. The object is given its particular individual identity and character, the nature or being it has, by its essential form. In knowing, the form of the external object (but not its matter) is received by the soul. More particularly, a material impression is first received by the sense organs from the object, usually by way of some medium. The imagination creates from this impression a sensory image, from which the active intellect then abstracts to form the intelligible species. This intelligible species is the essential form of the thing known. The mind, in thus receiving (becoming informed by) the essential form of the object, becomes identical *in character* with its object without becoming the object itself (that is, without *materially* becoming the object).[1] It must be stressed that the intelligible species, the essential form of the object which is received by the soul, is *not* a representative entity: it is not an intermediary standing between the knower and the object, and representing by proxy the object to the knower. The species is the object itself existing *intentionally* (i.e. cognitively, as something known) in the mind, as opposed to existing materially in the world. The object is present to the mind, is known, because the mind receives the form of, and thus becomes, its object.

By contrast, the theory of ideas in seventeenth-century thought, in all its variations, substitutes for this notion of the mind receiving the

---

[1] This brief account is abstracted from St Thomas, *Summa Theologiae*, Part I, Qs. 84–6. See also Aristotle, *De Anima*, 429a14ff., 429b20, 431b17f.

object itself a conception of representative knowledge, whereby objects are known or perceived because they are represented in the mind. The object itself is not present to the mind in any literal sense (the mind does not become identical with the object, as the Thomists argue), but it is present to the mind in the sense that the mind contains a representation of the object. In some versions of the theory, the representation is a part of the mind; in other versions, the representation is "present to" the mind (or "united" with it) without being a property of it. All parties agree, however, in calling these representations in the mind *ideas*. An object, then, is present to the mind when the mind has an idea representing that object.

It is possible to discern three tendencies in the use of the term 'idea' in seventeenth-century philosophy in connection with human knowledge.[2]

First, the term 'idea' is used to refer to non-physical objects present in and attended to by the mind, and representing to that mind objects external to it. This representative idea is something apprehended by a mental act of whatever sort (a perceiving, a remembering, a conceiving, etc.). The mind's relation to an idea, thus conceived, is generally discussed in perceptual terms, whereby the mind "perceives" or "sees" ideas. The idea may be something distinct from the mind, as Malebranche insists; or it may be considered to be a part of the mind, as the view traditionally attributed to Locke would claim. Although there has been much debate lately on just what an 'idea' is for Locke, he and Malebranche sometimes appear to agree on certain fundamentals of the theory. Locke states (*Essay Concerning Human Understanding*, I, i, 8): "I must here in the entrance beg pardon of my reader for the frequent use of the word 'idea' which he will find in the following treatise. It being that term, which, I think, serves best to stand for whatever is the object of the understanding when a man thinks."[3] Malebranche, too, notes that "by the word 'idea' I understand

---

[2]See Robert McRae, "'Idea' as a Philosophical Term in the Seventeenth Century", *Journal of the History of Ideas*, 26 (1965), 175–84.

[3]For the "traditional" reading of Locke, see R. I. Aaron, *John Locke*, 2nd ed. (Oxford: Oxford University Press, 1955), pp. 101–5; and Jonathan Bennett, *Locke, Berkeley, Hume: Central Themes* (Oxford: Oxford University Press, 1971), p. 69. It has been argued that Locke does not subscribe to this "object theory of ideas". See John Yolton's works, n. 17 below; and M. A. Stewart, "Locke's Mental Atomism and the Classification of Ideas", Part I, *The Locke Newsletter*, 10 (1979), 53–82. H. E. Matthews argues that Locke's position is, in several important respects, similar to Malebranche's, in "Locke, Malebranche and the Representative Theory",

nothing other than that which is the immediate object of the mind . . . when it perceives something", (*Rech.*, III, ii, 1; OC I, 413; LO, 217), although for Malebranche the ideas attended to in perception are not properties of the human mind but are in God.

The second version posits ideas not as objects perceived or otherwise apprehended, but rather as perceivings or apprehendings. Ideas, according to this view, are mental acts (*operationes*). They are, thus, necessarily properties of the mind. And, as all ideas must, they represent. But in this case, the idea of an object is not some representative proxy standing between the perceiver and the external object, serving as the immediate object of the act of perceiving. Rather, it is the act of perceiving itself in its representative capacity. This, as we shall see, is Arnauld's position. It is also Descartes' considered view, although he occasionally talks as if ideas are objects perceived, And Spinoza, in the *Ethics*, insists that an idea is not "some dumb thing like a picture on a tablet", but "a mode of thinking, to wit, the very act of understanding."[4]

A third position is expressed by Leibniz when he claims that "an idea consists, not in some act, but in the faculty of thinking, and we are said to have an idea of a thing even if we do not think of it, if only, on a given occasion, we can think of it."[5] An idea, in other words, is neither an object nor an act, but a disposition. I have an idea of an object if I have the power or faculty to think of that object, whether or not I do actually think of it. Leibniz followed the Arnauld–Malebranche debate with great interest.[6] He saw merits and problems in the positions of each, and did not commit himself to either side. The problem with an "act theory" such as Arnauld's, Leibniz felt, was that if an idea is reduced to an activity, then the idea of a thing is present only once, and endures in the mind only as long as the activity itself. At least if ideas were objects, they could persist even when not being perceived. But he objected to making ideas, as Malebranche did,

---

in *Locke on Human Understanding*, I. C. Tipton, ed. (Oxford: Oxford University Press, 1977), pp. 55–61. See also Michael Ayers, "Are Locke's 'Ideas' Images, Intentional Objects, or Natural Signs?", *Locke Newsletter*, 17 (1986), 3–36, for a third reading and a critique of Yolton.

[4] *Ethics*, Samuel Shirley, trans. (Hackett, 1982), II, 43, scholium.

[5] *non in quodam cogitandi actu*, from "Quid sit Idea?", in *Die Philosophischen Schriften von Gottfried Wilhwelm Leibniz*, C. J. Gerhardt, ed., 7 vols. (Hildesheim: Georg Olms, 1960–62), vol. 3, p. 263; translation quoted from "What is an Idea?", *Philosophical Papers and Letters*, Leroy E. Loemker, ed. (Dordrecht: D. Reidel, 1969), p. 207.

[6] See André Robinet, *Malebranche et Leibniz* (Paris: J. Vrin, 1955), pp. 133–241.

objects independent of the human mind: "There appears to be much against the sentiment of Father Malebranche concerning ideas. For there is no need ... to take them to be something outside of us. It is enough to consider ideas as Notions, that is to say as modifications of our soul. The School, M. Des Cartes, and M. Arnauld take them thus."[7]

The Arnauld–Malebranche controversy is, among other things, a debate between one who holds an "act theory" of ideas (Arnauld) and one who holds an "object theory". At least as an historical tendency, if not also as a philosophical truth, the object theory of ideas involves a commitment to a representationalist or *indirect* realist theory of perception, such as Malebranche (and, on the traditional reading, Locke) put forth. An act theory of ideas, on the other hand, forms the core of Arnauld's perceptual direct realism. If ideas are representational mental acts, then they can put the mind in direct cognitive contact with an external world – no intervening proxy, no *tertium quid*, gets in the way.

This is, first of all, a study of Arnauld's theory of ideas. My aim is to provide a philosophical and historico-philosophical analysis of Arnauld's account of our perceptual acquaintance with the external world. By 'philosophical' analysis I mean a detailed and critical examination of Arnauld's approach to certain metaphysical and epistemological problems of perception. The metaphysical problems include deciding what it means for something to be an "object of perception", what is involved in the veridical perception of an external object, and what the difference is between veridical and non-veridical perception. The epistemological problems include questions about the truth and justification of our perceptual beliefs (e.g. the belief that there is an external world having such-and-such properties); and about how something in the external world is "made known" or "rendered present to the mind" in perception. By 'historico-philosophical' analysis I mean placing Arnauld's concern with, and approach to, these issues in the context of both his philosophical and intellectual commitments and his theological agenda. Arnauld's account of perception cannot be understood apart from his Cartesianism, nor apart from his

---

[7]Leibniz to Rémond, November 4, 1715. See Robinet, *ibid.*, p. 481. See also a letter to Walter von Tschirnhaus, November, 1684 (Loemker, *op. cit.*, p. 275).

Jansenism and his general philosophico-theological debate with Malebranche.

Second, this is a study in the Cartesian philosophy of ideas. Several reasons for the downfall of Cartesianism have been proposed. On the one hand, it has been argued that crucial internal inconsistencies in the Cartesian system (most notably, between certain of its ontological assumptions and epistemological principles) led, in spite of efforts to save it, to the eventual breakdown of Cartesian metaphysics.[8] On the other hand, it seems that Descartes was placed on the Index in 1663 not because of any internal inconsistencies, but because of a perceived failure (and impiety) in the Cartesian attempt to account for transubstantiation without the substantial forms or real accidents of the Scholastics.[9] It was believed that on Cartesian terms the real presence of Christ's body in the Eucharist was impossible. This problem facing Cartesianism was exacerbated by the proposed solutions to transubstantiation offered by later Cartesians, such as Dom Robert Desgabets and Jacques Rohault.

I am concerned here, however, with what appears to be one of the more popular philosophical explanations of the ill-repute into which Cartesianism has fallen since the middle of the eighteenth century. Descartes, it is claimed, made ideas to be mental objects which serve as the immediate objects of perception. He thereby opened the way for skepticism, the argument runs, enclosing the mind with a "veil of ideas", leaving it forever cut off from perceptual or cognitive contact with the external world. Thus, in 1764, Thomas Reid claims that philosophers since Descartes have maintained that the mind's immediate objects in cognition and perception are ideas, not external objects:

Modern philosophers ... have conceived that external objects cannot be the immediate objects of our thought; that there must be some image of them in the mind itself, in which, as in a mirror, they are seen. And the name 'idea', in the philosophical sense of it, is given to those internal and immediate objects

---

[8]See Richard A. Watson, *The Downfall of Cartesianism* (The Hague: Martinus Nijhoff, 1966).

[9]For example, this objection is raised in a rather mild form in the Sixth Set of Objections: AT VII, 419; CSM II, 281. It was raised more agressively by others throughout the century. See J. -R. Armogathe, *Theologia Cartesiana: L'explication physique de l'Eurcharistie chez Descartes et Dom Desgabets*, International Archives of the History of Ideas, No. 84 (The Hague: Martinus Nijhoff, 1977); and Steven M. Nadler, "Arnauld, Descartes and Transubstantiation", *Journal of the History of Ideas*, 59 (1988), 229–46.

of our thoughts. The external thing is the remote or mediate object; but the idea, or image of that object in the mind, is the immediate object, without which we could have no perception, no remembrance, no conception of the mediate object.[10]

One of the problems with this view, Reid insists, is that, far from explaining how the world is known, it renders such knowledge problematic at best, impossible at worst: "Des Cartes' system of the human understanding, which I shall beg leave to call the ideal system, and which ... is now generally received, hath some original defect; that this skepticism is inlaid in it, and reared along with it."[11] Descartes and Cartesians (especially Arnauld and Malebranche) are, in Reid's mind, the real culprits here, having set up a theory of ideas and perception which was perpetuated into the eighteenth century by Locke, Berkeley and Hume.[12] All of these thinkers, according to Reid, are proponents of the "philosophical" view of perception, members of a cult from which Reid was the first to break.

The legacy of Reid's reading of the history of seventeenth- and eighteenth-century philosophy is the tendency among historians of philosophy to see a tradition here, a so-called "way of ideas" initiated by Descartes and finding its logical conclusion in Berkeley's immaterialism and Hume's skepticism. Cartesianism, in particular, has been singled out and vilified as involving a commitment to the object theory of ideas and, thus, a representationalist view of perception. Norman Kemp Smith, for example, claims that the doctrine of representative perception is a "fundamental tenet" of Descartes' system.[13] Other Cartesians (except Arnauld) were then compelled to follow Descartes on this matter. And Berkeley's theory of ideas and his immaterialism are, Smith insists, nothing more than "the outcome of a consistent development of Descartes' principles."[14] More recently, Richard Rorty

---

[10] *The Philosophical Works of Thomas Reid*, William Hamilton, ed., 2 vols. (Edinburgh: James Thin, 1896), vol. 1, p. 226.

[11] *An Inquiry Into the Human Mind on the Principles of Common Sense*, Chapter 1, Section 7, in *Works*, vol. 1, p. 103

[12] For the argument that Reid considers Arnauld among those who hold an object theory of ideas, see Steven M. Nadler, "Reid, Arnauld and the Objects of Perception", *History of Philosophy Quarterly*, 3 (1986), 165–74.

[13] Norman Kemp Smith, *Studies in the Cartesian Philosophy* (New York: Russell and Russell, 1902), p. 115.

[14] *Ibid.*, p. 216.

has perpetuated Reid's myth in his attempt to identify the historical roots of certain philosophical problems. Rorty uncritically but conveniently accepts what he calls the "more familiar account" of "the emergence of what is now thought of as the epistemological problematic created by Descartes" and passed on through Locke; namely, the problematic of the "veil of ideas".[15] The origin of this problem lies in the seventeenth century's "novel" picture of the mind, of

a single inner space in which bodily and perceptual sensations ... mathematical truths, moral rules, the idea of God, moods of depression, and all the rest of what we now call "mental" were objects of quasi-observation. Such an inner arena with its inner observer had been suggested at various points in ancient and medieval thought but it had never been taken seriously enough to form the basis for a problematic. But the seventeenth century took it seriously enough to permit it to pose the problem of the veil of ideas, the problem which made epistemology central to philosophy.[16]

One of the theses of this study of Arnauld is that such a reading of seventeenth-century thought on ideas and knowledge is mistaken. Few of the philosophers indicted by Reid, Rorty, *et al.* maintained the picture of the mind that Rorty suggests. Nor did they take such a picture very seriously. For example, Malebranche, whose doctrine of ideas appears closest to the theory caricatured by Rorty, was harshly judged by Arnauld, Locke and Régis (all for different reasons) for proposing such an "absurd" view. For many of these early modern thinkers, ideas are acts of the mind, not objects of quasi-observation. This is true of two of the central figures of the period: Descartes and Arnauld (see Chapter 5). John Yolton has argued that it is also true of Locke.[17] At the very least, there was sufficient variety and disagreement on this issue to warrant against the kind of broad generalizations made by Reid and Rorty.

Arnauld is particularly important here. In his debate with Malebranche, he offers the most fully articulated act theory of ideas of

---

[15] See Richard Rorty, *Philosophy and the Mirror of Nature* (Princeton: Princeton University Press, 1979), p. 50.

[16] *Ibid.*, pp. 50–51.

[17] See John Yolton, "Ideas and Knowledge in Seventeenth-Century Philosophy", *Journal of the History of Philosophy*, 13 (1975), 145–66; "John Locke and the Seventeenth-Century Logic of Ideas", *Journal of the History of Ideas*, 16 (1955), 431–52; and *Perceptual Acquaintance from Descartes to Reid* (Minneapolis: University of Minnesota Press, 1984).

the period, as well as an exhaustive and influential critique of the object theory of ideas and its model of the mind. Moreover, he argues persuasively that he is simply elaborating on Descartes' account. Arnauld is, thus, central to any attempt to bury the myth of the "way of ideas", at least as it is usually understood. Yolton's work, which, in general, is a healthy antidote to the traditional way of interpreting the seventeenth century, curiously omits any full-bodied analysis of Arnauld, such as he gives to Descartes, Malebranche and Locke.[18] This study fills in an essential part of the new story.

Furthermore, I hope to dispel the notion that a "problematic of the way of ideas" could have its origin in some strictly *Cartesian* picture of the mind. Rorty (again, after Reid) insists that *"the Cartesian mind ... made possible 'veil of ideas' skepticism."*[19] If "Cartesian" refers only to Descartes, then, as I show, the problem is simply that Rorty has not read Descartes closely enough. If, on the other hand, he is speaking of some picture of the mind shared by Cartesians generally, then the facts themselves argue against him. There is no such thing as "the Cartesian mind"; there is no consistent Cartesian position on the nature of ideas and their role in perception. To be sure, representational ideas do play a very important part in Cartesian epistemology. But Malebranche, Arnauld and Régis are all Cartesians.[20] And the latter two spent years trying to persuade the former that his particular theory of ideas was nonsense.

Now it is not clear that the position traditionally attributed to Descartes and Cartesians is necessarily a philosophically inferior one. That is, holding ideas to be mental acts of apprehending rather than apprehended mental (or non-mental) objects does not in itself seem to solve any epistemological problems. But it is, nonetheless, important to dispel the long- and widely- accepted belief that Descartes was, in fact, responsible for a theory of ideas thought by many to be so problematic and unacceptable. That reading of the history of seventeenth- and eighteenth-century philosophy according to which Descartes and later Cartesians uniformly proposed a picture of the

---

[18]In *Perceptual Acquaintance*, while Descartes and Malebranche each get a chapter to themselves, Arnauld receives only six pages (pp. 60–66).

[19]Rorty, *op. cit.*, p. 140, emphasis added.

[20]It should however be noted that Malebranche is, in many important respects, a self-avowed deviant from Cartesian orthodoxy. See Daisie Radner, *Malebranche* (Amsterdam: Van Gorcum, 1978), Chapter 1; and Ferdinand Alquié, *Le Cartésianisme de Malebranche* (Paris: J. Vrin, 1974).

mind's cognitive activity which had its logical conclusion in Hume is mistaken and simplistic, and does not give sufficient credit to the serious philosophical thought on perceptual acquaintance that is found in Arnauld and others.

Throughout this study of Arnauld's theory of perception, I often employ such terms as 'direct realism', 'direct-' and 'indirect perception', 'immediate perception', etc. These terms are vague, and there are several varieties of perceptual direct realism. I will use a rather simple and general definition of 'direct realism', one which covers what is common and central to all these varieties, some of which are discussed where they are relevant to clarifying Arnauld's position.

Before offering a definition of perceptual direct realism, I need to clarify what is to be understood by 'direct and immediate perception', or 'directly and immediately perceives'. There are two related claims involved in the assertion that A directly and immediately perceives x. First, there is what is mainly an ontological claim. A's relation R with x is direct if there is no entity y, not identical with x, standing between A and x towards which A is R-related and on A's R-relation to which is founded A's R-relation to x. Thus, A's perceptual relation with x is direct if there is no entity y standing between A and x which A perceives and on A's perceptual relation to which is founded A's perception of x. Stated less technically, my perception of x is direct if it is not causally or otherwise based on the perception of some y. The claim is mainly ontological in that it asserts that there is no *tertium quid* standing between myself and x. Direct perception is a dyadic relation; indirect perception is triadic, involving the perceiver, the intermediary object directly perceived, and the ultimately-intended, indirectly-perceived object.

The way in which an indirect perceptual relation to an object has often been said to be "founded" or "based" upon the direct perception of some other object brings me to the second claim involved in the assertion that A directly and immediately perceives x. When it is asserted that I indirectly or mediately perceive x, that I perceive x "by means of", "through", or "by virtue of" perceiving y, this is often understood as the claim that my perception of x is *inferentially* based on the direct perception of y.[21] The indirect perception is claimed to involve an inference from some direct perception. On the other hand,

---

[21] Although I concentrate here on an inferential relation between the direct perception

what is immediately perceived is perceived non-inferentially. (Berkeley, for example, in the First Dialogue, insists that "the senses perceive nothing which they do not perceive *immediately*; for they make no inferences.")[22] Thus, *A* immediately perceives *x* if *A*'s perception of *x* does not involve an inference from the perception of *y*. This brings out the epistemic side of direct and immediate perception.[23] Direct and immediate perception, then, is a dyadic, non-inferential relation between a perceiver and an object.

Direct realism is the view that the direct and immediate objects of normal veridical perception are external physical entities existing independently of any perceiving mind. Thus, on this general understanding, direct realism is a philosophical position on the nature of the direct and immediate objects of perception. By way of contrast, indirect realism (e.g. representationalism) is the view that the direct and immediate objects of perception are never independently-existing physical entities, but non-physical, and (on some versions of this theory) mind-dependent, representative entities; physical objects are perceived indirectly, by means of these immediately-perceived entities.[24] For the direct realist, on the other hand, the perceiver is (in veridical perception) in direct, non-mediated (non-inferential) perceptual contact with the objects of the physical world (chairs, human bodies, etc.). Proponents of direct realism usually differ with regard to the kinds of qualities they are willing to ascribe to these objects, and the basis on which such ascriptions can be made.[25] Yet they all agree

and the indirect perception, the indirect perception might be *causally* related to the direct perception, or related to it in some other way. In all cases, however, the structure of indirect perception involves a direct perception plus some further relation (inferential, causal, or otherwise).

[22] George Berkeley, *Three Dialogues between Hylas and Philonous*, in *The Works of George Berkeley*, A. A. Luce and T. E. Jessop, eds., vol. 2 (Londonz: Nelson, 1949), pp. 174–5.

[23] For the view that the immediate/mediate distinction comes down to a non-inferential/inferential distinction, see D. M. Armstrong, "Immediate Perception", in *The Nature of Mind and Other Essays* (Ithaca: Cornell University Press, 1981), pp. 119–31.

[24] For a good discussion comparing these two views, as well as phenomenalism, see James Cornman, *Perception, Common Sense and Science* (New Haven: Yale University Press, 1975), pp. 1–18. See also Roderick Chisholm, *Perceiving: A Philosophical Study* (Ithaca: Cornell University Press, 1957), p. 154; Brian O'Neil, *Epistemological Direct Realism in Descartes Philosophy*, (Albuquerque: University of New Mexico Press, 1974); and Richard Fumerton, *Metaphysical and Epistemological Problems of Perception* (Lincoln: University of Nebraska Press, 1985).

[25] For example, the naive realist is willing, on the basis of sense experience alone, to admit certain qualities really to belong to physical objects which other, more sophisticated forms of realism would not.

that in normal veridical sense perception the percipient has, as the direct and immediate object of perception, an independent external world, or whatever may be said "to occupy space and to have a career of its own",[26] and not some ideational copy (mental or otherwise).[27]

[26]Cf. O'Neil, *op. cit.*, pp. 7–8.

[27]Cornman gives a more sophisticated definition of direct realism, although the position is roughly the same as the one I describe. According to Cornman, the direct realist holds that "it is false that S would perceive p at t only if at t he were to experience something x which is different from p, which is neither a constituent of p nor has p as a constituent, and which S experiences at t because of the stimulation of a sense organ of S by p" (*op. cit.*, p. 10). For other definitions, see D. M. Armstrong, *Perception and the Physical World* (London: Routledge and Kegan Paul, 1961); and J. E. Turner, *A Theory of Direct Realism* (New York: Macmillan, 1925).

I I
Arnauld and Cartesian philosophy

It is often taken for granted that Antoine Arnauld is, in some sense of the term, a Cartesian. Yet the nature and extent of Arnauld's commitment to the fundamental tenets of Descartes' philosophical system has, for the most part, escaped close examination.[1] While some view Arnauld's Cartesianism as complete and unequivocal, others see it as only nominal and secondary. For example, it has been argued that Arnauld was attracted to Cartesian philosophy only conditionally, "for the purpose of arousing interest in Augustine as a philosopher among men who were already Augustinians in theology." He was, the argument runs, a reluctant defender of a philosophy which, for him, had only "apologetic value". Thus, on this view, Arnauld is a Cartesian "only in a limited sense": "to suppose that the point of view underlying [Arnauld's] writings is fundamentally Cartesian is to be dupe to a label."[2]

One cannot overestimate the importance of Augustine to Arnauld.

[1] An important exception here is Geneviève Rodis-Lewis's article, "Augustinisme et Cartésianisme à Port-Royal", in E. J. Dijksterhuis, ed., *Descartes et le Cartésianisme Hollandais* (Paris: PUF, 1950), pp. 131–82. Though Rodis-Lewis is not concerned with presenting a study of Arnauld's Cartesianism *per se*, she examines, among other things, several issues on which Arnauld's "enthousiasme immodéré" for the Cartesian philosophy is, she believes, apparent. See also Francisque Bouillier, *Histoire de la philosophie Cartésienne*, 3rd ed., 2 vols. (Paris: Delagrave, 1868), vol. 2, Chapter 9; and Charles Augustin Sainte-Beuve (1804–69), *Port-Royal* (Paris: La Connaissance, 1928), vol. VI, Chapter 5. Sainte-Beuve notes that "Arnauld & Bossuet ont cela du commun de se tenir sans craint au Cartésianisme" (p. 165). See also Ferdinand Brunetière, *Etudes critiques sur l'histoire de la littérature française*, 4 vols. (Paris: Hachett, 1904). In an essay titled "Jansenistes et Cartésiens" (vol. 4, pp. 111–78) he accuses Arnauld of a "naiveté doctorale" in his attachment to Cartesianism in not seeing the methodological opposition between *Augustinus* ("la Bible du Jansenisme") and Descartes' *Discours* (pp. 140–41).

[2] Jan Miel, "Pascal, Port-Royal and Cartesian Linguistics", *Journal of the History of Ideas*, 30 (1969), p. 262.

The Saint's word is the bottom line in matters of faith (and even in matters of metaphysics) for Arnauld, as it was for Jansenists generally. But Augustine is not Arnauld's only intellectual mentor. Arnauld's philosophical writings are fundamentally and consistently Cartesian: the methodological and metaphysical principles of Descartes' philosophy deeply inform Arnauld's thinking on both philosophical and theological issues. In fact, when compared with Malebranche, Spinoza, Cordemoy, and others who self-consciously deviated from Descartes, Arnauld must be classed among "orthodox" Cartesians. Like Régis, Rohault, and de la Forge, Arnauld was generally concerned with interpreting and developing Descartes' thought as faithfully as possible. Granted, such a devotion would not have been possible had Arnauld found anything of importance in the Cartesian philosophy inconsistent with Augustinian principles. But, unlike other Jansenists, he did not.[3] A perceived Augustinian affinity between Descartes' philosophy and Port-Royal doctrine facilitated Arnauld's whole-hearted and enthusiastic acceptance of Cartesianism.

1 *Life and religious works*

Antoine Arnauld was born in Paris on February 6, 1612.[4] He was the twentieth and youngest child (the tenth to survive infancy) of Antoine

[3]Louis-Paul Du Vaucel, for example, insists that in many important respects Cartesianism is opposed to the writings of St Augustine. See Du Vaucel's "Observations sur la philosophie de Descartes", in Dijksterhuis, *op. cit.*, pp. 113–30.

I do not take the opportunity here to examine the important issue of the Augustinian roots and motivations of Arnauld's commitment to Cartesianism. See Rodis-Lewis, *op. cit.*, pp. 133–6; Etienne Gilson, *Etudes sur le rôle de la pensée médiévale dans la formation du système Cartésien* (Paris: J. Vrin, 1930), pp. 191–2; Henri Gouhier, *Cartésianisme et Augustinisme au XVIIe siècle* (Paris: J. Vrin, 1978), pp. 123–32; and Jean Laporte, *Le Rationalisme du Descartes* (Paris: PUF, 1945). Laporte notes that "there is a striking concordance between the religious ideal of Descartes and that of the Augustinian Port-Royalists – of which several, moreover, were declared Cartesians" (p. 337). Arnauld himself notes, in his objections to Descartes' *Meditations*, that "the first thing that I find remarkable is that our distinguished author has laid down as the basis for his entire philosophy exactly the same principle as that laid down by St. Augustine – a man of the sharpest intellect and a remarkable thinker, not only on theological topics but also on philosophical ones" (AT VII, 197; CSM II, 139).

[4]Good sources for details of Arnauld's biography and for the history of Jansenism in France are Sainte-Beuve, *op. cit.*, especially vol. 6; Bouillier, *op. cit.*, vol. 2; and Alexander Sedgwick, *Jansenism in Seventeenth-Century France* (Charlottesville: University Press of Virginia, 1977).

Arnauld and his wife Catherine. Arnauld *père* was a lawyer in Paris, and had pleaded the case of the University of Paris against the Jesuits. The youngest Arnauld (later to be known as *Le Grand Arnauld*) thought of becoming a lawyer himself until the Abbé St Cyran (Jean Duvergier de Hauranne), the spiritual director of Port-Royal and a friend of the family, as well as a close associate of Jansenius (Cornelius Jansen, Bishop of Ypres), convinced him to follow the ecclesiastical life. After teaching philosophy for two years at the Collège de Mans in Paris, he was ordained and received his doctorate in theology in 1641. He was admitted to the Sorbonne two years later (after the death of Richelieu, who originally opposed his admission on a technical matter). Arnauld, however, immediately became involved in the religious controversy surrounding Jansenism and renounced his ambitions (and a lucrative ecclesiastical benefice) in order to use his intellectual powers in support of St Cyran's religious ideals.

In 1602, Arnauld's sister Jacqueline, the eldest daughter, became the abbess of the convent of Port-Royal of the Cistercian order situated in the valley of the Chevreuse (not far from Versailles) under the name of *Mère Angélique*. Because of her reforming zeal and the ideals and policies of St Cyran, her spiritual counselor, Port-Royal soon earned the enmity of Church and state alike, particularly of the Jesuits and Cardinal Richelieu. Devoted to the Augustinian doctrine of efficacious grace (whereby a person's salvation is not earned by his or her own acts, but only by the constant and irresistible grace of God) and a rigorous penitential discipline, which they saw propounded in Jansenius's *Augustinus* (1640), the Jansenists sought reform within the Roman Catholic Church, trying to direct it away from the worldliness and laxity into which they saw it falling. In 1641, Arnauld entered the controversy with a work supporting the contritionism of St Cyran against Jesuit condemnations. St Cyran argued that in order for a person to deserve absolution for his sins from a priest, he had to be genuinely contrite and repent his sin from his heart. Such repentance must come not from a fear of God's punishment (a selfish motivation), but from a pure love of God. In 1644, Arnauld wrote the *Apologie de Monsieur Jansenius* in response to attacks on *Augustinus* by Herbert of Notre-Dame de Paris. The most important of his religious works, *De la fréquente communion*, appeared in 1643. This was a defense of the ethical principles of St Cyran and an indictment of what he saw as the indulgent morals of the Jesuits. Arnauld felt that occasionally depriving oneself of the sacrament might be a more effective way for a sinner to develop his commitment to God's purpose, and a more beneficial means in the process of absolution, than the weekly communion recommended by the Jesuits. In this work, Arnauld presents the harsh Jansenist position on penitential discipline as the true and only viable Catholic position, and the only real bulwark against Protestantism.

In spite of the help provided by the University, Parlement and his Port-Royal colleagues, Arnauld was subject to much persecution for his views. Like all Jansenists, he was accused of Calvinism and political subversion. In 1656 he was excluded from the faculty of the Sorbonne for his refusal to submit to the Church on the issue of five propositions condemned as heretical in the encyclical *Cum occasione* (1653), and which the Pope (Innocent X) said were to be found in Jansenius. Arnauld granted that the Pope had the right to decide the former matter of faith (*question de droit*) but reserved for the individual himself judgment on the latter *question de fait*. Though the five propositions may be heretical (and it was for the Pope to decide this for all), he insisted that whether or not the propositions were to be found in Jansenius's work was a factual question which ought not to be decided by papal fiat but by means of empirical investigation. Each and every individual has the authority and ability to pursue such an investigation on his or her own. Arnauld denied that the propositions were in Jansenius's work.

The quarrel over the Five Propositions was the beginning of a long period of persecution for French Jansenists. The Church hierarchy, spurred on by the Jesuits, and the political elite of France felt threatened by these reformers. Over the next half-century, those who refused to renounce publicly their stand on the propositions and their "heretical views" were subject to constant harassment, even imprisonment. Those faithful who did make the public renunciation found the spiritual anguish just as hard to bear. In 1669, Clement IX and Louis XIV, fearing for the stability and unity of the French Church, agreed to what became known as the Peace of the Church. Further discussion of the issues touching the *Augustinus* was forbidden, the nuns of Port-Royal were once again allowed to partake of the sacraments, and Arnauld and other leading Jansenists were able to come out of hiding or were released from prison.

Although the Peace of the Church provided Arnauld with some

respite from intimidation, most of his later life was, nonetheless, spent in religious and philosophical polemic. Fearing renewed persecution by the Archbishop of Paris after the breakdown of the Peace and renewed constraints and threats issued by Louis XIV against Port-Royal (to which he, along with Antoine Le Maistre, Le Maistre de Sacy, Claude Lancelot, Pierre Nicole, Nicolas Fontaine, and others remained connected as *solitaires*), Arnauld, along with his longtime collaborator Nicole, went into exile in the Netherlands in 1679. He resided in Mons, Ghent and Brussels before finally settling in Liège, where he died on August 8, 1694. Nicole had already returned to France earlier on, seeking tranquility and peace in order to devote himself to introspection and his own spiritual well-being.[5]

2 *Jansenism and Cartesianism*

The tendency in intellectual history has been to see Port-Royal as a bastion of modern thought, with Cartesianism as its "official doctrine".[6] Careful investigation, however, reveals that the majority of those connected with Port-Royal professed an open hostility towards Cartesian philosophy. In fact, Arnauld appears to be one of only very few Port-Royalists of his generation to have had any sympathy towards this new philosophy.

Jansenists were divided over the value of philosophy, depending on the importance they variously accorded to reason. St Cyran was skeptical and distrustful of philosophy and of the ability of reason to improve man's condition. He maintained that reason was harmful to piety because it fostered pride, and that intellectual pursuits, particularly as exemplified in the contemporary scene, constituted an obstacle to the acquisition of virtue. Pascal, who (although not a

[5] See Sedgwick, pp. 150f.

[6] Marjorie Grene, for example, writes uncritically that "Cartesianism became, we are told, up to a point the official doctrine of Port-Royal". See her *Descartes* (Minneapolis: University of Minnesota Press, 1985), p. 183. Grene is in good company here. Among seventeenth-century commentators, Pierre Jurieu, the orthodox Protestant theologian, claims that "the theologians of Port-Royal are as devoted to Cartesianism as they are to Christianity" – see his *La politique de clergé de France* (2nd ed., 1681), p. 107. Pierre Daniel, in the *Voyage du Monde de M. Descartes* (Paris, 1961), insists that "there are very few Jansenists who are not Cartesians" (p. 285). See also Bouillier, *op cit.*, vol. 2, p. 234. Bouiller's mistake is to take the word of Jurieu, an anti-Cartesian *and* an anti-Port-Royalist. But see Steven Nadler, "Cartesianism and Port-Royal", *The Monist*, 71 (1988).

solitaire) was associated closely with Port-Royal (he identified with its spiritual ideals, and publicly defended Jansenism in his *Provincial Letters*), often belittled the self-sufficiency of reason, and strongly objected to the Cartesian philosophy in his *Pensées*, although he was himself a brilliant mathematician. Pyrrhonist arguments against reason and other human faculties as guides toward truth were often implicitly at work in the distrust many Jansenists felt for philosophy.[7] Le Maistre de Sacy, for example, preferred a simple faith to the Cartesian philosophy, which he saw as undermining true religion. Descartes' philosophy, he believed, demystified nature in its mechanistic picture of the material world and thereby emptied that world of its theological significance. In conversation with Nicolas Fontaine, he insisted that

God created the world for two reasons ... one, to provide an idea of his greatness, the other, to depict invisible things in the visible. M. Descartes has destroyed the one as well as the other. "The sun is a lovely piece of work", one says to him. "Not at all", he replies, "it is a mass of metal filings." Instead of recognizing invisible things in the visible, such as the god of nature in the sun, and seeing in all that he has produced in plants an image of his grace, he insists, on the contrary, on providing a reason for everything.[8]

Louis-Paul Du Vaucel felt that the mechanistic philosophy threatened the dignity and spirituality of humankind as well. Furthermore, he argued against his friend Arnauld, it undermined the doctrine of Eucharistic transubstantiation by making extension the essence of body. Since it was traditionally held that the *substance* of Christ's body, but not its extension, replaces the substance of the bread of the sacrament, Cartesianism, which identifies a body with its local extension, cannot account for the "real presence" of Christ's body in the Eucharist. This latter consequence, in du Vaucel's mind, aligned Cartesianism with Calvinism.[9] Having already been accused of Protestantism because of their views on grace, the last thing Jansenists needed was to provide more grist for the Jesuit mill by appearing to embrace a Cartesian philosophy carrying a Calvinist

[7] See Thomas M. Lennon, "Jansenism and the Crise Pyrrhonienne", *Journal of the History of Ideas*, 38 (1977), 297–306; and Sedgwick, *op. cit.*, p. 87.

[8] Nicholas Fontaine, *Mémoires pour servir à l'histoire de Port-Royal*, 2 vols. (Cologne, 1738), vol. 2, p. 54.

[9] Du Vaucel, *op. cit.*, pp. 113–16. For the traditional Scholastic view of Eucharistic transubstantiation, see St Thomas, *Summa Theologiae*, Part IIIa, Qs. 73–8.

theology. In fact, Arnauld's Cartesianism was a source of great anxiety to other Jansenists for just this reason, since he was seen by the public as their leading spokesman and apologist.

Finally, Cartesian philosophy represented to these deeply religious and puritanical individuals the arrogance and folly of human reason. Not only did Jansenists, on the whole, not share Descartes' optimism regarding the indefinite progress of science and the ability of reason to penetrate the mysteries of the universe, but they felt that Descartes and later Cartesians did not sufficiently respect the distinction between the realm of faith and the realm of reason. Rather than attempting to explain in naturalistic terms such divine matters as transubstantiation, they argued, reason should humble itself to a higher authority (preferably Scripture or the writings of the Church Fathers) on such questions. As Geneviève Rodis-Lewis has observed, "when Jansenists condemned the pride which sought to elevate reason to matters transcending the human mind, it was in order to humble *raison imbécile*."[10]

Ironically, in their hostility toward Cartesian philosophy, these Jansenists found themselves on the side of the Jesuits, and even of the Sorbonne and Parlement. Although I do not intend to impugn the sincerity of their distaste for Cartesianism, this is probably no coincidence but rather the result of prudent calculation. Descartes' works were placed on the Index in 1663 at the instigation of the Jesuits. And we know that just before Du Vaucel's warning to Arnauld, the Parlement of Paris, at the urging of the University, was seriously considering a resolution which would forbid the teaching of Cartesian philosophy and prescribe the exclusive teaching of that of Aristotle.[11] In fact, a decree against *la philosophie de Descartes* had already been passed by the University of Louvain in 1662. Port-Royal had a reputation for being full of Cartesians – it would certainly help their already troubled cause if they could shake this false but dangerous label.

[10] Rodis-Lewis, *op. cit.*, p. 136.

[11] Around 1671. See Victor Cousin, "De la persécution du Cartésienisme en France", *Fragments Philosophiques*, in *Oeuvres*, 3 vols. (Brussels: Société Belge de Librairie, 1841), vol. 2, pp. 181–91. Arnauld is the author of a short piece addressed to the Parlement of Paris entitled *Plusiers raisons pour empêcher la censure ou condamnation de la philosophie de Descartes* (dated 1679 by Cousin), wherein he argues against those (especially at the University) who would have Parlement issue a decree against *les opinions cartésiennes*. The text of this is presented by Cousin, pp. 183ff.

It should be noted, nonetheless, that in spite of their suspicion of philosophy, Pascal, De Sacy and most other Jansenists participated in intellectual activities, including teaching in the "Little Schools" run in conjunction with Port-Royal, and maintained an interest in philosophical developments. Even Descartes' philosophy was still the object of much discussion in Jansenist circles. This is particularly true of Nicole, who, while professing a skeptical view of the value of philosophy, collaborated with Arnauld on the Port-Royal Logic, which, as we shall see, is permeated by Cartesian principles. For Nicole, as for many of the other Jansenists, Cartesian philosophy was often distasteful, but reason and philosophy had their uses.[12] Of all the Jansenists, Arnauld is clearly the most enthusiastic toward philosophy and the most optimistic regarding the fruitful possibilities of philosophical (and scientific) inquiry. Although most of his time was taken up with religious controversy, he never ceased to take an active part in philosophical polemic.

One of the earliest works of philosophy by Arnauld is the thesis he completed at the end of his studies at the Collège de Mans, and which fulfilled the requirements for the licence which was a condition for acceptance into the Sorbonne. These *Conclusiones Philosophiae* were submitted, in Latin, on July 25, 1641. They comprise a short treatise which deals with various questions in logic, mathematics, morals, physics, and metaphysics. However, Arnauld's real introduction to the philosophical world, and the basis for his attraction to Cartesian thought, are his exchanges with Descartes in the 1640s concerning the latter's *Meditationes de Prima Philosophia*. Descartes circulated his *Meditations* among his friends after he had completed them, hoping to gather comments and criticisms. He passed the manuscript on to Marin Mersenne, asking him to solicit further responses and objections from theologians and scholars. The young doctor (soon to be of the Sorbonne) was invited to comment on the work.

Arnauld addressed his objections to Mersenne early in 1641, and they appeared to Descartes himself to be the most acute and serious of the responses he received.[13] In Descartes' reply to Arnauld's

---

[12] Sedgwick, *op. cit.*, pp. 140–45. For a general discussion of Cartesianism at Port-Royal, see Rodis-Lewis, *op. cit.* See also Nadler, "Cartesianism and Port-Royal", *op. cit.*

[13] Descartes was generally disappointed with the quality of the responses he had received heretofore. See his letter to Mersenne of January 28, 1641 (AT III, 292; Kenny 92).

objections, and in a letter to Mersenne on March 18, 1641, one sees a contrast between the impatience and condescension scarcely hidden in his replies to others and the sincere respect that he feels for Arnauld's intellect. In the letter, he presents Mersenne with the changes to be made in the *Meditations* based on Arnauld's objections, "to let it be known that I have deferred to his judgment" (to Mersenne, March 18, 1641: AT III, 334; Kenny, 95). To Descartes, Arnauld was "acute and learned, so that I shall not be ashamed to be worsted in argument or to learn from him" (a letter for [Arnauld] June 4, 1648: AT V, 192; Kenny, 231).[14]

The objections Arnauld makes are divided into three parts. The first, entitled "The Nature of the Human Mind", discusses the problem of how it follows from the fact that one is unaware that anything else except being a thinking thing belongs to one's essence that nothing else really does belong to one's essence. The most that can be concluded with certainty from such a premise, Arnauld insists, is "that I can obtain some knowledge of myself without knowledge of the body"; not, however, that there is a "real distinction in existence between mind and body" (Fourth Objections: AT VII, 197ff.; CSM II, 139ff.). In the section concerning God, after making several interesting and important remarks regarding the representational content of ideas (see Section 3 below, and Chapters 5 and 6), Arnauld goes on to argue, in reference to Descartes' proof for the existence of God in Meditation III, that God cannot be thought of as standing in relation to himself in a manner similar to that in which an efficient cause stands in relation to its effect. Descartes had argued that it is certain that he is not the cause of his own imperfect being, since he would have bestowed upon himself all the perfections of which he has an idea. But Caterus, in the First Objections, distinguishes between two senses of 'from itself'. In a positive sense, 'from itself' means "from itself as from a cause"; in a negative sense, it means "not from another" (AT VII, 95; CSM II, 68). Caterus insists that if the phrase is taken in the negative sense ("and this ... is the way in which everyone

---

[14] This was written in 1648 in response to Arnauld's Second Set of Objections to the *Meditations*. In a letter to Mersenne (March 4, 1641), he acknowledges Arnauld's objections to be *les meilleures de toutes* (AT III, 331). And in his Fourth Replies, Descartes is just as enthusiastic: "I could not possibly wish for a more perceptive or more courteous critic. He has dealt with me so considerately that I can easily perceive his goodwill towards myself and the cause that I defend" (AT VII, 218; CSM II, 154).

takes the phrase"), then it does not follow that something caused "from itself" derives its existence from itself as from a cause, existing prior to itself and choosing in advance what it should subsequently be. Thus, Descartes' argument will not work, resting as it does on a false understanding of being a cause from itself. Descartes counters that the phrase 'from itself' should be taken in "an absolutely positive sense" (First Replies: AT VII, 110; CSM II, 80), and that God, in the immensity of his power, stands "in a sense" in the same relation to himself as an efficient cause does to its effect.

Arnauld disagrees. Although, were such a thing possible, I could only derive my existence from myself in the positive sense, it is clearly impossible for one to stand in relation to oneself as an efficient cause stands in relation to its effect – indeed, such a notion is conceptually incoherent. Every effect depends on a cause and receives its existence from a cause, and one and the same thing cannot depend on itself or receive existence from itself. Moreover, every cause is the cause of an effect, and every effect is the effect of a cause. Hence, there is a mutual relation between cause and effect, a relation which involves *two* terms which are different from each other (Fourth Objections: AT VII, 208–9; CSM II, 146–7). This notion of being self-caused in a positive sense, so crucial to Descartes' argument, is thus untenable with regard to finite beings. Arnauld then goes on to argue that it is even clearer that God cannot be thought of as deriving his existence from himself in the positive sense, but only in the negative sense of not deriving it from anything else.

Arnauld closes this section of his response with his famous objection to the circularity of Descartes' demonstrations for the existence of God. We know that God exists because we clearly and distinctly perceive that this is so. But how, he asks, can the principle of the truth of clear and distinct perception be used to establish the certainty of God's existence when his existence is needed to guarantee the truth of clear and distinct perception?

In the section entitled "Points which may cause difficulty to Theologians", Arnauld's most important remark concerns the consequences of Descartes' theory of matter for the Catholic doctrine of transubstantiation. Descartes has emptied the material world of sensible qualities (colors, tastes, smells, etc.), leaving behind only shape, extension and motion – properties which, of necessity, inhere in a substance. His ontology thus appears to Arnauld to be inconsistent with faith, which has traditionally been aligned with the view that the substance of the bread of the Eucharist is either converted into Christ's body (the Thomistic account) or annihilated and replaced by Christ's body (the Scotist account), and only its accidents (including its sensible qualities) remain. Such a real existence of accidents, independent of any underlying substance in which they inhere, is ruled out on Cartesian principles. This objection elicits from Descartes one of his cautious formulations of a Cartesian theory of transubstantiation (Fourth Replies: AT VII, 248ff.; CSM II, 173ff.). It is on just this issue that Cartesianism will founder, helped along by the efforts of later Cartesians (such as Dom Robert Desgabets) to elaborate on Descartes' suggestions here and in his letters to Mesland in 1645.[15]

This set of objections by Arnauld was followed by two letters to Descartes in June and July of 1648 (*Novae Objections*).[16] In the first letter, he expresses his satisfaction with Descartes' responses to his earlier objections. Nonetheless, Arnauld has "two or three scruples" he would like to raise. He insists, contrary to Descartes, that the mind is not always thinking. Although the soul is a thinking substance, it suffices if it simply possesses in itself a faculty of thinking (*vis cogitandi* or *faculté de penser*). Concerning God, he reiterates his general approval of Descartes' proofs of God's existence ("the reasons which you use to prove the existence of God seem to me not only ingenious ... but also true and solid demonstrations" – Arnauld must have been satisfied with Descartes' response to the circularity charge), while raising some questions (and offering some clarifications) on the nature of time and duration. He then, once again, expresses a doubt that Descartes' view of matter is reconcilable with Catholic doctrine concerning the Eucharist. He is pleased with Descartes' treatment of the earlier question regarding the persistence of the accidents (i.e. the appearance) of the bread, although the bread itself is no longer

---

[15] See Descartes' letters to Mesland, February 9, 1645 (AT IV, 161ff.) and May, 1645(?) (AT IV, 215ff.). For discussions of these issues, see Richard A. Watson, "Transubstantiation among the Cartesians", in *Problems of Cartesianism*, ed. T. M. Lennon, J. M. Nicholas and J. W. Davis (Kingston and Montreal: McGill-Queen's University Press, 1982), pp. 127–48; Armogathe, *Theologia Cartesiana*; and Henri Gouhier, *La Pensée Religieuse de Descartes*, 2nd ed. (Paris: J. Vrin, 1970).

[16] These letters were collected by Elzevier in his edition of Descartes' letters, published in 1668. Cf. Arnauld, *Oeuvres*, 38: 67–83; Descartes, AT V, 184–91, 211–15.

present. But how can Christ's body be present in the sacrament (i.e. within the same dimensions as the bread) *without* its own local extension, as *la foi Catholique* teaches, if, as Descartes claims, a body is nothing distinct from its local extension? He is clearly looking, hoping even, for some satisfaction in this matter. Most of his other problems with Descartes' thought are minor philosophical quibbles or have been taken care of by Descartes' replies. But he cannot be entirely comfortable with the Cartesian system until he is convinced that it is not in conflict with so important an element of Church doctrine. Eventually, as we will see, he is convinced of this, and will defend Descartes whole-heartedly against accusations that Cartesian metaphysics renders impossible a sincere and pious belief in transubstantiation as the Catholic Church understands it.

In the second letter of 1648, in addition to enlarging on some points made in the first letter, and in the light of Descartes' reply, Arnauld reconsiders his opinion that the mind does not always think ("I strongly approve what you say, that the mind always thinks"). He then treats of some problems he believes can be raised if thought is considered to be the essence of mind. For example, since our thoughts are different from one another, is it not the case that the essence of the mind must also differ on occasion? But he is not a hostile opponent here, concerned with discovering serious flaws in the Cartesian system. Rather, he is playing *within* that system. And at the end of the letter, he again expresses pleasure in Descartes' responses ("As for the issue of duration, I have looked at the place you noted [*Principia Philosophiae*, I, 57], and it has greatly pleased me"). Arnauld was impressed with, and persuaded by, almost all of Descartes' replies to his objections. "[I] have read with admiration, and I approve almost entirely, all that you have written concerning First Philosophy" (letter to Descartes, July, 1648, 38:67).[17] He was convinced that the Cartesian system was of value in dealing with important philosophical

---

[17] The qualification seems to be due, still, to an uncertainty regarding the details of Descartes' explication of transubstantiation (see 38:83). Compare this qualified approval with Arnauld's earlier response to an inquiry by Mersenne. Mersenne writes to Voetius on December 13, 1964: "cum nobilem quartarum objectionum Autorem, qui totius Academiae Parisiensis subtilissimus habetur Philosophus et Theologiae Doctor, rogarem, num rursus vellet contra responsiones insurgere, *mihique respondisset se nihil prorsus habere, sibique penitus esse satisfactum* ..." (Descartes, AT III, 603; emphasis added). One can only conjecture that Arnauld, at the earlier date, was too busy to give Descartes' responses the attention he would give them in 1648.

and theological issues, while nonetheless respecting the essential distinction between "matters of reason" and "matters of faith". Arnauld's satisfaction with Descartes on this latter point was a crucial factor in his enthusiastic acceptance of Descartes' philosophy.

For Arnauld, there were two different and independent orders of truths: the natural and the Christian (or divine). Reason is the sole guide when it comes to judging of natural objects and matters of fact. Revelation and, thus, faith are to serve in considering Christian truths.

It seems to me that too much trouble is taken to adjust the belief in mysteries which depend only on the omnipotence of God with the knowledge that we have of nature ... these are things of entirely separate orders, and they must not be mixed together, the former revealing themselves by means of the divine light, the latter by the natural light of reason. (38:xx-xxi)

In his *Examen*,[18] Arnauld notes that in matters of science (i.e. in the realm of nature) one must allow oneself to be persuaded only by reason, not by authority. The latter is to be obeyed only in regard to "mysteries of faith". He cites St Augustine: *quod scimus, debemus rationi; quod credimus, auctoritati* (what we know, we owe to reason; what we believe, to authority) (38:94). Reason and authority are "different foundations for two kinds of knowledge: the former, science; the latter, human or divine faith" (38:94). Rational inquiry is to be contrasted with belief on faith, and it is as improper to employ the latter in the realm of nature as it is to employ the former in the realm of divine mysteries:

Nothing is more judicious than this rule – listen to reason when it comes to the human sciences, and to authority in matters of religion. Nothing has spoiled philosophy or theology more than the fact that this rule has not been followed, and that, indeed, people do just the opposite. They have insisted on believing when they should desire to know; and they have insisted on knowing when they should be content to believe. They have employed the authority, the antiquity, and the universality of opinions, as well as other grounds, to compel belief in the context of the human sciences, in which,

---

[18] In 1680, while in exile in Holland, Arnauld wrote his *Examen d'un écrit qui a pour titre: Traité de l'essence du corps & de l'union de l'Ame avec le corps, contre la philosophie de M. Descartes* (38:89–179). The work is a response to an attack against Cartesianism by M. Le Moine, Dean of the Chapter of Vitré.

according to St Augustine, they should only consult reason, because only reason leads to knowing. (38:94–5)

Arnauld makes an identical point in the *Logique*:[19]

The world cannot long remain in this deference [to authority] and move about indifferently in possession of a natural and rational liberty, which consists in accepting that which is judged to be true and rejecting that which is judged to be false. For reason does not consider it odd if it is subordinated to authority in those sciences which, dealing with matters which are above reason, must follow another light, which can only be that of divine authority. But it seems that reason is well within her rights not to tolerate being submitted to authority in the human sciences, which make a profession of appealing only to reason. (41:123)

Although some things are clearly above and beyond the grasp of reason (*Logique*, IV, i), a rational faculty and a philosophy *qui demeure dans ses propres bornes* will not go astray, and will submit absolutely to faith on those matters on which it ought.[20]

Arnauld took this distinction seriously, and it may be found in his own work in the divisions he often made between the kinds of problems with which he would deal. His objections to Descartes' *Meditations*, for example, are separated according to whether they deal with philosophical or theological matters: "Firstly I shall put foward what seem to me to be the possible philosophical objections regarding the major issues of the nature of our mind and of God; and then I shall set out the problems which a theologian might come up against in the work as a whole" (AT VII, 197; CSM II, 138). *Des vraies et des*

---

[19] *La Logique, ou l'art de penser* (41:101–412). First published in 1662, the *Logique* is a collaborative effort between Arnauld and Nicole, and is one of the most important works in the history of thought on language and grammar. It is the only work of Arnauld's to have been fully translated into English. Along with his objections to Descartes and his letters to Leibniz, Arnauld's fame in the Anglo-American philosophical world rests on the "Port-Royal Logic", as it is commonly called. It was written for the son of the Duc de Luynes, and embodies the pedagogical principles of the schools associated with Port-Royal. For a long time, it was considered an essential part of a young Frenchman's education.

[20] Sainte-Beuve notes that "Arnauld did not love only controversy, he loved philosophy in itself as long as it was not at variance with religion. He preferred the investigation of natural truths to be pursued, with the aid of reason, as far as it could be taken. From the beginning he had been for Descartes and he remained faithful to him" (*op. cit.*, p. 162).

fausses idées was intended purely as a work of philosophy, concerned with the nature of ideas and the analysis of perception and cognition, in which he would attack what he saw as the philosophical underpinnings (presented in Malebranche's *Recherche*) of the theological doctrines in Malebranche's *Traité de la Nature et de la Grace*. The theological doctrines concerning grace and providence would be dealt with in a separate work, *Réflexions philosophiques et théologiques sur le nouveau système de la nature et de la grace*.

It is important to note that Arnauld had great faith in the progress of the sciences. Writing against those who saw little to praise and much to condemn in modern science, he sincerely extolled the accomplishments of such men as Copernicus, Brahe, Huyghens, and Galileo (see *Examen*, 38:96–7) – certainly a risky stand to take in the seventeenth century for a man already under suspicion by the Church of holding heretical views. Although the division between the realm of nature and the realm of grace, and between the different epistemological (or fideistic) principles at work in each, is a strict one, that is not to say that for Arnauld philosophy is of no use to religion. Arnauld saw the primary threat to true religion as emanating from Pyrrhonism and the libertinage towards which many felt such a skepticism inevitably led.[21] What philosophy has to offer, in the first place, is a method and path towards certainty and knowledge. Arnauld felt that through correct and proper reasoning the threat of Pyrrhonism might be shown for what it truly is – an untenable and insincere position.[22] The Port-Royal Logic is intended to show that there is genuine knowledge, that we do have "cognitions founded on clear and certain reasons." There are some things, for example, that it is impossible to doubt: that one exists, that one thinks, that one lives. These, at least, constitute "clear, certain, and indubitable knowledge." There is certainty, for Arnauld, both in the mind and in the senses. It is one of the goals of philosophy, and particularly of logic, to direct and guide the mind toward this knowledge by means of method.

In the second place, philosophy is to serve religion directly. Logic "has been developed only to serve as an instrument to the other sciences" (*Examen*, 38:117), such as physics, metaphysics, morals and,

---

[21] See Richard H. Popkin, *The History of Skepticism from Erasmus to Spinoza* (Berkeley: University of California Press, 1979), Chapter 5.

[22] Cf. *Logique*, IV, i.

most important, theology. It is Arnauld's opinion that many theological disputes are not, in fact, over matters of faith or other subjects which, being in the "realm of grace", are properly left to authority to decide. For example, we have seen how in the quarrel over the Five Propositions Arnauld makes use of the distinctions between *questions de droit* and *questions de fait* (*Mémoire sur les décisions des conciles & des Papes,* 10:705). The central issue at hand, whether or not the propositions are to be found in the *Augustinus,* is not a matter of doctrine at all.

Similarly, in order to clear up many theological problems, all that is needed, Arnauld insists, is clear thinking. Logic and philosophy can make an enormous contribution to religion by instilling correct principles of reasoning. In this way, matters such as the immortality of the soul, say, or the true conception of God, can be resolved by clearly distinguishing thought from extension, the soul from the body. It is significant that the mystery of the Eucharist, for example, should be discussed in a work such as the *Logique.* In Part II, Chapter xii, Arnauld attempts to clear up any misunderstanding as to how something can be bread at one moment and the body of Christ at another by reference to the use made in common speech of a single subject, or "common idea", to refer to two things which have some sensible resemblance to each other and succeed each other in the same place. All disputes regarding this question are "no better than a frivolous wrangling ... and must all be clarified through this way of conceiving many separate subjects under a single idea" (41:229). Likewise, the "problem" of whether the sense of the Eucharist is figurative or literal may be cleared up by reference to certain principles regarding the use of names in propositions (41:236–40).

The philosophical method and system which Arnauld sees as most compatible with (and supportive of) Christian truth, and as most likely to resolve certain philosophical and theological disputes, is Cartesianism. He rejects both the Aristotelian and the Epicurean philosophical systems (particularly as they appeared in their Scholastic forms and in the works of thinkers such as Gassendi) in favor of an orthodox Cartesianism which he saw as faithfully representing, in many important respects, the thought of St Augustine. Clearly, the motivation, in part, for his adherence to Cartesianism was that it seemed to serve well the purposes which he thought philosophy ought to serve. That is, he was convinced that Cartesian philosophy not only did *not* prejudice Christian truths, but that it in fact supported them, and would provide Christian solutions to many seemingly interminable theological debates.[23] For example, Arnauld notes in several contexts that the immortality of the soul is well grounded in Cartesian ontological dualism.[24] And he is particularly impressed with Descartes' proofs for the existence of God ("There is no other philosophy which gives as many demonstrations of the existence of God, and whose followers should be less suspected of having only feigned to establish it, such as the Epicureans are suspected of doing"). Moreover, Cartesian philosophy serves well to clear up certain issues in the realm of nature. Most important, however, is his conviction that this philosophy could accomplish these tasks without overreaching the proper bounds of rational inquiry. That is, Arnauld was certain that Descartes' philosophy respected the distinction between *questions de droit* and *questions de fait*. In defense of Descartes on this point, he cites Principle 76 from Part I of Descartes' *Principia Philosophiae*:

But above all else we must impress on our memory the overriding rule that whatever God has revealed to us must be accepted as more certain than anything else. And although the light of reason may, with the utmost clarity and evidence, appear to suggest something different, we must still put our entire faith in divine authority rather than in our own judgement. But on matters where we are not instructed by divine faith, it is quite unworthy of a philosopher to accept anything as true if he has never established its truth by thorough scrutiny ... (AT VIII-1, 39; CSM I, 221; quoted in the *Apologie pour les Catholiques*, II, vi, 14:626).

[23] See Bouillier, *op. cit.*, vol. 2, p. 160: "Nul n'a été plus fermement convaincu des services rendus à la religion par la nouvelle philosophie."

[24] "You insist that what I say in favor of M. Descartes will be appreciated only by those who are attached to the doctrine of this philosophy; as for myself, I believe that it will be appreciated by all who are persuaded (as it seems to me that everyone must be) that it is very important to be able to prove the immortality of the soul by natural reasons. For we must either despair of proving it by reason, or agree that M. Descartes has proven it better than anyone" (Letter to M. Du Vaucel, November 13, 1962; cited by Sainte-Beuve, *op. cit.*, p. 162). Cf. also *Examen* (38:138): "If there is anything for which M. Descartes should be commended, it is for having so well separated our soul from our body, and having so well established that these are two totally distinct substances." Arnauld's enthusiasm for Descartes is in particular evidence in this curious passage, found in various forms, in several of his writings: "It must be regarded as a singular effect of God's providence that M. Descartes has written what he has in order to stop the dreadful inclination shown by many persons of late towards irreligion and libertinage..." (see Bouillier, *op. cit.*, vol. 2, pp. 168ff.).

In the *Notae in Programma*, as well, Descartes distinguishes between matters which are to be believed on faith alone and those which can be investigated by natural reason (*ratio naturalis*) (AT VIII-2, 353; CSM I, 300). Arnauld insists that Descartes is sincere in his professions here – Descartes has a perfect respect and reverence for *tous les mystères de la foi*, and deals philosophically only with those matters which may legitimately be treated by *les lumières de la raison* (*Examen*, 38:90).

An important example here is Arnauld's defense of Cartesianism against the charge of being contrary to what the Catholic Church teaches concerning the Eucharist. The issue, for Arnauld, is that "whatever philosophy one subscribes to, it is necessary to acknowledge that the manner in which Jesus Christ is in the sacrament is incomprehensible, as the Council of Trent proclaims" (letter to Du Vaucel, April 29, 1683, 2:245). He demands that Cartesianism, as well as any other philosophical system, observe the distinction between those matters which are proper for philosophical investigation and those which, like the miracle of transubstantiation, are matters of faith alone. In a letter to Du Vaucel on April 29, 1683, Arnauld insists:

> I have nothing to say to you concerning the Cartesians except that it seems to me that it is beneficial to the Church that those who profess to follow this philosophy declare publicly that it is not inconsistent with what the Church teaches concerning the Eucharist (since it is difficult to understand the route they take to reconcile faith with their opinions), provided that they remain in agreement with everything in this mystery which is a matter of faith. (2:245)

Du Vaucel raises one of the standard problems for the Cartesian concerning the Eucharist. If extension is the essence of body, and inseparable from it, then there appears a *grand difficulté* for the Cartesian concerning the real presence of the body of Christ in the host. It is certain that his body is not present there with its own extension.[25] Thus, for Christ's body to be really present in the sacrament, where the local extension (i.e. dimensions) of the bread remains, its own extension must be separable from it. But on Cartesian principles, he insists, it is impossible to explain how the body of Christ can be present in the bread of the Eucharist without its extension (which, according to Descartes, is identical with body).

---

[25] See St Thomas, *Summa Theologiae*, Part IIIa, Q. 76, Arts. 4, 5. Arnauld raised a similar question with Descartes years earlier (*Nov. Objs.*, 38:73).

Hence, the Cartesian is committed to denying the real presence of Christ's body in the host.[26] This was a chief concern among Jansenists regarding Cartesian philosophy, and they saw in this apparent ramification the strain of Calvinism and impiety. This "incompatibility" between the Cartesian account of matter and *la foi Catholique* concerning the Eucharist is an accusation leveled against Cartesians by Catholics and Protestants alike.

Generally distrustful of philosophical speculations on such mysteries, Arnauld is not interested in elaborating on or propagating Descartes' "conjectures" concerning the Eucharist, particularly those found in the letters to Mesland in 1645 and 1646 ("However much I may be attached to the principles of this philosophy, I do not think that I am obliged to exhaust my mind by trying to accord these principles with what I very firmly believe regarding this mystery" [*Examen*, 38:123–4]). He was, no doubt, aware that such speculations are probably what got Descartes placed on the Index in 1663. And he was certainly aware of the problems this issue was causing for Cartesians generally.

Arnauld is satisfied simply to know that Cartesian principles *do not conflict* with Catholic dogma. And in the *Examen* and elsewhere, he stoutly defends Descartes on just those points raised by Du Vaucel, Le Moine and others. On the one hand, he insists that Cartesianism does not necessarily render impossible a pious and sincere belief in real presence. He claims that the opinion that extension is the essence of matter is not in itself contrary *à la foi de ce mystère* [*de l'Eucharistie*] (*Examen*, 38:105). It is a philosophical opinion that in no way determines what may or may not be an article of faith. Nor is what Descartes asserts regarding body condemned by any Council. In fact, many of the Church Fathers held the same opinion – most importantly, St Augustine (38:105). Thus, there is no reason why a Cartesian cannot consistently maintain that there is a "real presence" of Christ's body in the Eucharist. Although one may reject substantial forms and real accidents, this is no indication that one does not conform to *les vérités de la foi*. Those who attack the Cartesian theory of matter for being contrary to certain dogmas of religion are the ones who threaten the true Catholic faith by attaching it to a single set of

[26]Du Vaucel, "Observations sur la philosophie de Descartes", in Dijksterhuis, *op. cit.*, pp. 113–30.

untenable philosophical opinions: "It is very dangerous to have the verity of our faith concerning this mystery depend on the philosophical consequences which the Scholastics drew from it" (*Examen*, 38:107).

Moreover, it is *préjudiciable à l'Eglise* to insist that those who reject the Aristotelian account and seek to explain the nature of body solely by means of *les idées naturelles que nous en avons* are suspect of not believing in the miraculous nature of Eucharistic transubstantiation (*Examen*, 38:107). This is to confuse what properly belongs to the articles of faith with an explanation of the mystery which has traditionally been used by theologians; that is, it is to breach the crucial distinction between that which is a *vérite de foi* and that which, although derivable from an article of faith *par une conséquence évident*, must not be included among the dogmas of the Church. Arnauld firmly believes that it is Descartes who in this issue respects the distinction between matters of faith and matters of rational inquiry. The naturalistic explanation of the Eucharist that Descartes offers in his replies to Arnauld's Fourth Set of Objections is, Arnauld feels, compatible with a pious respect for the miracle accomplished therein by God. He allows that an acknowledgement of the incomprehensibility of the miracle that takes place at the moment of consecration may exist side by side with a philosophical explanation (in this case, in Cartesian mechanistic terms) of what is in fact happening in nature behind our sensory experience (i.e. that by means of God's miracle a certain substance, bread, is replaced by a different substance, Christ's body, within the same "superficies", hence occasioning the same sensations in, and appearances to, the mind as the bread formerly occasioned).[27] The miracle of how the body of Christ is *physiquement* substituted for the bread is completely inexplicable and outside the scope of philosophical investigation. On the other hand, what God accomplishes in this miracle (i.e. that such a substitution *does* take place), what changes in the natural world do in fact occur in this incomprehensible act of

---

[27] Fourth Replies: AT VII, 249ff., CSM II, 173ff. This is not Descartes' only response concerning the Eucharist. See Descartes' letters to Mesland cited above, n. 15. See also Armogathe, *Theologia Cartesianna*; and Watson, "Transubstantiation among the Cartesians". For a discussion of Arnauld's defense of Descartes on this issue, see Gouhier, *Cartésianisme et Augustinisme*, pp. 133ff.; and Steven M. Nadler, "Arnauld, Descartes and Transubstantiation: Reconciling Cartesian Metaphysics and Real Presence", *Journal of the History of Ideas*, 59 (1988), 229–46.

transubstantiation and how they relate to our experience, is a legitimate field of rational inquiry. For Arnauld, Descartes respects this distinction in *une manière très Christienne* (*Examen*, 38:113). The issue of the Eucharist is naturally an important one for Arnauld, and his satisfaction with Descartes regarding this point is essential in his acceptance of the method and metaphysics of Cartesian philosophy (see *Novae Objectiones*, 38:73).

Arnauld would remain committed to *la pensée cartésienne* for the rest of his life. In fact, he is found at the forefront of those trying to stem the persecution of Cartesianism in France. In a letter to Du Vaucel (October 19, 1691), for example, he criticizes the congregation of the Index (who had condemned the works of Descartes in 1663) for censoring an author so valuable to true religion and yet not censoring so dangerous a libertine as Gassendi (3:396). As Bouillier suggests, "of all the great men of the seventeenth century, there was not one whose attachment to the philosophy of Descartes was more secure and more profound".[28]

3 *Cartesian method*

The first issue in assessing Arnauld's Cartesianism is the question of method. Descartes' break with scholastic philosophy was (at least to his mind) methodological as well as metaphysical. One professing to be a Cartesian would be expected to follow Descartes self-consciously here, even if trained in traditional Scholastic philosophical method. In VFI, Arnauld offers seven rules to be followed *pour chercher la vérité* and *pour éviter dans les sciences naturelles beaucoup d'erreurs* (VFI, 38:181–3; the *Logique* is, likewise, an excellent source for Arnauld's thoughts on philosophical method.) He is clearly indebted to Descartes' *Regulae ad Directionem Ingenii* for these principles of method.

1 Begin with the most simple and clear things, which are such that they cannot be doubted when attention is given to them. This rule, of course, is Rule V of the *Regulae* and is reiterated in the *Discours de la méthode*: "to direct my thoughts in an orderly manner, by beginning with the simplest and most easily known objects ..." (*Discours*: AT VI, 18; CSM I, 120).[29]

---

[28] *Op. cit.*, vol. 2, p. 160; for a good discussion of Arnauld's role in the defense of Cartesianism, see Chapters 9 and 10.

[29] Cf. also *Logique*, IV, ii.

2 Do not mix up what is known clearly with what is known only confusedly (*des notions confuses*); and do not employ confused notions to try to explain clear notions: "this would be like trying to illuminate light by means of shadows" (VFI, 181). Arnauld notes later, as an axiom to be regarded, that "it is clearly an inversion of the mind to want to explain that which is clear and certain by obscure and uncertain things" (VFI, 200).

3 Do not seek reasons *ad infinitum*, but rest with what is known to be "the nature of a thing ... or a quality of it". This is a strange maxim to come from one professing to be a Cartesian in method in so far as it seems, *prima facie*, in its use of the phrase *la nature d'une chose*, to recall Aristotelian "natures" or forms, and the occult qualities offered as explanations by Scholastic thinkers. Nevertheless, one must not, for example, demand a reason why extension is divisible or why the mind is capable of thinking. It is sufficient in these cases to state that it is the nature of extension to be divisible, and that it is the nature of mind to think.

4 Do not demand definitions of terms which in themselves are clear, and which would consequently only be made more obscure by any attempt to define them; any *explanans* would be less clear than the *explanandum*. This is the case with words such as 'thought' and 'being', which in themselves are so clear that "there is no one who does not at least know what it is to think or what it is to be" (VFI, 181). This follows Descartes' claim in *Principia* (I, 10) that it is unnecessary to explain terms which are "sufficiently self-evident": "philosophers make the mistake of employing logical definitions in an attempt to explain what was already very simple and self-evident; the result is that they only make matters more obscure" (AT VIII-1, 8; CSM I, 195–6).

5 Do not confound questions to which one must respond with a formal cause with questions to which one must respond with an efficient cause; and one must not seek the formal cause of a formal cause, but respond in this case with an efficient cause. If one were to be asked why a certain object is round, it would be possible to respond with a definition of roundness, that is, to give the formal cause and say it is because if one were to draw straight lines from the surface of the object to a point in its center they would all be equal. But if one were pressed and asked why the exterior surface of the object is such as it was just described, one ought not to respond with another

formal cause ("a Peripatetic will look for another formal cause, saying that this ball is round because it has received a new quality called roundness, which has been drawn from the bowels of its substance to make it so" [VFI, 182]) but with an efficient cause (e.g. it was fabricated with a concave mould).

6 Do not treat or conceive of minds or souls as bodies; nor bodies as minds or souls. Do not attribute to one what applies only to the other. Thus, one ought not to ascribe beliefs to material bodies or extension and divisibility to minds. In other words, the strict dualism of Cartesianism demands the methodological principle that one should not mix categories and predicate of one kind of object what can be predicated only of another.

7 Do not multiply beings without necessity. Arnauld, who saw the mechanistic view of nature as sufficient to explain natural objects and phenomena (see Section 5 below), was particularly concerned here with substantial forms which are "really distinct from everything which can be imagined concerning the arrangements and configurations of the parts of matter" (VFI, 182).

Arnauld supplements these seven Cartesian *règles* with several *axiomes*. He is most Cartesian in accepting clarity and distinctness as criteria of truth. Thus, he notes as an axiom that, "when seeking to know things by way of science, one must accept as true only that which can be clearly conceived" (VFI, 200). This, of course, is the rule Descartes "discovers" in Meditation III and formulates in the *Discours* as "never to accept anything as true if I did not have evident knowledge of its truth ... and to include nothing more in my judgements than what presented itself so clearly and so distinctly that I had no occasion to doubt it" (*Discours*: AT VI, 18; CSM I, 120. Med. III: AT VII, 35; CSM II, 24). Arnauld expresses this rule with equal confidence in the *Logique*, explicitly acknowledging Descartes as his source: "never to _ accept anything as true which cannot be evidently known to be so" (41:367–8). It is interesting to note that, unlike Descartes, Arnauld feels no need to justify the reliability of clarity and distinctness as criteria of truth. To dispute this principle, that the clarity and distinctness of an idea are a reliable guide to its truth, is "to destroy all the evidence for human knowledge, and to establish a ridiculous Pyrrhonism ... if the judgements which we make while attending to these [clear and distinct] ideas do not bear at all on the things in themselves but only on our thoughts ... it is clear that we will have no knowledge of these things, but only of our thoughts; and, consequently, we will know nothing of those things which we think we know with the most certainty ... this obviously would destroy all the sciences" (*Logique*, 41:379).

It is not clear how far Arnauld is ultimately willing to distinguish clarity from distinctness. Initially, a distinction is made: clarity regards the forcefulness of an idea (or, in Humean terms, its vivacity): "it might be said that an idea is clear for us when it strikes us forcefully" (*Logique*, 41:156). Distinctness, on the other hand, seems to be a matter of content: a distinct idea is one whose representational content is presented in a "non-confused", well-defined, and accurate manner. The idea of pain, for example, strikes us very sensibly, and thus may be called clear. But it is not distinct to the extent that it appears vaguely to represent the pain as being, for example, in the hand which is wounded, although it is actually only in the mind.

This is made clearer in Arnauld's discussion with Descartes concerning the material falsity of ideas in his objections to the *Meditations*. Every positive idea, he notes, "displays" (*exhibeat*) something real. That is, every idea has some representational content. Descartes seems to agree with Arnauld's point. It is not that materially false ideas do not represent anything to the mind, but that they (their representational contents) are so "obscure and confused" that one cannot tell exactly what they display or represent to the mind; in other words, as representations they are faulty and fail to represent their objects adequately. Hence, they "furnish material for error", for false judgement (Med. III: AT VII, 43; CSM II, 29f. Fourth Replies: AT VII, 232f.; CSM II, 162f.). This seems to be what Arnauld is concerned with in his discussion of "distinctness" in the *Logique*. The pain, for example, although it lacks nothing in forcefulness, is not sufficiently determinate as a representation to inform us that it is not in the hand but in the mind. Thus, we judge it to be in the hand. The point is not that it has no representational content, but that this content is "obscure and confused". This seems to agree with Descartes' definitions of clearness and distinctness in the *Principia* (I, 45): "I call a perception clear when it is present and accessible to the attentive mind – just as we say that we see something clearly when it is present to the eye's gaze and stimulates it with a sufficient degree of strength and accessibility" (AT VIII-1, 22; CSM I, 207); an idea is distinct when it is "so sharply separated from all other perceptions that it contains within itself only what is clear" (AT VIII-1, 22; CSM I, 208). For Descartes, as for Arnauld, clearness is a matter of forcefulness and vivacity. Distinctness seems to be bound up with discreteness, whereby the "boundaries" or limits of an idea (what exactly it represents and what it excludes) are easily determined, and the idea is not easily confused with another. This, in turn, is a function of the fullness and determinacy of its representational content. A conception is distinct because we can distinguish accurately that which it does comprehend from all other notions (*Principia*, I, 63: AT VIII-1, 31; CSM I, 215).

Elsewhere, however, the distinction between clarity and distinctness tends to become blurred for Arnauld. First, he often sees distinctness as so bound up with clarity that "it might be said that every idea is distinct in so far as it is clear, and that its obscurity derives only from its confusion" (*Logique*, 41:156). He is willing, he says, to take the clearness of an idea and the distinctness of an idea *pour une même chose* (*Logique*, 41:156). Second, "clearness" is no longer simply the force and vivacity of an idea, but seems to refer (like "distinctness") to an idea's representational content. The idea of an object "is clear when it represents [that object] to us sufficiently for conceiving it clearly and distinctly" (*Logique*, 41:157). In VFI, an idea is clear if "it allows us to perceive manifestly that of which it is the idea" (VFI, 325).[30]

Arnauld is careful, like Descartes (in his reply to Arnauld's Fourth Set of Objections), to insist on the distinction between a clear and distinct idea, and an adequate or comprehensive idea, "which contains all the properties of the object" (VFI, 306). A clear and distinct idea need not contain all the actual and possible properties of its object, nor all its relations to other objects.[31] A clear and distinct idea need only tell one "what [the idea] contains and what it excludes".

The second axiom Arnauld proposes as essential to the "proper direction of one's reason" is closely related to the above: reject as imaginary those entities which cannot be clearly conceived, and which serve not at all to explain what they have been "invented" to explain. This rule is particularly to be observed, he notes, when "an

[30] For Arnauld (as for other Cartesians, such as Malebranche), clarity also produces an "inner conviction ... [which] cannot be denied." In other words, the clarity of an idea is bound up with indubitability and psychological certainty (cf. *Logique*, IV, i).

[31] VFI, 306, 314f., 323. Cf. Descartes, Fourth Replies: AT VII, 219ff.; CSM II, 155ff.

explanation is much better without these invented beings ..." (VFI, 200–201).

Finally, he insists on two rules which, as he acknowledges, are proposed by Descartes in the *Regulae* (Rules VI and VII) and in the *Discours*:[32] to divide each of the difficulties we examine into as many parts as possible, and as may be necessary for resolving it; and to make in relation to everything enumerations so complete that we may be assured of having omitted nothing (*Logique*, 41:368).

Together, the rules outlined above constitute, for Arnauld, the method of analysis, of "finding out some truth". This is to be contrasted with synthesis, which is the method for "explaining what is found":

> Thus, there are two kinds of method: one for discovering the truth, which is called "analysis", or the method of resolution, and which may also be called the method of discovery; and another for explaining it to others when it has been discovered, which is called "synthesis", or the method of composition ... analysis is used only to resolve some question. (*Logique*, 41:362)

The distinction is, in most respects, the one made by Descartes in his reply to the Second Set of Objections:

> Analysis shows the true way by means of which the thing in question was discovered methodically and as it were [from effect to cause] ... Synthesis, by contrast, employs a directly opposite method where the search is, as it were [from cause to effect.] (AT VII, 155–6; CSM II, 110)

Analysis, in other words, is the method of philosophical or scientific investigation; synthesis is the method of exposition or demonstration. In both methods one always moves from "that which is better known [*plus connu*] to that which is less known. For there is no true method which can dispense with this rule" (*Logique*, 41:366).

Analysis, for Arnauld, regards the resolution of questions. "Questions of things" are of four types: when we seek causes through effects; when we seek effects through causes; when through the parts we seek the whole; and when, having the whole and some part, we seek another part (*Logique*, 41:362). In all questions there is something unknown which is sought. The purpose of analysis, of

---

[32] *Regulae:* AT X, 381; CSM I, 21–8. *Discours:* AT VI, 18; CSM I, 120.

course, is to discover this unknown x. "Analysis consists principally in the attention which is given to that which is known in the question which we desire to resolve; the whole art consisting in drawing from this examination many truths which may lead us to the knowledge of that which we seek" (*Logique*, 41:362–8). Synthesis, on the other hand, lays out in "geometric" fashion the results of investigation for the purposes of "persuasion". "This method consists principally in beginning with the most general and simple things, in order to move on to those which are less general and more complex" (*Logique*, 41:368). If the end of analysis is discovery, the end of synthesis is demonstration. Each represents an essential part of "method", of "disposing well a series of many thoughts, either for discovering truth when we are ignorant of it, or for proving it to others when it is already known".

It is important to note here Arnauld's insistence on introspection and the certainty of the *cogito* as the positive starting-points of the process of rational inquiry:

St Augustine realized, long before M. Descartes, that in order to arrive at the truth we cannot begin with anything more certain than this proposition: I think, therefore I am. And ... from there, in order for the soul to know itself, it need only separate those things which can be separated from its thought, and what remains will be what the soul is. (VFI, 183)

What the mind thereby discovers *par une sérieuse attention à ce qui se passe en nous* is that it is a substance whose essence is to think. At this point, several truths become apparent regarding the nature of thought (e.g. that "every thought has its object") and ontology (e.g. the distinction between a mode and a substance). From here, in accordance with the rules and axioms outlined above, it is possible to construct a science of the mind and to discover the nature of perceptual and cognitive awareness of the external world, much as Arnauld has done in VFI. Arnauld's method for discovering "truth" is clearly a Cartesian one.

4 *Cartesian metaphysics: substance/modification*

In Descartes' system the ontology of substance and modification is exhaustive: every thing is either a substance or a mode of a substance. A substance is that which is self-subsistent, which "exists in such a way as to depend on no other thing for its existence" (*Principia*, I, 51:

AT VIII-1, 24; CSM I, 210). Strictly speaking, there is only one substance which fits this definition: God, for only God can exist without anything else. All other things that do or can exist need the concourse of God to exist. However, Descartes allows that, relatively speaking, the two kinds of created substance can be subsumed under the concept of substance, for they are "things that need only the concurrence of God in order to exist" (*Principia*, I, 52: AT VIII-1, 25; CSM I, 210). There are thus three kinds of substance in the Cartesian universe: one uncreated infinite substance, God, and two created substances: finite mind and finite body. The term 'substance' is applied equivocally between God and finite substances, but univocally among finite substances. The two created substances are "really distinct" in that "each of them can exist apart from the other" (Second Replies: AT VII, 161; CSM II, 114).

Furthermore, substance functions as that in which all other things inhere. "This term [substance] applies to every thing in which whatever we perceive immediately resides, as in a subject, or to every thing by means of which whatever we perceive exists. By 'whatever we perceive' is meant any property, quality or attribute of which we have a real idea. The only idea we have of a substance itself, in the strict sense, is that it is the thing in which whatever we perceive ... exists, either formally or eminently" (Second Replies: AT VII, 161; CSM II, 114). A substance is thus that which depends on nothing (except God) for its existence and on which every thing which is not a substance (e.g. a mode) depends for existence.

Finally, it is possible to conceive of a substance "by itself". Two substances are really distinct from each other in that "we can clearly and distinctly understand one apart from the other" (*Principia*, I, 60: AT VIII-1, 28; CSM I, 213). We can also clearly conceive substance "apart from the mode which we say differs from it" (*Principia*, I, 61: AT VIII-1, 29; CSM I, 214), that is without any modifications (e.g. pure extension).

Modes, for Descartes, on the other hand, are simply "attributes or qualities" of substances. A mode is a substance existing in a certain manner. Modes diversify substances and make each of them of "such and such a kind" (*Principia*, I, 56: AT VIII-1, 26; CSM I, 211). Consequently, unlike substances, modes are not independently subsisting entities, but depend for their existence upon the substances they modify. "Nothingness possesses no attributes or qualities. It follows that, wherever we find some attributes or qualities, there is necessarily some thing or substance to be found for them to belong to" (*Principia*, I, 11: AT VIII-1, 8; CSM I, 196). Although there is no necessary relationship between a substance and a particular quality which may actually modify it, there is a necessary relationship between any one modification and the substance it modifies. There is no modification without a substance modified. In a letter to Hyperaspistes (August, 1641) Descartes notes:

There is no doubt that if God withdrew his cooperation, everything which he has created would go to nothing; because all things were nothing until God created them and provided his cooperation. This does not mean that they should not be called substances, because when we call a created substance self-subsistent we do not rule out the divine cooperation which it needs in order to subsist, we mean only that it is a thing of a kind to exist without any other creature; and this is something that cannot be said about the modes of things, like shape and number. (AT III, 429; Kenny, 116).

A mode cannot be thought of apart from a substance, cannot be independently conceived in the way a substance can. Although we can clearly conceive the substance without the mode, we cannot conversely understand the mode apart from the substance (*Principia*, I, 61: AT VIII-1, 29; CSM I, 214). As Daisie Radner notes, the impossibility here is logical, not psychological.[33] It is not simply that, as a matter of fact, the human mind is not fit to make a distinction which, were its abilities different, it otherwise could. The definition of a modification makes reference to substance. Roundness is defined in terms of extension; imagining in terms of thought. Neither extension nor thought are defined in terms of anything else.

Finally, the kinds of qualities which are capable of modifying one kind of substance are as radically distinct from the kinds of qualities which are capable of modifying another kind of substance as the two substances are distinct from each other. That is, the real distinction in essence between substances is paralleled by a difference in kind between modes.

Arnauld was never concerned with ontology in a purely philosophical manner. There is no work of his in which he explicitly examines substance ontology as a viable system in philosophical and

[33]*Malebranche*, p. 2.

scientific terms. Yet it is clear that he wholeheartedly accepted the Cartesian ontological distinction between substance and modification as exhaustive[34] and, more important (to his mind), not prejudicial to true religion. In fact, all of Arnauld's "philosophical" works are permeated by the assumptions of Cartesian substance. In the *Logique*, for example, he insists that all that we conceive is represented to the mind as either a *chose*, a *manière de chose* or a *chose modifiée* (41: 134). In the *Examen* he is concerned with proving that it is impossible for the kind of modification which is proper to one kind of substance (mind) to be transferred to, or even possessed by, another, radically distinct kind of substance (body).[35]

Following Descartes, Arnauld defines a substance or a "thing" as "that which is conceived as subsisting by itself, and as the subject of everything which is conceived of it": "When I consider a body, the idea which I have of it represents to me a thing or a substance, because I consider it as a thing which subsists by itself, and which needs no other subject in order to exist" (*Logique*, 41:134). A mode, or *manière de chose*, is "that which, being conceived in the thing and as not able to subsist without it, determines it to be of a certain kind, and to be so named". A *chose modifiée* is "the substance as determined by a certain manner or mode" (*Logique* 41:134). Again, the logical distinction between mode and substance is the Cartesian one:

> It is, thus, the nature of a true mode that the substance of which it is a mode can be conceived clearly and distinctly without it; but the mode, in turn, cannot be clearly conceived without conceiving, at the same time, its relation to the substance without which, naturally, it cannot exist. (*Logique*, 41:134)

In VFI, the same principles are at work. Those changes which occur in a substance (e.g. the different thoughts of a mind, the motions of a body) are simply that substance modified in different ways (VFI, 184). That which distinguishes "things or substances from modes, or manners of being, which may also be called modifications", is that the latter cannot be conceived "without conceiving the substance of which they are modifications": "in order that I may think about diverse things without [undergoing] a change of nature, these diverse

---

[34] Cf. VFI, 187. In VFI, Arnauld often reasons in a manner which clearly suggests that something must be either a substance or a modification of a substance.
[35] Cf. *Examen*, 38:172–3.

thoughts must be only different modifications of the thought which makes up my nature" (VFI, 184).

5 *Cartesian metaphysics: mind/body dualism*

Arnauld fully accepted the absolute Cartesian distinction between mind, or mental substance, and body, or corporeal substance. This dualistic division of substances is comprehensive: every thing (*chose*) is either a mind or a body, thinking substance or extended substance. "If there is anything for which M. Descartes is to be commended, it is for having so well separated our soul from our body, and having so well established that these are two totally distinct substances" (*Examen*, 31:138). Mind is the created substance whose essence or essential attribute is thought; body is the created substance whose essence is extension. Similarly, for Arnauld as for Descartes, mind is unextended, and extended body cannot think. The division is thus not only exhaustive but also exclusive, and extends to the modifications of which each substance is capable. The modes which pertain to one kind of substance are necessarily incapable of modifying the other. The sixth of Arnauld's principles of method (in VFI: see Section 3 above) proscribes attributing to minds what pertains only to bodies, and vice versa. The fourth part of the *Examen* is devoted to proving that extended substance is incapable of receiving spiritual properties as its modifications, and (more particularly) that the body, *qua* extended matter, is essentially incapable of thought or sensation. In this work, he defends Descartes' "real distinction" of mind and body against the view that the mind imparts some of its *spiritualité* to the body, thus allowing the body to sense. He finds it inconceivable that a spiritual quality can become a modification of a material body (38:143):

The word 'thought' indicates so distinctly and so clearly *conscientiam sui*, that it is sufficiently clear ... that it is only applicable to a substance distinct from extended substance. For subtilize as much as you want, taking the word 'body' as it is understood by all who know what they are talking about, even if an Angel divides a body into as many parts as he desires, moving it and turning it around in all imaginable ways, will it be possible for this body or this matter, which hitherto did not think, suddenly to begin to think, to know, and to have what the Latins call *conscientiam suae operationis* (38:107)

He notes in the *Logique* that "it is impossible to imagine that there is any relation between the motion or figure of matter, subtile or gross, and thought" (41:161). Likewise, the soul is incapable of assuming the properties of matter. It is unextended thinking: "our soul is not corporeal ... it is not figured" (*Examen*, 38:165). As Descartes avers in his reply to the Fifth Set of Objections, "the whole nature of the mind consists in the fact that it thinks, while the whole nature of the body consists in its being an extended thing; and there is absolutely nothing in common between thought and extension" (AT VII, 358; CSM II, 248).

Descartes sees thinking substance as capable of being modified in several ways: doubting, conceiving, understanding, affirming, denying, refusing, imagining, and feeling are all modifications of "a thing which thinks"; all are modes of thought.[36] Arnauld accepts Descartes' enumeration (and, thus, his extensive picture of the mind): the mind, *qua* thinking substance, is modified in various ways when it senses, imagines, conceives, wills, doubts, judges, and perceives. Perceptions, imaginings, sensations (including feelings such as pain and pleasure), conceptions, etc. are all modifications of mental substance (cf. *Examen*, 38:166f.). Furthermore, for Descartes the defining characteristic of thought is its reflexivity, or self-awareness: "I use this term [thought] to include everything that is within us in such a way that we are immediately aware of it [*ejus immediate conscii simus*]" (Second Replies: AT VII, 160; CSM II, 113).[37] Arnauld, too, notes that "our thought ... is essentially reflective on itself, or (as it is more aptly put in Latin) *est sui conscia*. For I never think without knowing that I am thinking ... at the time when I am conceiving, I know that I am conceiving" (VFI, 371). In his *Examen*, he states his agreement with St Augustine that the properties of the soul "all involve thought", and, consequently, all contain *conscientiam sui* (38:167). Whenever the mind is modified in any

---

[36] Med. II: AT VIII, 28; CSM II, 19. Second Replies: AT VII, 160; CSM II, 113.

[37] In the *Principia* he seems to modify this to mean that of which we are *capable* of becoming immediately conscious, perhaps in order to avoid the problematic implication that we are conscious of everything that happens in the mind: "Cogitationis nomine, intelligo illa omnia, quae nobis consciis in nobis fiunt, *quatenus eorum in nobis conscientia est*" (*Principia*, I, 9: AT VIII-1, 7; my emphasis). But elsewhere he insists that "there can be nothing in the mind ... of which it is not aware ... we cannot have any thought of which we are not aware, at the very moment when it is in us" (Fourth Replies: AT VII, 246; CSM II, 171). He notes, however, that this applies only to acts and operations of the mind, not its powers or faculties.

way whatsoever, whenever it thinks, doubts, wills, etc., it is always aware of that mode. Conversely, if the mind is unaware of any thought taking place, no such thought exists (letter for Descartes, July 1648, 38:82).

Mind, for Descartes, is also distinguished from matter by its activity. Many of its modifications are "operations" (*operationes*). Not only is it capable of forming ideas for itself, but also of willing, judging, affirming or denying, doubting, etc., all of which are actions taken upon ideas. In a letter to Regius (May, 1641), Descartes distinguishes between the "activity [*actio*] and passivity [*passio*] of one and the same substance" – understanding is the passivity of the mind, willing is its activity (AT III, 372; Kenny, 102). The former is the mind's capacity to receive ideas, which relate to the soul as the various shapes it can assume relate to a piece of wax.[38] Volitions, on the other hand, are the mind's activity. The soul is also capable of acting on the body by means of the animal spirits, which travel from the brain to the muscles by way of the nerves. In *Les Passions de l'Ame*, this division translates into the distinction between the "actions of the soul", which "proceed directly from our soul and appear to depend on it alone", and its passions, which "the soul always receives ... from the things that are represented by them" (AT XI, 342; CSM I, 335).

For Arnauld, likewise, mind is active. Contrary to Malebranche, Arnauld insists that there is no reason to believe that the soul is purely passive with regard to its perceptions; indeed, it is demonstrable that it has received from God the faculty to produce them (VFI, Chapter XXVII). In his response to the *Recherche*, he insists that the soul is capable of producing its modifications not only in acts of willing and desiring, but also with regard to perceptions. "To insist that the soul is active with regard to one of its faculties, the will, is to insist that it is absolutely and by its nature active" (VFI, 343). Arnauld thus parts company with Descartes here. Whereas Descartes was willing to distinguish an active and a passive aspect of the mind, Arnauld rejects this division on the grounds that the mind is a simple substance. Being a simple substance, it is incapable of being divided into parts *distinctes réellement*. But, he argues, to insist that the mind is both active will and passive understanding (as Malebranche also insists) is to destroy this simplicity and regard "the diverse faculties of

[38] *Regulae*, XII: AT X, 412; CSM I, 40.

the soul as really distinct things." In fact, willing and understanding are both *activities* of the mind, "the same thing considered differently" (VFI, 343).

Descartes did not see the issue of the simplicity of the soul as bound up with the question of the soul's distinct faculties in this way. As noted above, he was willing to differentiate between an active faculty of the mind (the will) and a passive faculty (the understanding). Yet he still maintained the simplicity of the soul. This simplicity, for Descartes, is a matter of indivisibility. Being unextended, the soul is not composed of parts, that is, it cannot be divided into smaller elements. Descartes notes that "the mind is utterly indivisible [*indivisibilis*]": "when I consider the mind or myself in so far as I am merely a thinking thing, I am unable to distinguish any parts within myself; I understand myself to be something quite singular and complete" (Med. VI: AT VII, 85–6; CSM II, 59). The soul's faculties of willing, feeling, conceiving, etc. are not its parts, but the same substance (the same mind) employing itself in different ways. On the question of indivisibility, Arnauld concurs: that substance which thinks, being unextended, neither fills any space nor has parts; such things *ne conviennent qu'au corps* (*Logique* 41:210). Hence it is indivisible; and that "intelligible extension" of which Malebranche speaks, which (having parts) is divisible, can in no way be admitted to be an attribute either of our soul or of God (infinite thinking substance) (VFI, 254).

Matter, on the other hand, is both entirely passive and divisible, being composed of parts. In Meditation VI, Descartes insists that "there is no corporeal or extended thing that I can think of which in my thought I cannot easily divide into parts; and this very fact makes me understand that it is divisible" (AT VII, 86; CSM II, 59). In fact, Descartes rejects atomism and opts for the indefinite divisibility of matter (*Principia*, I, 26). Whatever is extended is divisible into parts; each of these parts is extended and, hence, further divisible, and so on.

Furthermore, Descartes' matter is devoid of any qualities save length, breadth, depth, and motion, and bodies are composed solely of "various differently shaped and variously moving parts" (*Principia*, II, 1: AT VIII-1, 40–41; CSM I, 223). Descartes has thus emptied the material world of all non-geometrical, non-quantifiable properties such as color, taste, etc. This follows from having identified matter with its essential attribute: extension. Matter, being pure extension, contains no properties which cannot be the properties of extension. "The nature of matter, or body considered in general, consists not in its being something which is hard or heavy or coloured, or which affects the senses in any way, but simply in its being something which is extended in length, breadth and depth" (*Principia*, II, 4: AT VIII-1, 42; CSM I, 224). All natural phenomena, "all the variety in matter, or all the diversity of its forms", depend solely on the motions of matter figured, configured and compounded in various ways. "All the properties which we clearly perceive in it are reducible to its divisibility and consequent mobility in respect of its parts, and its resulting capacity to be affected in all the ways which we perceive as being derivable from the movement of the parts" (*Principia*, II, 23: AT VIII-1, 52; CSM I, 232).

Arnauld's account of matter is purely Cartesian. In the *Logique*, he rejects Aristotelian substantial forms and real accidents in favor of a non-atomistic, corpuscularian, mechanistic view of nature. Arnauld insists on both the passivity and the indefinite divisibility of matter.[39] "Effects of nature" are explained solely by "the imperceptible parts of which bodies are composed, and by their different situation, size, figure, motion or rest, and by the pores which are found between these parts and which provide or allow passage to other materials" (*Logique*, 41:381). In the *Examen*, Arnauld presents a defense of the Cartesian conception of matter and the mechanistic explanation of nature. He compares God's work in creation with that of a mechanic, and his creation with an artificial machine (e.g. a clock). Arnauld insists that the mechanistic explanation of natural phenomena, of *la végétation des plantes, & ce qui se passe dans les bêtes*, is *le plus satisfaisant*. All such events and effects in material bodies can be explicated "mechanistically; that is, by the disposition, configuration and movement of their parts, or of the fluids which run through an infinity of small perceptible and imperceptible channels ... without recourse to powers, faculties and virtues, which are only indeterminate words by which ... philosophers disguise their ignorance" (*Examen*, 38:151-3). The Cartesian picture of the material world as a machine, with all its entities and effects being simply the result of extended matter (composed solely of quantifiable properties) in motion, is enthusiastically accepted and defended by Arnauld.

[39] *Logique*, I, ix; VFI, 422.

There is, however, one notable (and important) difference. Descartes argued against the existence (real or possible) of a vacuum. This follows from his having identified matter solely with extension: corporeal substance, being only extension in length, breadth, and depth, is consequently not different from space: "the extension constituting [*constituit*] the nature of a body is exactly the same as that constituting the nature of a space ... nothing remains in the idea of a [body] except that it is something extended in length, breadth, and depth. Yet this is just what is comprised in the idea of space, not merely a space which is full of bodies, but even a space which is called 'empty' [*vacuum*]" (*Principia*, II, 11: AT VIII-1, 46; CSM I, 227–8). Thus, there is no such thing as a vacuum (i.e. a space in which there is no substance) because the extension of space is no different from that of body. Since in every space there is extension, there is necessarily also material substance.

At first, one would expect Arnauld to agree with Descartes on this point, since he accepts the Cartesian notion of matter solely as extension in three dimensions. Indeed, his words often suggest as much. In the *Logique*, he notes that there is no more matter in a box full of gold than in one full of air: "Reason makes us judge that, each part of matter never occupying anything but its place, equal spaces are always filled by the same quantity of matter" (41:160). But in his *Novae Objectiones*, he sees Descartes' view on the impossibility of a vacuum in nature as detracting from the omnipotence of God:

What? God is not able to reduce to nought the wine which is contained in a barrel without producing any other body in its place or allowing any other to enter there (although the latter is not necessary, since once the wine has been annihilated, no other body can take its place without leaving another place in nature empty)? From which it follows that either God necessarily preserves all bodies, or if he is able to annihilate one, he can also leave a vacuum there. (38:74)

If one removes a quantity of wine from the inside of a barrel, is it any wonder if the concavity of the barrel remains as it is? The body contained in the barrel did not contribute to this concavity; it was merely contained within it. The vacuum created therein has itself no properties; what remain are solely the same properties (wide, depth, etc.) of the same concavity of the barrel.

Descartes, in his response (June 4, 1648), insists that Arnauld's objection is not to the point. What Arnauld calls the dimensions (length, breadth, depth) of the concavity of the barrel are exactly what, for Descartes (and, one would think, for Arnauld), constitute (*constituit*) a material body: "I have hardly anything to say about the void, which is not already to be found somewhere or other in my *Principles of Philosophy*. What you call the hollowness of a barrel seems to me to be a body with three dimensions, not to be identified with the sides of the barrel" (38:77, AT V, 194; Kenny, 233). In a later letter (July 29, 1648) Descartes insists that since the space in the empty barrel has the properties of length, depth and breadth (i.e. true extension, *veram extensionem*), hence "all the properties necessary for the nature of body, we would not say that it is wholly void . . . for wherever extension is, there, of necessity, is body also [*ubicunque extensio est, ibi etiam necessario est corpus*]" (38:87-8; AT V, 223-4; Kenny, 236).

Arnauld responds with a simple reiteration of his first point: it is hard to believe that God is not able to destroy a body without being obliged at the same time to create another of similar dimensions; or that the space formerly occupied by the destroyed body is *véritablement & réellement* a body without a new act of creation having taken place.[40] His opposition on this issue is paradoxical, given his acceptance of the Cartesian picture of matter, whereby extension is the *essence* of body.

A person, for Arnauld, is a being composed of both a mind and a body. His account of the union and interaction of the two substances in a human being, particularly as exemplified in sensation, is the Cartesian one. In sensation, motions are communicated from the object to the body, where they come into contact with a sense organ and stimulate the extremities of the nerves located there. The motion is then communicated to the brain by means of the small fibers in the nerves. When these fibers are stirred at the extremity of the nerve, the part of the brain in which they originate (or terminate) is likewise stirred. This motion in the brain serves as the "cause" or occasion for the soul (which has its "seat" in the brain) to have a perception of color, sound, light, pain, etc. Thus, sensation comprises two elements: the motions in the body (most notably, in the brain) which are communicated in a purely mechanical fashion; and certain *perceptions confuses* which exist in the mind.[41] All sensations are purely mental,

[40] *Nov. Objs.*, 38:83.
[41] *Examen*, 38:144, 148; *Logique*, 41:158-9. Cf. Descartes, *Principia*, IV, 189: AT VIII-1, 315; CSM I, 279ff.

and simply correspond to certain parts of extended matter in motion.

Arnauld was certainly aware of the problems inherent in Cartesian dualism. How is the union and interaction of two substances so radically and essentially different in nature as mind and body possible? That interaction, in some sense of the term, does take place is indubitable – we have the evidence of the senses, the imagination, and the passions and emotions to confirm this. In all these cases, "nature" informs us of the union and interaction of the mind and body. Thus, Descartes notes in a letter to Regius (January, 1642), the mind and the body are "united in a real and substantial manner [*mentem corpori realiter & substantialiter esse unitam*]", as attested by sensation (AT III, 493; Kenny, 127). Yet two questions need to be answered. What is the nature of this union? And how is mind/body interaction possible on Cartesian dualistic principles? If mind and body are so essentially different, how can we explain the fact that union and interaction occur?

The question of the nature of the union arises for two reasons. On the one hand, dualism demands an answer to the problem of the manner in which an unextended substance can be united to an extended substance. On the other hand, Descartes' answers to the question, as I show below, are inconsistent and ambiguous, stating in one place that the soul is present throughout (or "coextensive with") the body and in another that it has its "principal seat" in the pineal gland (i.e. that it is "located" in the brain).

The question of interaction arises when the dualism is taken in conjunction with the Cartesian view of causation. Although Descartes remarks, in a letter to Clerselier (Janaury 12, 1646: AT IX, 213), that there is no reason to believe that two substances of diverse natures cannot act on one another, he does appear committed to a general theory of causation which rules out mind/body interaction. Descartes claims that a necessary condition for a causal relationship between two entities, for one to be able to act upon (produce an effect in) the other, is that the cause must contain in itself, either formally (i.e. actually) or eminently (i.e. "in some higher form"), what it produces in the effect:

Where, I ask, could the effect get its reality from, if not from the cause? And how could the cause give it to the effect unless it possessed it? (Third Med.: AT VII, 40; CSM II, 28)

The fact that 'there is nothing in the effect which was not previously present in the cause, either in a similar or in a higher form' is a primary notion which is as clear as any that we have. (Second Replies: AT VII, 135; CSM II, 97)

If mind is to act causally on body, the bodily effect must exist previously, in some form, in the mental cause. There must, in other words, be something in the mind similar to that which the mind causes in the body. "For if we admit that there is something in the effect that was not previously present in the cause, we shall also have to admit that this something was produced by nothing. And the reason why nothing cannot be the cause of a thing is simply that *such a cause would not contain the same [idem] features as are found in the effect*" (Second Replies: AT VII, 135; CSM II, 97, emphasis added). But given the radical difference in nature between mind and body, such a preexistence of the effect in the cause is incomprehensible. There is no respect in which mind resembles matter – not in the kind of substance each is, nor in the kind of modifications of which each is capable. Thus, there is no respect in which anything mental can resemble anything physical. How, then, could a physical effect (e.g. motion in a certain direction at a certain velocity) be found "in a similar form" in a non-extended substance? Perhaps there is a way in which a physical effect can preexist "eminently" in a mental substance. But unless Descartes makes clear what this amounts to (and I do not see that he does), he has a problem explaing how mind and body interact causally.[42]

The question was raised for Descartes by Princess Elizabeth in her letter of May 6, 1643: "How can the human soul determine the spirits of the body, in order to initiate voluntary actions (since it is only a thinking substance)?" (AT III, 661). How can an immaterial thing cause physical movement? Simon Foucher, in his critique of Malebranche, formulates the problem in a more systematic manner, raising a critical problem for any Cartesian metaphysics.[43]

[42] See Daisie Radner, "Is there a Problem of Cartesian Interaction?", *Journal of the History of Philosophy*, 23 (1985), 35–49. Not everyone agrees that there is such a problem for Descartes: see R. C. Richardson, "The 'Scandal' of Cartesian Interactionism", *Mind*, 91 (1982), 20–37; and Louis E. Loeb, *From Descartes to Hume* (Ithaca: Cornell University Press, 1981). Loeb and Richardson reply to Radner's article in *Journal of the History of Philosophy*, 23 (1985), 221–48.

[43] Simon Foucher, *Critique de la Recherche de la vérité* (Paris: Martin Coustelier, 1675). Cf. Watson, *The Downfall of Cartesianism*.

Descartes' response to the question of mind/body union is often inconsistent. It is possible to discern in his writings two conflicting views. According to the first view, the mind has its "principal seat" in the brain (more particularly, in the pineal gland): "It must be realized that the human soul, while informing the entire body, nevertheless has its principal seat [*praecipuam sedem*] in the brain; it is here alone that the soul not only understands and imagines but also has sensory awareness" (*Principia*, IV, 189: AT VIII-1, 315; CSM I, 279). In the Sixth Meditation he states that "the mind is not immediately affected by all parts of the body, but only by the brain" (AT VII, 86; CSM II, 59). The union of the mind and the body is simply the correspondence that takes place between motions in the brain and thought processes (sensations, etc.). On the occasion of certain motions in the brain (caused by similar movement in the nerves) the mind "will necessarily feel" certain sensations. The union of the mind and the body is this brain-state/mind-state correspondence, and the mind is "located" in the brain.

This is to be contrasted with a second view often expressed by Descartes (sometimes on the same page), whereby the mind is "coextensive" (*coextendatur*) with the body, present throughout its extremities and "immediately" in contact with every part of the body:

Nature also teaches me, by these sensations of pain, hunger, thirst and so on, that I am not merely present in my body as a sailor is present in a ship, but that I am very closely joined and, as it were, intermingled with it, so that I and the body form a unit ... [All] these sensations of hunger, thirst, pain and so on are nothing but confused modes of thinking which arise from the union and, as it were, intermingling of the mind with the body. (Med. VI: AT VII, 81; CSM II, 56)

A similar view is expressed in the replies to the Sixth Set of Objections and in a letter to Elizabeth (May 21, 1643). In these two contexts, he compares the relation of the mind to the body with the Scholastic conception of the relation of gravity to body (which, of course, is, for Descartes, a mistaken view of the nature of gravity):

The mind, even though it is in fact a substance, can nonetheless be said to be a quality of the body to which it is joined. And although I imagined gravity to be scattered throughout the whole body that is heavy, I still did not attribute to it the extension which constitutes the nature of a body. For the true extension of a body is such as to exclude any interpenetration of the parts. (Sixth Replies: AT VII, 442; CSM II, 297–8)

The mistaken view of gravity that Descartes himself once held, whereby it is a property "coextensive with the heavy body", is "exactly the way in which I now understand the mind to be coextensive with the body – the whole mind in the whole body and the whole mind in any one of its parts" (Sixth Replies: AT VII, 442; CSM II, 298). The mind is both coextensive with the whole body, and wholly present in each of its parts. Naturally, the extension of thought throughout the body is different from the extension of matter "because [matter] is determined to a definite place, from which it excludes all other bodily extension, which is not the case with [thought]".[44] He is not very clear on just how we are to conceive the soul as extended, nor on how such extension differs from bodily extension. Perhaps it is this problem which leads him to say in the reply to the Fifth Set of Objections that "even though the mind is united to the whole body, it does not follow that it is extended throughout the body, since it is not in its nature to be extended, but only to think" (AT VII, 388–9; CSM II, 266).

These two views of the union of mind and body are proposed successively in *Les Passions de l'Ame*, although Descartes seems here to bring them together into a single account. In Part I, Article xxx, he insists that "the soul is really joined to the whole body, and that we cannot properly say that it exists in any one part of the body to the exclusion of the others." Article xxxi, however, states that "although the soul is joined to the whole body, nevertheless, there is a certain part of the body where it exercises its functions more particularly

---

[44] AT III, 694; Kenny, 143. In this letter to Elizabeth (June 28, 1643), he further insists on the usefulness of the gravity analogy, in spite of the falsity of such a conception of gravity (AT III, 694; Kenny, 142). Descartes "beg[s] her to feel free to attribute ... extension to the soul because that is simply to conceive it as united to the body. And once she has formed a proper conception of this and experienced it in herself, it will be easy for her to consider that ... the extension of the matter is of a different nature from the extension of thought" (AT III, 694; Kenny, 143). In a letter to Hyperaspistes, he insists that "the mind is co-extensive [*coextendatur*] with an extended body even though it itself has no real extension in the sense of occupying a place and excluding other things from it. How this can be I explained ... by the illustration of gravity concieved as a real quality" (August, 1641: AT III, 434; Kenny, 119–20).

than in all the others ... the brain" (AT XI, 351; CSM I, 339–40).[45]

Arnauld appears also to waver between two views of mind/body union. On the one hand, in his first set of responses to the *Meditations*, Arnauld is afraid that Descartes might have opened himself to the objection that his argument for the real distinction between mind and body proves too much and commits him to the view that "the body [is] merely a vehicle for the soul [*vehiculum animi*]; a view which gives rise to the definition of a person as 'a soul that makes use of a body'" (Fourth Objs.: AT VII, 203; CSM II, 143). He insists on a more substantial union between the two substances. Thus, as it was for Descartes in several contexts, the direct experience that each and everyone has of the union of the mind and the body by means of the sensations, emotions, etc., is evidence for the fact that the mind is "intermingled" with the body:

The mutual and natural correspondence of thoughts in the soul with impressions in the brain, and emotions of the soul with the movements of spirits, suffices to convince us that our soul is not to our body as a sailor is to his vessel; but that these two parts are united together in an extremely great and intimate union, such that they together form a single whole. (*Examen*, 38:141)

Arnauld acknowledges his obvious indebtedness to Descartes for this view – it is the same one found in the Sixth Meditation. Arnauld elaborates: the sailor in his vessel, should it be damaged, will certainly be saddened by this fact; but the saddness in this case presupposes a knowledge of the damage on the part of the sailor. This, Arnauld insists, is different from the experience of pain one feels on breaking one's arm: "Bodily pain is a distressing feeling that does not at all require that the soul knows what it is happening in the body; but which, on the contrary, causes the soul to perceive it" (*Examen*, 38:141).

On the other hand, as Arnauld's account of sensation outlined above indicates, he seems committed to the view that the brain is the "principal seat" of the mind. It is on the occasion of certain

---

[45] For a more thorough discussion of this issue, see Margaret D. Wilson, *Descartes* (London: Routledge and Kegan Paul, 1978), pp. 204–20. That Descartes held two views on mind/body union is well argued by Ruth Mattern, "Descartes' Correspondence with Elizabeth: Concerning Both the Union and Distinction of Mind and Body", in Michael Hooker, ed., *Descartes: Critical and Interpretive Essays* (Baltimore: Johns Hopkins University Press, 1978), pp. 212–22.

movements in the brain, communicated thereto by the nerves from the sense organs and nerve-endings, that the mind has certain "perceptions". It is clear, however, as the above passages indicate, that on either view, for Arnauld (as for Descartes) mind/body union is simply the "natural correspondence" between thoughts in the soul and motions in the brain. Whether the soul is extended throughout the body or "localized" in the brain, to say that a soul is "united" with a body is simply to say that there is a correspondence between motions in that body and *cogitationes* in that soul.

When pressed by Elizabeth on the *causal* issue, Descartes either begs the question or offers obscure and condescending suggestions. It seems, however, that if one takes Descartes' view to be that the brain (in particular, the pineal gland) is the "seat" of the soul (and this seems to be the view most clearly and consistently formulated by Descartes, as well as being the more "scientific" one [cf. *L'Homme*: AT XI, 176-7; CSM I, 106]), while the union consists simply in the correspondence between certain bodily (brain) states and certain mental states, Descartes' answer to the causal question seems to be that it is by "natural institution", by the will of God, that such correspondence occurs.[46] The causal relationship (i.e. correspondence) between body and mind is the result of an arrangement by God:

My final observation is that any given movement occurring in the part of the brain that immediately affects the mind produces just one corresponding sensation; and hence the best system that could be devised is that it should produce the one sensation which, of all possible sensations, is most especially and most frequently conducive to the preservation of the healthy man. And experience shows that the sensations which nature has given us are all of this kind; and so there is absolutely nothing to be found in them that does not bear witness to the power and goodness of God. (Med. VI: AT VII, 87; CSM II, 60)

Later, in the same Meditation, he notes that God is responsible for the fact that certain movements in the brain are associated with certain thoughts (sensations, pains, etc.) (Med. VI: AT VII, 87-8; CSM II, 60). It is important to note that Descartes maintains in these contexts that there is a real causal interaction between mind and body. "[God] does not transmit the ideas to me either directly from

[46]Cf. Wilson, *op. cit.*, pp. 207ff.

himself, or indirectly ... they are produced by corporeal things" (Med. VI: AT VII, 79; CSM II, 55).[47]

When confronted with this question of mind/body causality in the context of a strict dualism of substances, most orthodox Cartesians, like Descartes, simply referred the interaction to God. Seeing that, on Cartesian principles, an explanation of causal interaction was problematic, and that such interaction (in some sense of the term) nevertheless obviously takes place, Cartesians such as Rohault, Le Grand, and others called upon God to support "interaction".[48] Arnauld, in this general respect, is no different: "The body and the soul are united together by the will of the Creator. It is a consequence of this union that their modifications are reciprocal, which is necessary if they are together to form but a single whole" (*Examen*, 38:140). However, he empties the notion of "interaction" of any real causal import. On the question of mind body interaction, Arnauld turns occasionalist.

In the *Examen*, he firmly states that the movements of the body do not cause sensations (*perceptions*) in the soul: "since the motion of a body cannot have any other real effect than to move another body ... it cannot cause any effect in a spiritual soul" (38:146). On the question of whether, then, it is the soul itself which forms its sensations on the occasion of bodily movements, or whether God provides them on such occasions, he strongly argues that God provides them. How can it be that the mind produces its own *perceptions* when clearly it does not always have them at will and when it wants them? Many are involuntary and appear whether we want them or not; other times, try as hard as we may, certain perceptions are just not forthcoming. Moreover, for the soul to be able to produce its own sensations on the occasion of certain bodily movements, it would first be necessary for the mind to have knowledge of these movements, to "perceive" the motions before producing the sensation. But clearly this is not what happens. There is no intervening cognitive act which takes place between the bodily motions and the sensation (*Examen*, 38:147). Finally, on the supposition that the mind has the power to provide itself with all its sensations, it would be impossible "for it to give them to itself so opportunely and with so marvelous a promptitude" (*Examen*, 38:147). The mind would not know when it ought to produce which sensation, since it does not know which perceptions do and

[47] Cf. Letter to Clerselier, Jan, 12, 1646: AT IX-1, 213.
[48] See Watson, *The Downfall of Cartesianism*, Chapter 5.

ought to follow (*par l'ordre établi dans la nature*) which corporeal movements in the sense organs.

Since there is clearly no cause "in nature" of the mind's sensations (both the mind itself and extended bodies being ruled out as causes), God must be the cause of such *perceptions* on the occasion of certain movements in the brain:

> Now it is certain, on the one hand, that our soul never fails, at least ordinarily, to have perceptions of light, colors, sounds and odors when certain corporeal objects strike our senses; that is to say, as we are informed by anatomy, when they cause motions which travel to the brain. And it is clear, on the other hand, that things being thus, no other natural causes could be assigned to these perceptions which our soul has of sensible objects than either these disturbances which occur in our sense organs, or our soul itself. Now, I am able to say that it can be neither the one nor the other, as we have just shown. It only remains for us to understand that it must be that God desired to oblige himself to cause in our soul all the perceptions of sensible qualities every time certain motions occur in the sense organs, according to the laws which he himself has established in nature. (*Examen*, 38:147–8)

Arnauld reiterates this position in VFI: "It can hardly be doubted that it is God who gives us our perception of light, sound and other sensible qualities, as well as of pain, hunger, and thirst, although this is on the occasion of what take place in our sense organs or in the constitution of our body" (VFI, 349). He notes that the body is not a "real" or physical cause, but only a "moral" cause of effects in the soul, "a certain and infallible occasion for what happens in our soul" (*Examen*, 38:150).

Thus, on the issue of mind/body interaction, Arnauld is an occasionalist. Whereas Descartes and other Cartesians maintained the reality of a causal mind/body relationship and simply had recourse to God in establishing this interaction, Arnauld denies the reality of mind/body *causal* interaction and insists that such "interaction" is merely as correspondence continuously maintained by God.[49] Whereas

---

[49] Cf. also *Logique*, I, ix. He presents a somewhat different view of what the occasionalist position is in a letter to Leibniz, March 4, 1687. See Leibniz, *Discourse on Metaphysics/ Correspondence with Arnauld/Monadology*, George R. Montgomery, trans. (LaSalle Open Court, 1980), p. 173. Arnauld, however, was not a complete occasionalist. He did maintain that there is real causal activity between bodies, and even attacked the theory of occasional causes in his *Dissertation sur les miracles* and in the *Réflexions philosophiques et théologiques*. See Bouillier, *op. cit.*, vol. 2, p. 192.

Descartes saw God as having instituted once and for all a causal relationship (i.e. correspondence) between the body and the mind, Arnauld demands God's recurring activity on the occasions of bodily motions.[50]

6 Conclusion

Arnauld clearly accepts both the method and the metaphysics of Cartesianism in a manner that precludes seeing him as a reluctant defender of a philosophical system for which he has no real sympathy. Indeed, Arnauld's commitment to Cartesianism is whole-hearted and enthusiastic, and Cartesian philosophy deeply informs his thought on important philosophical issues, and even on many theological questions. His debate with Malebranche on the nature of ideas and the correct analysis of perceptual acquaintance is a debate between two who saw themselves as "Cartesians", who accepted the fundamental principles of Descartes' philosophy. Malebranche makes certain important modifications in the Cartesian system, particularly with his theory of ideas (see Chapter 3).[51] Arnauld's theory of perception (Chapters 5 and 6) is more orthodox. Arnauld himself insists that his conception of ideas (and the corresponding perceptual direct realism) is in line with what Descartes has to say about ideas and perception. Before turning to Arnauld's theory, however, it is important to look first at the view against which he is arguing.

---

[50]Cf. VFI, 209: "I insist ... that it is God who has provided [perceptions] on the occasion of corporeal motions which occur in the sense organs and in the brain." Also, cf. *Défense*, 38:395–8. Arnauld does not seem to think that this is at all in conflict with what he has said regarding the soul as a substance entirely active. When the soul is considered as it is united to and interacting with the body, hence in regard to sensations (which are still mental operations or *activities*), Arnauld holds this occasionalist position. With regard to the soul in itself, however, its activity is entirely its own: "Our soul is able to give itself new modifications with regard to its ideas as well as with regard to its inclinations" (VFI, 346). God has given it the *pouvoir de se donner quelques' unes de ses idées* (VFI, 347). Nonetheless, Arnauld's position regarding the perception of an external object by an "entirely active substance" is thus confusing: it appears to include both the active production of perceptions by the mind itself (VFI, 290–91) as well as the passive reception of *perceptions* (sensations) caused by God on the occasion of motions in the brain.

[51]For a study of Malebranche as a Cartesian, see Alquié, *Le Cartésianisme de Malebranche.* See also Radner, *Malebranche*, pp. 1–14.

III
Ideas and perception in Malebranche

The doctrine of ideas put forth by Nicholas Malebranche in *De la recherche de la vérité* has been subjected to various interpretations since the work's initial publication in 1674.[1] It appears, *prima facie*, to lead to an awkward, high problematic, even "visionary" theory of perception, whereby the mind, cut off from any kind of contact with the external world, lives in and knows only a realm of intelligible (non-material) entities. More acute interpreters have seen his account of the role of ideas in perception as a representationalism similar in many respects to certain "causal" or sense-data theories. On both of these readings (each of which has some basis in the texts), ideas are, for Malebranche, the direct and immediate objects of perception: direct and immediate, in the sense that the mind's apprehension of the idea is not inferentially based on the non-inferential apprehension of some *tertium quid* standing between the mind and the idea. Arnauld himself, as we shall see, appears to waver between the two readings in his critique of the *Recherche*; a critique which, more generally, focuses on Malebranche's notion that an idea can be a perceptual object distinct from both the mental act of perceiving and the mind itself.

7 Ideas and sensations in perception

Malebranche's doctrine of ideas is ambiguous from the beginning. In Book I, Chapter i of the *Recherche*, the term 'idea' refers to two kinds of entities: those which represent objects external to the mind and allow us to see their properties; and "sensations", which are merely modifications of the mind and do not represent anything in the external world.

[1] The *Recherche* was published in several editions, the sixth (1712) being the last one to appear in Malebranche's lifetime.

We can likewise say that the ideas of the soul are of two kinds. The first, which are called pure perceptions, are, as it were, accidental to the soul; they do not make an impression on it and do not sensibly modify it. The second, which are called sensible, make a more or less vivid impression on it. Such are pleasure and pain, light and colors, tastes, odors, and so on. For it will be seen later on that sensations are nothing but modes of the mind, and it is for this reason that I call them *modifications* of the mind. (*Recherche*, Book I, Chapter i, Section 1: OC I, 42; LO, 2 [translation modified])

Later in the work, however, Malebranche draws a distinction between ideas proper and sensations; a distinction which, as we shall see, is both ontological and eptistemological. In Book I, Chapter ii, he notes that sensations often distract the mind from its contemplation of ideas. In Book III, Chapter vi, he differentiates the two elements which compose perceptual awareness:

When we perceive something sensible, two things are found in our perception: *sensation* and pure *idea*. The sensation is a modification of our soul, and it is God who causes it in us. He can cause this modification even though He does not have it Himself, because He sees in the idea He has of our soul that it is capable of it. As for the idea found in conjuction with the sensation, it is in God, and we see it because it pleases God to reveal it to us. God joins the sensation to the idea when objects are present so that we may believe them to be present and that we may have all the feelings and passions that we should have in relation to them. (*Rech.*, III ii, 6: OC I, 445; LO, 234)

Arnauld recognizes the ambiquity in Malebranche's definition of 'idea': "It is troublesome to give the name of the genus to one species and not to give it at all to the other species" (VFI, 187). Malebranche himself is aware of the equivocation:

The word *idea* is equivocal. Sometimes I take it as anything that represents some object to the mind, whether clearly or confusedly. More generally I take it for anything that is the immediate object of the mind. But I also take it in the most precise and restricted sense, that is, as anything that represents things to the mind in a way so clear that we can discover by simple perception whether such and such modifications belong to them. (*Rech.*, Eclaircissement III: OC III, 44; LO, 561)

The ambiguity thus stems from several different senses of 'idea'. Taken broadly to mean *tout que l'esprit aperçoit immédiatement*, it includes both pure ideas and sensations (I refer to this as 'broad sense *A*'). Yet, as the paragraph immediately above indicates, there is another broad sense of 'idea' according to which it signifies *tout ce qui représent à l'esprit quelque objet, soit clairement, soit confusement.* That is, whatever has a representational content, however minimal and obscure, can be called an idea in this second broad sense of the term ('broad sense B'). In the strict sense of 'idea' (*le sens le plus précis et le plus réservé*), only that which represents in a clear and distinct manner is an idea.

All sensations qualify as "ideas" in broad sense A. As for broad sense B, Malebranche is not entirely clear regarding the representational character and value of sensations. There seem to be three possibilities which need to be distinguished here.

On the one hand, he sometimes *identifies* sensation with a certain *jugement naturel* which is, in effect, a mental modification or correction of a corporeal image located in the fundus of the eye (this view of natural judgement in sensation is found in the first edition of the *Recherche*). The sensation is just that judgement which, in the sense perception of a cube, for example, allows one to perceive a three-dimensional object with all its angles equal on the occasion of a two-dimensional image with unequal angles occuring on the retinal nerve (*Rech.*, I, vii, 4: OC I, 96–7; LO, 34). *Je parle quelquefois des sensations comme des jugements naturels.* By identifying this corrective and modifying judgement with sensation, he thereby gives a sensation a representational content, one which, moreover, possesses a modicum of truth regarding the external world: it seems to tell us something about what is happening in external space. *Ils sont plus fidèles qu'en toute autre recontre.* This seems, however, to apply only to such judgement-sensations regarding distance, size, and figure:

> It is certain, then, that the judgements we make concerning extension, figure, and motion of bodies include some measure of truth. But the same is not true of those concerning light, colors, tastes, odors, and all the other sensible qualities, for truth is never encountered here. (*Rech.*, I, x: OC I, 122; LO, 48)

And the representational content here, this sensuous geometry, is certainly less clear and precise than the geometry based on the pure perception of external ideas in God. Thus, these sensations also warrant the label 'idea' in broad sense B; but they do not warrant the label in the strict sense.

With regard to sensations such as lights, colors, tastes, sounds, odors, pain, etc. (i.e. 'sensation' in the more ordinary sense of the term), however, a further ambiguity appears. Malebranche distinguishes betwen the sensation proper and a sensation/judgement complex. The former is "the passion, sensation, or perception of the soul, i.e. what each of us feels when near fire" (*Rech.*, I, x, 6: OC I, 129; LO, 52). What Malebranche has in mind here is the sensuous phenomenon itself, or what he calls the *qualité sensible*. These sensations proper contain no element of truth regarding the external world, and possess no representational content. They are only what happen in the mind on the occasion of certain bodily (brain) motions. (It will be in this very strict sense that I use the term 'sensation' in my discussion below.) Malebranche, however, notes that every sensation (e.g. pain, heat) is accompanied by an involuntary *jugement naturel* that, e.g., "what [the soul] perceives is in the hand and in the fire" (*Rech.*, I, x, 6: OC I, 130; LO, 52). (This account of natural judgement is found in the second and all later editions of the *Recherche*). The spontaneous judgement that the sensation (*passion*) which modifies the mind is in the sense organ or in the external object itself so closely and constantly accompanies the sensation that it is often "confounded" with the sensation proper and the two are taken for one and the same thing (*Rech.*, I, xiv, 2: OC I, 157; LO, 68-9). This natural judgement (which must be distinguished from, but is often followed by, a "voluntary judgement") is always false (*Rech.*, I, xiv, 1: OC I, 156; LO, 67). The sensation/judgement compound itself, often called a *sensation* by Malebranche (*Rech.*, I, x 6: OC I, 130; LO 52), clearly possesses a representational content of some kind, however false and obscure. The judgement, in a sense, attaches a content to the sensation proper, to the *qualité sensible*, thereby making it an intentional (or object-directed) phenomenon, e.g. 'this pain is in that hand'. With this extended conception of *sensation*, sensations might be called "ideas" in broad sense B: they *représentent à l'espirit ... confusement*.[2]

However, in the two above cases where sensations represent (i.e. sensation *qua jugement naturel* and sensation *qua passion/jugement* complex), they do not do so in a way that is "so clear that one can discover, from an ordinary survey, whether such-and-such modifi-

[2] For a discussion of sensation and natural judgement in Malebranche, see Thomas M. Lennon, "Philosophical Commentary" to his translation (with Paul J. Olscamp) of the *Recherche: The Search after Truth* (Columbus: Ohio State University Press, 1980), pp. 773ff.; and, by the same author, "Representationalism, Judgement and Perception of Distance: Further to Yolton and McRae", *Dialogue*, 19 (1980), 151–62.

cations belong [to the objects]." And sensations proper (i.e. the *passions de l'ame* which form part of the *passion/jugement* complex), such as heat, pain, etc., do not represent at all. Thus, strictly speaking, on this epistemic basis, ideas are to be distinguished from sensations.

Sensations are no more than modifications of the soul which occur in relation to what takes place in the body to which that soul is joined. More specifically, these modifications are caused by God, who acts on the occasion of an external body being present to and affecting the body. Pleasure, pain, heat, sadness, colors, our "passions and natural inclinations" are all *modalitez ou modifications de l'âme* (*Réponse*, Chapter VI: OC VI, 55). They are perceived solely by "inner sensation" (*sentiment interieur*), being simply modes of being of the mind itself. They are, in effect, "but the soul itself existing in this or that way." It follows from this, Malebranche believes, that sensations cannot represent anything external to the mind. Our perceptions of heat, color, etc. do not represent anything real in the external object; they tell us less about the world than about the mind itself (that it is capable of such-and-such modifications).

Ideas, on the other hand, are not modifications of the soul, but are in God.[3] Thus, they differ ontologically from sensations. Furthermore, ideas are capable of representing to the mind to which they are revealed objects external to the mind (their epistemic difference). This is made possible by identifying them with the ideas present in God's mind. God, being the creator of the universe, must contain within himself the ideas (intelligible archetypes) of all that he creates. Hence the veracity and representational value of *our* ideas (i.e. the ideas God chooses to reveal to us) of the objects making up the created world is assured. Through the idea of a body one is capable of knowing the nature of that body *qua* finite extended matter: its properties (both actual and possible) as a body extended in three dimensions. "A thing is known by its idea when, while examining this idea, it is possible to know by an ordinary survey its general properties, what it contains and what it excludes; and, when applying oneself to examining its general properties, it is possible to discover therein particular properties to infinity" (*Réponse*, Chapter XXIII, Section ii: OC VI, 160).

---

[3] I do not examine in this chapter Malebranche's argument that the ideas which allow us to perceive external objects are God's ideas. He reaches this conclusion by considering and eliminating various alternative theories (including the traditional Cartesian account). Cf. *Recherche*, III, ii, 1–6.

It is important to note that the properties and qualities of objects represented by ideas are strictly properties of extension: quantifiable properties (length, breadth, figure, etc.), the geometric features of things which Locke and others referred to as "primary qualities". Sensations, on the other hand, are in no way similar to those properties in the object which cause them. Thus, ideas represent real qualities of extended objects external to the mind; sensations do not, but are merely effects in the soul of motions in the body. In order to know the modifications of which a body is capable, one need only consult the idea representing it (*Réponse*, XXIII, iii: OC VI, 161). The knowledge that one obtains of objects via ideas is "clear and perfect"; the information that one obtains via sensations is "confused" and imperfect, and tells one only what is happening within oneself:

The mind knows objects in only two ways: through illumination [*par lumière*] and through sensation. It sees things through *illumination* when it has a clear idea of them, and when by consulting this idea it can discover all the properties of which these things are capable. It sees things through *sensation* when it finds no clear idea of these things in itself to be consulted, when it is thus unable to discover their properties clearly, and when it knows them only through a confused sensation, without illumination and without evidence. Through illumination and through a clear idea, the mind sees numbers, extension, and the essences of things ... The things the mind sees through illumination or through a clear idea it perceives in a very perfect fashion ... But what the mind perceives through sensation is never clearly known to it ... because of the inadequacy of the idea, which is extremely obscure and confused. (*Rech.*, Ecl. X: OC III, 141–2; LO, 621)

Note that by identifying knowledge by idea with clear, true and "adequate" knowledge, Malebranche has definitionally combined notions which, for Descartes, were distinct until proven otherwise. The idea of an object, for Malebranche, is necessarily a clear and *true* idea of it. It seems that certain skeptical problems that Descartes found necessary to deal with by proving God's existence and veracity are hereby circumvented. For example, Descartes' "evil genius" of Meditation I impugns the reliability of the clear and distinct conception of mathematical truths and of essences. Clarity and distinctness of conception, on this radical skeptical hypothesis, may not be a reliable guide to truth. Malebranche, on the other hand, disarms the "evil genius" hypothesis from the start by identifying the clear and distinct conception of a thing with the "true" and "perfect" conception of it.

The sense perception of an object necessarily involves both a clear idea of extension and sensations. Upon the presence of an object to the body, God both reveals to the mind an idea, "which represents its essence", and causes some sensations "that make us judge that it exists – for there is always a *pure idea* and a *confused sensation* in the knowledge we have of the existence of beings" (*Rech.*, Ecl. X: OC III, 142; LO, 621). The sensations, in a manner of speaking, "color" the idea (which is general), particularize it, and make it the idea of this or that object. Malebranche's favorite example is the perception one may have of the sun: "when we have a vivid sensation of light attached or related to an intelligible circle, distant through a certain intelligible space, and rendered sensible by different colors, we see the sun" (*Réponse*, VI, iii: OC VI, 55). In the *Résponse*, he further notes that "in our perception of material objects, two things are found: a confused sensation, and a clear idea ... [this] clear idea of extension ... is rendered sensible or visible by the color" (*Réponse*, VI, i: OC VI, 55–6; cf. also TL, Letter I, Remark xiv: OC VI, 241).

In Eclaircissement X, in what may be either a modification of or an elaboration upon his theory, Malebranche speaks of an infinite intelligible (i.e. non-material) extension located in God, and of bounded (or limited) parts of this infinite extension. He denies that there is in God a multiplicity of particular, discrete ideas, one for each object in the world:

It should not be imagined that the intelligible world is related to the sensible, material world in such a way that there is an intelligible sun, for example, or an intelligible horse or tree intended to represent to us the sun or a horse or a tree, or that everyone who sees the sun necessarily sees this hypothetical intelligible sun. (*Rech.*, Ecl. X: OC III, 153; LO, 627

He makes this point in response to the anticipated objection that if there were a particular intelligible sun in God, it would have to be able actually to move and change its size in order to account for the fact that the sun appears greater when it is near the horizon than when it is high in the sky. But such *real* motion and figure in God is impossible. Malebranche suggests, instead, that God "contains in Himself" an infinite, homogenous, non-material extension which can be divided and bounded into finite, intelligible, extended figures. And *any* finite extended figure can be represented on this infinite intelligible extension: "Since the mind can perceive a part of this intelligible extension that God contains, it surely can perceive in God all figures; for all finite intelligible extension is necessarily an intelligible figure, since figure is nothing but the boundary of extension" (*Rech.*, Ecl. X: OC III, 152; LO, 626).

The ideas of particular extended things are, thus, finite parts of a single infinite Idea of extension in God. With regard to a single and isolated act of perception, these finite intelligible parts of the one infinite intelligible extension function in fundamentally the same way as might discrete, individual ideas of particular extended bodies. Essentially, the components of perception remain the same: an idea, an intelligible extended figure (a bounded sector of the infinite intelligible extension), is particularized through sensation, and serves as the direct and immediate object of the mind.

We see or sense a given body when its idea, i.e. when some figure composed of intelligible and general extension, becomes sensible and particular through color or some other sensible perception ... Thus, when I said that we see different bodies through the knowledge we have of God's perfections that represent them, I did not exactly mean that there are in God certain particular ideas that represent each body individually, and that we see such an idea when we see the body; for we certainly could not see this body as sometimes great, sometimes small, sometimes round, sometimes square, if we saw it through a particular idea that would always be the same. But I do say that we see all things in God through the efficacy of His substance, and particularly sensible things, through God's applying intelligible extension to our mind in a thousand different ways, and that thus intelligible extension contains all the perfections, or rather, all the differences of bodies due to the different sensations that the soul projects on the ideas affecting it upon the occasion of these same bodies. (*Rech.*, Ecl. X: OC III, 152–4; LO, 626–7)

Malebranche's theory of intelligible extension was a great source of conflict between himself and others, especially Arnauld. The *Eclaircissements*, in fact, were added to the third edition of the *Recherche* (1677–8) after Malebranche had received various objections to the original six books of the text. It is not necessary to examine here whether, as Malebranche insists, he always understood ideas to be bounded sectors of an infinite intelligible extension; or whether this represents a subsequent modification of his theory, having previously determined ideas to be discrete intelligible entities in God's mind having a one-to-one correspondence with objects (or kinds) in the world. I am interested here in Malebranche's theory of the role of ideas in perception, and it is sufficient that the distinctions and differences between ideas and sensations have been made clear, and the importance of each to perception noted.

Malebranche offers two arguments for the necessity of ideas in the perception of external objects. The first argument is based on the possibility of existential error in perceptual judgement, and clearly foreshadows the "argument from illusion" (or hallucination) that later representationalists were to offer on behalf of sense-data theory. The argument uses the principle that every perception (and every thought) has an object. That is, whenever the mind perceives or knows or thinks, it is always the perception or knowledge or thought of something. To perceive is to perceive some thing: *voir le néant, voir rien, c'est ne point voir* (TL, I: OC VI, 202; RLA: OC VIII, 910). Malebranche takes the statement 'every perception is the perception of something' to mean that every perception must be the direct and immediate perception of some entity, that there is something ontically present with which the perceiving mind has direct acquaintance. Now it is occasionally the case that one perceives an external object which, in fact, does not actually exist. The point is, as Malebranche notes, that perceptions, in general, do not have any necessary relationship with external objects: "We often have perceptions of certain objects, even though they do not actually exist: our perceptions do not essentially have any relation to them" (RLA: OC VIII, 915). This becomes clear, he continues, in dreams, hallucinations from fevers and madness, and ordinary errors of sense. The perception is there, but there is no corresponding external object: "The sensible view of objects necessarily involves a judgement which might be false ... objects which do not actually exist are really seen, and it is a contradiction that nothingness can be seen. It is evident that to see nothingness, to see nothing, is not to see at all" (TL, I: OC VI, 202). Thus, "what is perceived ... is not nothingness ... It is to our ideas ... that our perceptions have an essential relation" (RLA: OC VIII, 916). Every act of perception must have a direct and immediate object which is really present to the mind. Material bodies cannot be the kind of objects which fill this role, however: if they were, we would never be able to perceive bodies which do not exist (since every perception of a body would have that external body as its immediate object), which contradicts experience. If *A* has a perception of an external object *x*, there is always the possibility that *x* does not exist. But there must always be some *y* present that is immediately and directly perceived by *A*. Otherwise, in the case that *x* does not exist, *A* would be perceiving nothing, which, for Malebranche, is not to perceive. (All perceptions, then, would be veridical and reliable). This *y* is the idea of *x*.

When we think about possible beings, beings which do not actually exist, for example, a flat sun, a square earth, a golden mountain, the circle of the geometers, it is not true that we are thinking of nothing: for ... to think of nothing is not to think at all. Thus, although the soul thinks indirectly about things which do not actually exist, it directly and immediately perceives their ideas. And since these ideas are not nothing, it cannot be said that the soul is thinking of nothing. (RLA: OC VIII, 910)

Thus, to preserve the logical possibility of existential (and qualitative) error in every case of perception; and to explain how it is that one still perceives something, still has a perception, when no external object for that perception actually exists, Malebranche introduces representative ideas distinct from both the mental act of perceiving and the external object (when there is one).[4] The possibility of illusion is preserved by these entities of a special ontological sort: every perception will be the perception of something (an idea), whether or not some corresponding external object exists.

Malebranche's second argument[5] is based on a variation of the principle, prevalent in sixteenth- and seventeenth-century physics, of no action at a distance.[6] Malebranche's application of this principle to

---

[4] The case for qualitative error (to see a square tower in the distance as round) is handled by assimilation to the case of existential error. To see a square tower as round is to see something (roundness) where it does not, in fact, exist; to see something as containing "more reality" than it actually has is, likewise, to see more than exists. Yet if there is not *some* object containing the "greater reality", if there is no "round tower", then there is a perception of nothing ... (cf. RLA: OC VIII, 946–7; *Recherche*: OC II, 100).

[5] There are a number of variations on, and sub-arguments within each major argument. For a thorough discussion of Malebranche's arguments here, see Martial Gueroult, *Malebranche*, 3 vols. (Paris: Aubier, 1955), vol. 1, Chapter 4.

[6] For a discussion of the application of the scientific principle to epistemology, see Yolton, *Perceptual Acquaintance*.

the case of knowledge and perception states, in effect, that the mind cannot know or perceive an object immediately unless that object is "intimately" united with, or present to, the mind; there is no cognition at a distance: "My soul must be united in some manner to whatever it perceives, it must be touched [*touchée*] or affected by it" (TL, I, ii: OC VI, 212). That is, *présence* is a necessary condition for (*préalable à*) perception. But material bodies are not, and cannot be, united with or present to the mind in the necessary manner. Thus, they cannot be the *immediate* objects of perception.

"Present to the mind" is taken by Malebranche, in a literal-minded way, to mean an *ontic* presence. The mind must be where its immediate object is; or that immediate object must be in the mind: "I think everyone agrees that we do not perceive objects external to us by themselves. We see the sun, the stars, and an infinity of objects external to us; and it is not likely that the soul should leave the body to stroll about the heavens as it were, in order to behold all these objects" (*Rech.*, III, ii, 1. 1: OC I, 413; LO, 217). Elsewhere, he speaks of the soul's inability to travel from its body towards distant objects (*Rech.*, I, xiv, 1: OC I, 156; LO, 67).[7] Thus, on the one hand, there is the contingent problem that, "even if it be agreed our souls are extended", the mind is not where the objects of its perceptions are; nor do these objects travel to the mind (Malebranche explicitly argues against this Epicurean alternative).

But Malebranche, being the Cartesian that he is, realizes that there is also – on the other hand – a metaphysical (and not merely a contingent, spatial) barrier between the mind and external objects, and that a local presence would not help in the mind's immediate perception of a material body. One needs ideas to perceive even one's own body (cf. *Recherche* III, ii, 7). "Material things ... certainly cannot be joined to our soul in the way necessary for it to perceive them, because with them extended and the soul unextended, there is no relation between them" (*Rech.*, II, ii, 1. 1: OC I, 417; LO, 219). He presents as an example the mind and the brain: though these are in some sense "united", and locally present to one another, the latter is not perceived by the former. Thus ideas (intelligible, non-material representative entities) are required to supply the "absence" of the

---

[7] Yolton (*ibid.*, Chapters 2 and 3) provides a good discussion of this "walking mind" argument.

material body. These ideas are ontically "present" to the mind in the manner requisite for perception, a manner not possible for material bodies.

Later in the *Recherche*, it seems as if the presence required were a causal presence: only objects which are capable of entering into a causal relationship with the mind can be "united" with the mind in the manner necessary for direct cognition. For something to be perceptible, he notes, *il pût agir immédiatement dans l'ame* (*Rech.*, IV xi, 3: OC II, 100; LO, 320. Cf. also RLA: OC VIII, 961). He often claims that ideas alone can "affect" the soul. This, of course, ties in with, and supports, the metaphysical reading of 'presence': Malebranche insisted on the impossibility of a real causal relationship between extended matter and unextended mind. Hence, again, only unextended ideas can be "present" to mind in the requisite manner (i.e. causally related), and for the same reason.[8] In either case, the kind of union or presence (ontic or causal) necessary for perception is possible only between entities of the same ontological kind. Material bodies are incapable of being immediately present to, or intimately united with, the mind because of the radical difference between mind and matter.[9]

Note that the second argument, like the first, incorporates the principle that every act of perception must have some present object which it directly and immediately perceives. Since we obviously do have perceptions of material objects (the sun, the stars, etc.); and since these material objects cannot be united to the mind in the manner requisite for *immediate* perception; and since every act of perception must be the direct and immediate perception of some really-present object (*voir le néant, voir rien, c'est ne point voir*), there must be some

---

[8] This notion of causally active ideas does not appear in the *Recherche* until the fifth edition (1700). For a fuller critical exposition of Malebranche's view of the causal efficacy of ideas, see Alquié, *Le Cartésianisme de Malebranche*, pp. 208ff.; André Robinet, *Système et existence dans l'oeuvre de Malebranche* (Paris: J. Vrin, 1965), p. 259ff.; Gueroult, *Malebranche*, vol. 1, Chapters 9, 10.

[9] This skirts the question of the ontological status of ideas in Malebranche's system. Since they are neither minds nor modifications of any mind (Malebranche insists that ideas are modifications neither of God's mind nor of the human mind), in what sense, then, are ideas of the right ontological type for "intimate union" with the human mind? For a discussion of this, see Watson, *The Downfall of Cartesiansim*, pp. 99–100. And for a discussion of this second argument for ideas, see Watson, p. 101; Yolton, *Perceptual Acquaintance*, Chapter 3; and Radner, *Malebranche*, p. 13.

non-material object present to the mind which supplies the absence of the material object and which is the direct and immediate object of perception. What Malebranche is concerned with here is not simply the possibility of existential error, but the possibility of perception of bodies in general. It is, in a manner of speaking, a "transcendental" argument for representative entities (*êtres représentatifs*) as the conditions for the possibility of the perception of external objects. The perception of an actually-existing external object is, in this argument, assumed (see the passage above from *Rech.*, III, ii, 1. 1: OC I, 413). Such a perception cannot be direct and immediate, because of the impossibility of the requisite kind of union. But there must be some direct object: hence, ideas.

Malebranche thus introduces *être représentatifs* into perception for a variety of philosophical reasons. They provide a solution to the problem of illustion and hallucination (now a standard issue in the philosophy of perception, one with which any theory of perception must deal). And they account for the fact that we actually do come to perceive external bodies, given what, at least to Malebranche, appear *prima facie* to be serious obstacles to such perception (no perception at a distance, etc.). These ideas, then, serve as representative proxies, standing in the mind for the external objects which it cannot perceive *en eux-mêmes* and serving as its direct and immediate objects in perception. And the ideas which perform this function are in God, a position Malebranche holds, as we saw, in order to insure their veracity and, thus, counteract any skeptical problems that might arise (see *Rech.*, IV, xi, 3: OC II, 100; LO, 320).

8 *Malebranche's representationalism*

It is clear from the foregoing that the ideas necessary for perception are distinct from both the perceiving mind and the external object, yet "present" to the former. But Malebranche appears, *prima facie*, to have constructed a theory of perception which precludes perceptual contact of any kind (direct or indirect) with the external world. He seems, that is, to have surrounded the perceiving mind with what Arnauld was to call a "palace of ideas". This is, however, a superficial reading of Malebranche's doctrine of the vision in God and the role of divine ideas in perception, one that ignores much of what Malebranche says regarding the perception of material bodies. A careful reading of Malebranche reveals that he holds, for the most part, a theory of representationalism very much like the causal or sense-data theories of perception, according to which external objects *are* perceived, albeit indirectly.

The "simplistic" (first) reading of Malebranche can be reconstructed as follows. Ideas (which exist in God's mind), once they have become particularized through accompanying sensations (or, alternatively, once a segment of the infinite intelligible extension has become bounded and particularized by means of sensation), are the sole objects of perception. Because of their representative value (guaranteed by their divine nature), it is possible, by a form of inference, to discover what the external world created by God is like. But we never perceive this world. One perceives (sees, hears, etc.) only intelligible representative entities, not external objects. In perception, the finite perceiving mind is in contact solely with a world of divine ideas "colored" by sensations. God's mind, being "the place of finite minds", contains the objects of perception.

A better idea of this account, often imputed to Malebranche, can be obtained by examining the charges leveled against him by some of his critics. It is clear that Arnauld sometimes opts for this reading of Malebranche. He notes that Malebranche

suddenly transports us to unknown lands, where men do not have any true knowledge of one another, nor of their own bodies, nor of the sun and the stars which God has created; but where each sees, instead of the men toward whom he turns his eyes, only intelligible men; instead of the sun and the stars which God has created, only an intelligible sun and intelligible stars; and, instead of the material spaces which are between us and the sun, only intelligible spaces. (VFI, 227–8)

After much philosophizing on the nature of these representative entities, after having marched them around everywhere and having been able to place them only in God, the only fruit that he gathers from all this is not an explanation of how we see material things, which alone was what was sought, but rather the conclusion that our mind is incapable of perceiving them, and that we live in a perceptual illusion in believing that we see the material things that God has created when we look at them, that is to say when we turn our eyes toward them; and meanwhile seeing, instead of them, only intelligible bodies. (VFI, 229)

Malebranche, according to Arnauld, holds that the mind sees nothing, nor is it able to see anything, besides the intelligible entities intimately united to it. In Chapter XI of *Des vraies et des fausses idées* he accuses Malebranche of completely cutting the mind off from the material world which God intended it to perceive and know and act upon. "It is material food and material beverage that I need to take through a material mouth in order to maintain the body which I animate . . . and not intelligible food and intelligible beverage, which my mind would see being received by an intelligible mouth in an intelligible body" (VFI, 231).

John Locke, in his *Examination of P. Malebranche's Opinion,*[10] offers a similar interpretation of Malebranche's theory of ideas and its epistemological ramifications. According to Malebranche, Locke notes, "we see nothing but God and ideas; and it is impossible for us to know that there is anything else in the universe; for since we see, and can see nothing but God and ideas, how can we know there is any thing else which we neither do nor can see?"[11] On this theory, one never sees the sun, or any external body, but only the idea of the sun.[12] The point of this line of criticism is not that Malebranche has, in spite of his intentions, closed off the perceiving mind from any kind of perceptual contact with the external world, but rather that such a radical skepticism regarding the perception of the external world was a necessary and (to Malebranche) acceptable consequence of the account of ideas he wished to put forth.

Malebranche himself seems to furnish ample evidence to support this simplistic reading of his theory of ideas. He notes that "the material world we animate is not the one we see [*voyons*] when we look at it [*regardons*], i.e. when we turn the body's eyes toward it. The body we see is an intelligible body and there are intelligible spaces between this intelligible body and the intelligible sun we see [*voyons*], just as there are material spaces between our body and the sun we look at [*regardons*]" (*Rech.*, Ecl. VI: OC III, 61; LO, 572–3). "The objects we immediately see [*voit*] are very different from those we see externally, or rather from those we think we see or look at [*regarde*]; for in one sense it is true that we do not see these latter" (*Rech.*, IV, xi, 3: OC II, 99; LO, 320). In Eclaircissement X, Malebranche states that "the soul

---

[10] *The Works of Johna Lock*, 10 vols. (London: Tegg, 1823), vol. 9, pp. 211–55.
[11] *Ibid.*, p. 239.
[12] *Ibid.*, p. 221.

can only see the sun to which it is immediately joined, only that sun that like it occupies no place" (*Rech.*, Ecl. X: OC III, 149; LO, 625). Theodore, Malebranche's spokesman in the *Entretiens sur la Métaphysique et sur la Religion*, insists that "there is as much difference between the desk which I see [*voi*] and the desk which you think you see as there is between your mind and body ... while our bodies walk in a corporeal world, our minds for their part are unceasingly transported into an intelligible world" (*Entretiens*, I, iv-v: OC XII, 36).[13] "It is the intelligible world which we contemplate, which we admire, which we sense. But the world which we look at [*le monde que nous regardons*], or which we consider when we turn our heads on all sides, is simply matter" (*Entretiens*, I, v: OC XII, 38).[14]

The distinction Malebranche is working with here rests on the difference between *voir*, to see, to perceive, and *regarder*, to look at or to turn one's attention towards. In the passages cited above, *voir* is used with respect to intelligible entities, representative ideas; *regarder*, on the other hand, appears in conjunction with external bodies. Hence, it seems as though the only objects of perception are ideas: only intelligible entities are ever perceived (seen, heard, etc.). One merely turns one's attention (or sense organs) towards, or looks at, external objects. Those who believe that they are in perceptual contact of any kind with the external world are mistaken; what is actually seen differs essentially from that toward which the eyes are turned. *Les corps qu'on voit ne sont nullement ceux qu'on regarde* ("The bodies which are seen are in no way those which are looked at"). Ideas are perceived *instead of* bodies.

It is clear, however, that Malebranche does not intend to assert that there is no perception whatsoever of external objects. He is emphatic in asserting that we do perceive them, *mais non en eux-mêmes*. The passages quoted above need to be taken in conjuction with a distinction that, for Malebranche, parellels and works upon his use of *voir* and *regarder*; the distinction, that is, between direct and indirect (or immediate and mediate) objects of perception. Malebranche often refers to ideas as the direct objects of perception and external things as the indirect objects of perception. Perception involves "two kinds of

---

[13] Quoted from *Dialogues on Metaphysics*, Willis Doney, trans. (New York: Abaris Books, 1980), p. 29.
[14] *Ibid.*, p. 31.

beings: those our soul sees immediately, and those it knows only by means of [*par le moyen de*] the former" (*Rech.*, I, xiv, 2: OC I, 159: LO, 69). In one of his responses to Arnauld, Malebranche distinguishes, as he does in the *Recherche*, between *l'objet immédiat et direct* of the mind and *l'objet . . . exterieur que l'idée représente* (RLA: OC VIII, 910). Thus, although one always perceives directly (*voit*) ideas, and only looks at (*regarde*) external objects, external objects are, in perception, the mind's indirect and ultimate objects. This is accomplished by means of the representative character of ideas, which allows them to mediate between the mind of the perceiver and the external world.

Malebranche's use of the terms 'direct' and 'indirect' to describe objects of perception appears to commit him to something like a causal or sense-data theory of perception (making the necessary adjustments for his occasionalist theory of causation).[15] When an external body is present to (or in contact with) the perceiver's own body, God reveals to the perceiver's mind the idea (or a part of the infinite intelligible extension) representing that body, "colored" (or made particular) by the sensation which he has produced in the mind on the same occasion. This idea/sensation complex is what is directly perceived when the body's senses are turned towards an external object. Yet the latter is still *indirectly* perceived. And although Malebranche is rather vague on just how this *indirect* acquaintance is achieved, on the inferential (or other cognitive) processes that take place in the presence of a representative idea, he is clear on the fact that an object indirectly perceived is still an object perceived. In other words, while ideas, in non-reflective veridical perception, are claimed to be the direct and immediate objects of the mind, they are not claimed to be the *ultimate* objects of perception. Malebranche notes that "bodies are seen [*on voit les corps*] but not in themselves immediately and directly . . . It is not wrong to believe that they are seen; it is only wrong to believe that they are seen directly and in themselves: for they are often seen, but only indirectly" (RLA: OC VIII, 959). If the perception of an external object involves inference from mental entities "intimately united to our mind" and immediately seen, it remains, nonetheless, the *perception* of an external object. On Malebranche's view, the (ultimate) object of perception is that which

[15] For a characterization of the causal theory, see H. H. Price, *Perception* (London: Methuen, 1932), Chapter 4; R. J. Hirst, *The Problems of Perception* (London: George Allen and Unwin, 1959), Chapter 6.

the idea represents, not the idea itself. *L'esprit apperçoit ce qui lui est representé* (RLA: OC VIII, 920). Naturally, whether or not such a position is tenable will depend on the proponent's success in explaining or justifying the move from the directly-perceived ideas to the ultimately- and indirectly-perceived external world.

The essential difference between this reading of Malebranche's theory and that offered by Arnauld and Locke is that on this reading, but not on that of Arnauld and Locke, Malebranche uses the distinction often found in medieval and early modern theories of perception between what one perceives and that by means of which one perceives it.[16] On this reading, Malebranche distinguishes between what one ultimately (though indirectly) *perceives* and that initial, direct *perception* which is necessary for accomplishing the former ('perceives' and 'perception', it seems, used univocally and qualified as either "direct" or "indirect").[17] Ideas ("intelligible objects") are what are

---

[16] See St Thomas, *Summa Theologiae*, Part I, Q. 85, Art. 2, where he distinguishes between *id quo intelligitur* and *id quod intelligitur*.

[17] The general representationalist interpretation of Malebranche's theory of perception outlined above is favored by most recent commentators. See Gueroult, *Malebranche*, vol. 1, pp. 88–9; A. O. Lovejoy, "Representative Ideas in Malebranche and Arnauld", *Mind*, 32 (1923), 449–61; Ralph W. Church, *A Study in the Philosophy of Malebranche* (London: George Allen and Unwin, 1931), pp. 226–30; Geneviève Rodis-Lewis, *Nicholas Malebranche* (Paris: PUF, 1963); J. M. Gaonach, *La théorie des idées dans la philosophie de Malebranche* (Brest, 1908); Yolton, "Ideas and Knowledge in Seventeenth-Century Philosophy"; McRae, "'Idea' as a Philosophical Term in the 17th Century"; Lennon, "Philosophical Commentary" to *The Search after Truth*, p. 795; and Radner, *Malebranche*, p. 107.

Harry Bracken ("Berkeley and Malebranche on Ideas", *The Modern Schoolman*, 41 [1963], 1–15) does not dispute the essentially representationalist structure of Malebranche's doctrine of ideas, whereby ideas are perceived directly and immediately, external objects only indirectly and by the mediation of ideas. But he prefers to see in the peculiar Malebranchian form of this structure an example of epistemological and perceptual direct realism. He bases his claim on Malebranche's insistence that for an object to be the object of knowledge, two conditions must be fulfilled: the object must be independent of the knower, and it must be immediately known (p. 2). Bracken sees these principles as indicative in Malebranche of an epistemological direct realism with regard to (God's) ideas existing independently of the knower's mind.

Alquié and Robinet, on the other hand, see Malebranche as moving away from the notion of the mind attending to static ideas. Alquié (*Le Cartésianisme de Malebranche*, pp. 208ff.) insists that Malebranche's doctrine moves from affirming *une Vision dans Dieu* to affirming *une Vision par Dieu*; moves, that is, from seeing God's ideas (or intelligible extension) as the inert objects of perception to seeing them either as agents themselves bringing about perception by modifying the mind or as that by means of which God affects us. See also Robinet, *Système*, pp. 259ff.; and Gueroult, *Malebranche*, vol. 1, Chapters 9 and 10. According to Robinet, this modification appears for the first

directly perceived; external things are indirectly perceived by means of the perception of representative ideas serving as proxies before the mind.[18]

As we shall see in the following chapters, Malebranche's doctrine of representative ideas and the theory of perception it involves were energetically attacked by Arnauld on several fronts. He objected to Malebranche's notion of the vision in God for both philosophical and theological reasons; he thought the account of an infinite intelligible extension to be utter nonsense; and he frequently complained of Malebranche's reasoning, which, to his logically rigorous mind, often seemed weak at best, fallacious at worst. Above all, however, he attacked the notion that a representative idea, that that by means of which we perceive and know the world, could be some entity distinct from the human mind and serving as its direct and immediate object in perception.

---

time around 1695 in the preface to the *Entretiens*. The notion of a "causal presence" of the idea, discussed earlier with regard to Malebranche's arguments for representationalism, does not surface in the *Recherche* (Book IV, Chapter x, Section 3) until the fifth edition (1700).

[18] I argue elsewhere for a third possible reading of Malebranche's theory of ideas, whereby he holds what would now be called a "direct realist" account of perceptual acquaintance with the external world. See "Ideas and Perception in Malebranche", *Studies in Early Modern Philosophy* (forthcoming).

I V
Arnauld's critique of Malebranche

9 History of the debate

The polemic between Arnauld and Malebranche concerning the nature of ideas was initiated by Arnauld with the publication in 1683 of *Des vraies et des fausses idées*. The work is a systematic critique of Malebranche's *Recherche*, particularly his representationalism (*idées comme êtres représentatifs*), the theory of intelligible extension, the doctrine of the vision in God, his views on one's knowledge of one's own soul, and his position on the issue of whether or not a demonstration of the existence of the external world is possible. Malebranche responded in 1684 with his *Réponse de l'auteur De la Recherche de la Vérité au livre de M. Arnauld, des vrayes et des fausses Idées*, in which he defends himself point by point against the charges and arguments presented by Arnauld. This was followed, in June of the same year, by Arnauld's *Défense de M. Arnauld contre la réponse au livre des vraies et des fausses idées*. Malebranche replied with three letters on Arnauld's *Défense* in 1685 (TL). Arnauld's response to this correspondence is contained in nine letters sent to Malebranche between 1685 and 1686, to which Malebranche responded in 1686 with another series of letters. After a break of several years, during which Arnauld defended himself against Jesuit and Protestant attacks and Malebranche was busy composing the *Entretiens sur la Métaphysique et sur la Religion* and arguing with Régis, the public debate reappeared with Arnauld's four letters of 1694, two of which appeared in the *Journal des Savants* of that year (Nos. XXV and XXVI). Malebranche replied with two letters in the same issue (XXVI), and in a third letter (RLA, a response to Arnauld's third letter) which is dated 1699, after Arnauld's death.[1]

[1] For a comprehensive survey and collation of the written debate, see Robinet's introduction to OC VI, pp. vi-xxvii. See also Bouillier, *Histoire de la philosophie Cartésienne*, vol. 2, p. 179, n. 1.

Such is the general outline of the written debate between Arnauld and Malebranche regarding the issues raised in VFI and the *Réflexions*. My discussion will be limited to those parts of the debate which are directly and philosophically relevant to the issue of Arnauld's theory of perception. In particular, the emphasis will be on Arnauld's critique of Malebranche's representationalism and the role of *êtres représentatifs* in perception. Arnauld's problems with the vision in God and the infinite intelligible extension, as well as with Malebranche's position on knowledge of the soul, are indeed important, but they are not central to the question of Arnauld's anti-representationalism and the more general epistemological issues raised thereby; they relate more to certain idiosyncratic features of Malebranche's version of a representationalist theory of perception. It is clear that Arnauld saw the two sets of issues as distinct: the early chapters of VFI are concerned with *êtres représentatifs* in general; only later (Chapters XIIff.) does he consider the modifications peculiar to Malebranche's theory.

10 *Malebranche and the object theory of ideas*

From the examination of Malebranche's theory of perception in the last chapter, certain salient features emerge regarding the nature of ideas and their role in perception.

First, on Malebranche's analysis of perceptual acquaintance, ideas are entities distinct from both the mind of the perceiving subject (they are not modifications of that mind) and the objects which they represent. More particularly, ideas are *objects* ontologically distinct from both the perceptual act (which is a property of the mind) and the external material body (which, it seems, is the ultimately-intended object of perception). As Malebranche's arguments for the necessity of ideas in perception indicate, these idea-objects serve as non-material representative surrogates for material objects, taking the place of those objects in the mind.

Second, these idea-objects are what are directly and immediately perceived. The ideas ontically present to the mind are the direct objects of the mind in perception, cognition and other mental processes; they are, for Malebranche, entities toward which the operations of the mind are immediately directed. (As we saw in the last chapter, Arnauld occasionally reads Malebranche as saying that one sees, hears, and in general perceives *only* representative non-material entities: ideas.) In the perception of a chair, the operation or act of the mind is immediately directed towards a bounded expanse of the infinite intelligible extension (or, alternatively, an idea of the object *qua* extended body) in God. This idea is "colored" by the sensations of the perceiver on the occasion of the presence of the object (the chair) to the perceiver's body. Again, although one may look at, or turn one's sense organs towards (*regarder*), the external object, it is only this intelligible object (the idea) which is directly and immediately seen. This theory regarding the objects of perception, this form of representationalism, has generally been referred to as the "object theory of ideas": ideas are representative intermediary entities distinct from both the operations of the mind (its perceptions) and the external objects they represent. Such idea-entities function as the direct *objects* of perception.

11 *The Arnauld–Malebranche debate: what is at issue?*

According to Arnauld, the general position regarding the perception of external objects that he is attacking in *Des vraies et des fausses idées* is this "object theory of ideas": the view that ideas are "entities which are representative of objects and really distinct from both perceptions and objects, and which we need to perceive things" (VFI, 187).[2] Such entities are the primary objects of perception. They represent in the mind material bodies which, it is argued, are incapable of being immediately present to the mind and, hence, incapable of being immediately and directly perceived. This theory thus supposes that there are three elements in the perception or knowing of any external object: "the object, which needs to be known, and which is not intelligible by itself; the representative entity, which puts the object in a condition for being known; and the perception of our mind, by which it is actually known" (VFI, 336). Note that, for Malebranche, neither of the first two items are properties of the mind (although the *être représentatif* is "intimately present to the mind"), while the third item, *la perception*, is a part of the mind, a *modalité de l'âme*. Arnauld is generally concerned with combating this tripartite view of the nature of perception.

There is an interesting problem, however, in deciding just what

[2] Cf. also VFI, pp. 188–9, 195–6, 199 (Rule 7).

exactly is at issue between Arnauld and Malebranche. The problem arises from Malebranche's characterization of the debate:

What is the issue at hand? Mr. Arnauld insists that the modalities of the soul are essentially representative of objects distinct from the soul; and I maintain that these modalities are nothing but sensations, which do not represent to the soul anything different from itself. (*Réponse*, V: OC VI, 50)

According to Malebranche, the issue is whether representative ideas are modifications of the mind, or external to it. Alternatively stated, the issue is whether or not modifications of the mind represent objects external to the mind. In a recent article, Monte Cook argues that "Malebranche's statement of the disagreement between Arnauld and himself is misleading and, more important, inaccurate."[3] There is reason, however, to believe that although Malebranche's statement may be misleading, it is not misleading for the reason Cook alleges. Furthermore, there are two ways of looking at the Arnauld–Malebranche issue – on one interpretation, Cook is right and Malebranche's statement is inaccurate; on the other reading, however, this is not the case.

The statement is misleading, Cook argues, because "Arnauld admits that some modifications of the soul, namely sensations (what Malebranche calls *sentiments*), are non-representative."[4] If by 'non-representative' Cook means "not presenting or displaying a content to the mind" (that is, not representing anything to the mind), and this clearly seems to be the sense in which Arnauld understands 'non-representative', then it appears inaccurate to hold that for Arnauld "some modifications of the mind, namely sensations, ... are non-representative". In his Fourth Set of Objections to the *Meditationes*, Arnauld insists that every positive idea "displays [*exhibet*] [something] real" to the mind, where 'idea' refers to clear and distinct conceptions of essences and of objects *qua* extended bodies, as well as to sensations such as heat, color, pain, etc.:

It cannot be imagined that the idea [of an infinite being] does not represent anything real to me. The same can plainly be said of any positive idea. For although it can be imagined that cold, which I suppose to be represented by a

[3] "Arnauld's Alleged Representationalism", *Journal of the History of Philosophy*, 12 (1974), p. 54.
[4] *Ibid.*, p. 54.

positive idea, is not something positive, it cannot be imagined that the positive idea does not represent anything real and positive to me. For an idea is called 'positive' not in virtue of the existence it has as a mode of thinking (for in that sense all ideas would be positive), but in virtue of the objective existence which it contains and which it represents [*exhibet*] to our mind. (Fourth Objections: AT VII, 206–7; CSM II, 145)

Sensations are clearly capable of representing, of presenting or displaying a positive content to the mind. Granted, as Descartes notes in his reply, this content may be so obscure and confused that it furnishes us with material for errors (*materiam erroris*) of judgement (Fourth Replies: AT VII, 232ff.; CSM II 162–4); but it nonetheless possesses a representational content of some degree (see Chapter 6). Thus, Malebranche's description is not misleading in this regard – all of Arnauld's "modalities of the soul" *are* essentially representative, and none of Malebranche's are (see Chapter 6, Section 19 below).

Actually, Arnauld occasionally seems to go so far as to say that, in a sense, our sensations do display a content to the mind in a clear and distinct manner:

It is only a matter of showing that the idea which we have of sensible qualities, such as colors, sounds and odors, in so far as they are modifications of our soul, is a clear idea. And for this it is only necessary to show that we know them clearly. For since we know them by an idea, in the general sense of the term, as the author avows, if this idea does not represent them to us clearly and distinctly, it will be a confused idea; but if it represents them to us clearly and distinctly, it will be a clear idea. Now, I appeal to everyone's experience. (VFI, 316)

This appeal to the authority of each and every individual, if they were to "think it over and tell me whether or not it is true that they believe that the different colors which they see, and the diverse sounds which they hear, are known clearly", would reveal that we do, indeed, know such things (*les couleurs, la douleur*) *clairement* (VFI, 316). When I consider my sensations without forming any judgement regarding their causes, that is, when I consider them simply as displaying a certain content to my mind, I know them *clairement et distinctement* (VFI, 318).

Cook's second, and "more important", claim is that Malebranche's statement is inaccurate because "although they [Malebranche and Arnauld] do disagree on whether modifications of the soul can be essentially representative (on whether ideas are modifications of the soul) they also disagree on whether ideas are objects of perception or acts of perception."[5] Cook believes that "there are two basic differences" between Arnauld's and Malebranche's theories: "First, as Malebranche recognized, in Malebranche's theory ideas are mind-independent, whereas in Arnauld's theory they are mind-dependent. Secondly, what Malebranche failed to recognize, in Malebranche's theory ideas are objects of perception, whereas in Arnauld's theory they are acts of perception."[6] In fact, the two differences Cook sees between the two theories are one and the same difference. That is, the issue of whether or not representative ideas are modifications of the soul is the same issue, at least for Arnauld, as the issue of whether ideas are objects of perception or acts of perception. Thus, Malebranche's statement is not all that inaccurate.

Clearly, what Arnauld is attacking is the theory that *êtres représentatifs* are distinct from acts of perception and external objects, and serve as the immediate objects of perception. It is, moreover, clear that Arnauld is attacking Melabranche's theologized version of this theory, whereby these idea-objects are in God. But an ambiguity enters at this point, in that there are two ways of reading what is at issue.

On the reading offered by Cook, there are three relevant theories regarding the nature of ideas and their role in perception; Arnauld chose one of these theories while attacking the other two, one of which Malebranche held. The first position (Arnauld's) is that representative ideas are identical with those modifications of the mind which are its operations (e.g. acts of perception). In this case, then, modifications of the mind are essentially representative (see Chapters 5 and 6). The second position, the one held by Malebranche (see Chapter 3), is that there is a distinction between non-representative modifications of the mind (its operations, e.g. acts of perception, sensations) and representative ideas, which are outside the mind but are capable of being "intimately present" to it without modifying it (*Il faut des idées differents des modifications* [*Réponse*, V: OC VI, 54]). Malebranche makes this move because, among other reasons, it is inconceivable to him how a modification of a finite and particular mind (which modification is, thus, itself finite and particular) could do the cognitive work it would need to do. We have an idea of infinity. This objective reality, or representational content, being infinite, cannot be a modality of a finite being, i.e. the human mind. Similarly, we have an idea of a circle in general. But this idea, this objective reality, which is general, cannot be a property of a particular being (see *Recherche*, III, ii, 5; *Réponse*, VI). A third theory is that there is a distinction between non-representative acts of the mind and representative ideas (which, as in the second theory, are the immediate objects of these acts), but that such mental operations and idea-objects are *both* modifications or properties of the mind. Something like this is basically the claim made by most representationalists, including many recent sense-data theorists. Ideas, sensa, etc. are *mental* entities which are perceived or sensed by the mind (i.e. by an act of perceiving or sensing). Locke, it is often claimed, places ideas in the mind and makes them the direct objects of perception (cf. *Essay Concerning Human Understanding*, II, i, 1).[7] This also seems to be the view often ascribed to Descartes (for whom ideas are modifications of the mind) by those who see him as holding a representationalist view of perception.[8]

Is Arnauld concerned with attacking not just Malebranche's idiosyncratic version of the "object theory of ideas", but also a representationalism in which idea-objects are modifications of the mind distinct from acts of perception, i.e. are mental entities? Cook seems to think so. He insists, wanting to correct Malebranche's reading of Arnauld, that Arnauld is attacking not only the view (held by Malebranche) that modifications of the soul cannot be representative (that is, the view that representative idea-objects cannot be modifications of the soul), but also any theory in which representative ideas are *objects* of perception. Malebranche's description of the debate, Cook insists, is inaccurate because it is too narrow: Malebranche fails to see that Arnauld is arguing not only against the Malebranchian position that representative idea-objects cannot be modifications of the mind, but also against any "object theory of ideas", including that in which such idea-objects *are* modifications of the mind. The debate, according to Cook, is not only over "whether ideas are modifications of the soul", but also about whether ideas are *objects* of perception (be they in God or in the mind of the perceiver) or *acts* of perception.

[7] See Chapter 1, n. 3.
[8] See Chapter 5, n. 36.

If, indeed, Arnauld is concerned with combating a more inclusive, general view whereby ideas as *objects* of perception can be either modifications of the mind or not; that is, if he saw a third position which, together with Malebranche's position, belongs to the class "object theories of ideas", then Cook is right and Malebranche's characterization of what is at issue between himself and Arnauld is too narrow. Malebranche overlooks the fact that Arnauld was concerned with attacking several versions of "object-theory-of-ideas" representationalism – not just the one in which idea-objects are not modifications of the soul. But there is evidence that such a third position was not something Arnauld considered. That is, for Arnauld, ideas are either modifications of the mind or they are not; and if they are modifications of the mind, then they are identical with its acts or operations. If they are not modifications of the mind (and this is the view Malebranche holds), then they are objects of perception distinct from the mind's acts. In other words, the act-of-perception/object-of-perception issue is equivalent to the modification-of-mind/non-modification-of-mind issue. In this case, Malebranche's description is not inaccurate, but merely one (correct) way of characterizing what is at issue. This claim rests on the fact that Arnauld, in *Des vraies et des fausses idées*, seems incapable of recognizing that a modification of the mind could be anything other than an act or operation of that mind; in his view it certainly could not be an inert idea-object.

Arnauld is arguing against any *êtres représentatifs distingués des perceptions*. However, whenever he argues against *êtres représentatifs* distinct from acts of perception, he does not ever consider the possibility that although not perceptions they might still be modifications of the mind: if they are distinct from the mind's operations, he reasons, they are distinct from the mind itself. Put another way, if they are not modifications of the mind in the sense of being its acts or operations, they are not modifications of the mind at all.

Some examples will help to establish this point. Arnauld argues that at one point in *De la recherche de la vérité* Malebranche does in fact take ideas to be identical with perceptions, with acts of the mind. As evidence he notes that Malebranche is willing to grant that to receive the idea of an object is to receive a modification of the soul (VFI, 187–8). From the fact that (according to Arnauld) Malebranche here holds that ideas are modifications of the soul, Arnauld infers that he holds that they must be identical with perceptions. Arnauld must be assuming that the operations of the soul (i.e. acts of perception, taken in the broad sense of the term, as well as acts of will) exhaust the possible ways in which it can be modified.[9] Later, Arnauld's evidence for the argument that Malebranche does not ultimately admit ideas to be "in the soul" and to be modifications thereof is the fact that he does not identify ideas with perceptions (VFI, 195–6). Again, if Arnauld had recognized that a modification of the soul need not necessarily be an operation or act of the soul, his use of such an argument would not make sense. There are other passages which support this view. In Chapter X, Arnauld identifies *faire nouvelle modification dans mon âme* with *recevoir nouvelle perception* (VFI, 223). Moreover, in his demonstrations against *êtres représentatifs distinguées des perceptions* he argues against two representationalist positions: Malebranche's, and the doctrine of species. In each theory, according to Arnauld, a representative entity is present to the mind without being a modification of the mind.[10] He seems to feel that to argue against *êtres représentatifs* is to argue only against these two views.

Throughout these passages, and others, Arnauld consistently refuses to recognize or mention any way that the soul might be modified except by its operations, in particular its perceptions (although willings are equally acts of the mind, hence modifications). One finds the same position in Arnauld's *Défense*: the issue is whether or not ideas are modifications of the soul; if they are, then they are perceptions (acts). In arguing that Descartes himself holds ideas to be identical with perceptions, Arnauld deems it sufficient to show that for Descartes *les idées sont des modalités de notre âme* (38: 386–8). If Descartes holds ideas to be modifications of the soul, then he must take *les idées pour les perceptions* (38: 386), for acts or operations of the mind. Again, there is no indication that Arnauld considered the possibility that ideas could be modifications of the soul *and* be idea-objects towards which acts of mind are directed. This reading is supported by Arnauld's view that the mind is entirely active. For in that case, all its modes will be

---

[9] The range of possible particular modifications is not exhausted by the range of *kinds* of acts or operations of which the soul is capable. Thus, for example, the perception of a particular chair differs from (modifies the soul differently than) the perception of a table, which in turn differs from the conception of a table, and so forth. Thus, although the soul is capable of only a limited number of *kinds* of modifications (perceivings, willings, rememberings, doubtings, etc.), they are further determinable *ad infinitum* according to their particular contents (which in turn are determined by their objects).

[10] For example, cf. VFI, Chapter VIII.

activities or *opérations*. It would be inconceivable to him that there is room in an entirely active substance for a passive, inert idea-object (see Section 5, Chapter 2 above).

Thus, for Arnauld, the issue of whether or not ideas are *êtres représentatifs distingués des perceptions*, that is, whether ideas are objects of perception or acts of perception, is the same issue as whether or not "modalities of the soul are essentially representative of objects which are distinct from the soul" (that is, the issue of whether representative ideas are modifications of the soul or not). In Arnauld's eyes, to deny the mind-dependence of representative ideas, to deny their being modifications of the soul, is to be committed to holding ideas to be objects of perception; to affirm their mind-dependence, to admit that ideas are just modifications of the soul which represent, is to be committed to holding them to be identical with perceptual acts. Although it is true, as Cook insists, that the issue between Arnauld and Malebranche is whether ideas are acts of perception or objects of perception, it is equally true that for Arnauld the issue is also whether or not modifications of the soul are representative, whether ideas are nothing more than such modifications. In fact, as the evidence cited above shows, for Arnauld the issues are identical.

12 *Arnauld's critique of Malebranche's representationalism*

Arnauld's critique of Malebranche, and of representationalism in general, is a critique of "representative entities distinct from perceptions [*des êtres représentatifs distingués des perceptions*] and objects which are needed to perceive things." Arnauld is arguing, that is, against the view that "we never immediately see objects by themselves [*par eux-mêmes*]", in the sense that *par eux-mêmes* is to be contrasted with *par ces êtres représentatifs des objets distingués des perceptions* (VFI, 211–12). He offers several arguments and *démonstrations* against this position, and presents some phenomenological evidence which, he believes, discredits such a view of perception.

1 As we saw in the last chapter, one of Arnauld's foremost concerns is that such a theory surrounds the mind with a "palace of ideas" and cuts it off from external objects. If it is the case that *êtres représentatifs* are the immediate objects of perception, then Malebranche seems to have foreclosed the possibility of perceptual contact with the external world, which (even Malebranche admits) was the initial *explanandum*.

Arnauld argues that there is something wrong with an *explanans* that not only fails to explain the *explanandum*, but also ultimately leads to the conclusion that the *explanandum* is impossible:

Ideas taken in this latter sense [as entities distinct from perceptions and representative of objects] are truly chimeras which, having been invented only to help us better understand how our soul, which is immaterial, is able to know the material things God has created, so poorly allow us to understand this fact, that the fruit of these speculations is that we are persuaded, after a long detour, that God has not given to our souls any means of perceiving the real and veritable bodies which he has created, but only intelligible bodies which are outside of our souls, and which resemble real bodies. (VFI, 189)

Arnauld reiterates this point in Chapter XI:

At first, he supposes that our mind does perceive material things. The trouble is only in explaining *how*: whether it is by means of ideas or without ideas, taking the word 'idea' to mean a representative entity distinct from perception. After much philosophizing on the nature of these representative entities, after having marched them around everywhere and having been able to place them only in God, the only fruit that he gathers from all this is not an explanation of how we see material things, which alone was what was sought, but rather the conclusion that our mind is incapable of perceiving them, and that we live in a perpetual illusion in believing that we see the material things that God has created when we look at them, that is to say when we turn our eyes toward them; and meanwhile seeing, instead of them, only intelligible bodies that resemble them. (VFI, 229)

The point here, Arnauld insists, is that the doctrine of *êtres représentatifs* leads one into *des erreurs tout à fait absurdes*, and he provides a *reductio* of the doctrine to demonstrate this. Malebranche initially assumes that "we see an infinity of bodies, and that our mind perceives them". But as a consequence of admitting "these ideas which are needed to see external objects", Malebranche (by his own admission) is condemned to holding that we have no true perception of our own bodies, "nor of the sun and the stars which God has created" (VFI, 227–8); that one sees only "intelligible" bodies: an intelligible sun, intelligible stars, etc. This unfortunate conclusion, Arnauld argues, contradicts the initial assumption (that we perceive material bodies), which was just what needed explaining in the first place. Far from explaining it, Malebranche has shown it, on his theory, to be impossible.

Not only does Malebranche's theory lead to absurdities, but it is also completely contrary to what would seem to be God's desire. Why would God join the soul to a body and yet not allow that soul to perceive that body; why would God surround the body (and, thus, the soul) with material bodies, some of which are necessary for the life and maintenance of that body, and yet not allow for the perception of those bodies (VFI, 231–2)? Nonetheless, Arnauld continues, this is exactly the conclusion one must draw from Malebranche's doctrine of representative idea-objects: the perceiving mind is completely cut off from the material world God intended it to perceive, and is instead surrounded by a "palace of ideas", a world of intelligible entities. The same concern is expressed several times in the *Défense*: "According to him, we do not ever see the bodies which God has created, but only intelligible bodies, which he says are God himself, and thus, we see only God" (38: 390); "According to your system of Ideas, our soul in no way sees the bodies which God has created" (38: 408).

It is not clear, as we saw in the last chapter, that Arnauld presents a fair reading of Malebranche here by claiming that Malebranche does not provide, *en aucune sorte*, for the perception of external objects. Malebranche did, for the most part, consider the perception of external objects to be indirect. (I will return to Arnauld's interpretation of Malebranche's theory, and consider its relevance to his critique, at the end of this chapter). Furthermore, it is not clear what epistemological ramifications, if any, Arnauld believes to follow from the view that we are never in perceptual contact with the external world. The issue of skepticism is not irrelevant to the debate. In fact, Arnauld's criticism is based on worries regarding what might be called "skepticism about perception" (the claim that perception of the world is not possible). But the same objection does *not* appear to be based on *epistemological* concerns, or worries regarding a 'skepticism about knowledge" (*knowledge* of the world is not possible). Arnauld realizes that no skeptical problems of the latter sort are necessarily solved by direct realism in itself (see Chapter 5). Nor is it clear that "skepticism about perception" entails "skepticism about knowledge".

2 Arnauld claims that the object theory of ideas is based on false principles which, although taken as "first truths", are actually nothing more than residues of childhood prejudices. The first principle is that which requires an object to be ontically present to the mind in order to be capable of being perceived (VFI, 190–91). Malebranche clearly relies

on this principle in his arguments for the necessity of ideas in perception: presence to the mind is a necessary condition for the perception of any object. The second principle asserts that since we often see objects reflected in mirrors or in water, or represented in paintings or other images, what is seen in each of these cases is, in fact, not the object itself but its representative image.

Arnauld insists that when these two principles are taken together, one is led into the theory of ideas by the following train of reasoning: We often perceive things (the sun, stars, and other material bodies) which are distant from the soul. It is inconceivable that these objects have actually traveled to the soul (to render themselves immediately present to the soul and, hence, in a state conducive to direct perception) or that the soul has left the body to travel to the object.

How, then, will the soul be able to see [these objects], since an object cannot be seen if it is not present? In order to solve this difficulty, they have had recourse to the other manner of seeing ... which is to see things not in themselves, but by means of their images, as when we see bodies in mirrors. (VFI, 191)

There must be some object immediately present to the mind for perception to occur. This is where the first principle operates, and it raises the problem that is resolved by the second principle. Since the material body itself cannot be present to the mind in the manner necessary for perception, a representative proxy takes its place there, and serves as the direct object of perception (which is possible due to the *présence* of such a proxy to the mind). This way out of the predicament is suggested by the second principle, which offers examples whereby a representative proxy (e.g. a portrait or a reflection in a mirror) is perceived instead of the object itself.

According to Arnauld, there are several problems with such reasoning, most importantly with the two principles on which it is based.

As for the first principle, *la présence de l'objet, qu'ils disent devoir être uni intimement à l'âme*, Arnauld remarks that it is based on a false analogy between, on the one hand, perceiving (which is an act of the mind) and, on the other hand, bodily (optical) "seeing" – the reception of certain motions by the eye and optic nerves, which motions are then communicated to the brain – and the physics of the material world. (To avoid confusion, I will hereafter use quote marks to indicate the physiological processes which constitute corporeal vision – the operations of the eyes, nerves, brain, etc. – as opposed to true seeing by the mind. Thus, "see", "seeing", "sight", etc. will refer to *la vue corporelle*, corporeal vision; without the quotes, these words will refer to *la vue spirituelle*, mental vision.) Arnauld notes that philosophers have sought to explain how we perceive with the mind (through which all perception takes place) by analogy with *la vue corporelle*, with optical mechanisms:

> They have wanted, in spite of everything, to draw a comparison with the body, in order to make it better understood ... how our mind is able to see material things. For this is what they found difficult to understand, and which is now found to be even more difficult to understand ... The same name had been given to both corporeal vision [*la vue corporelle*] and mental vision [*la vue spirituelle*], and this is what made them reason thus: There must be some similarity between the seeing of the mind and the seeing of the body. (VFI, 192)

Because it is supposed that in *la vue du corps* one can only "see" what is present to and in front of the eyes (just as a physical object can act directly only upon what is contiguous to it – "no action at a distance" was a principal maxim of Cartesian physics), it is assumed that the same must be true of the mind, which is responsible for perceiving (seeing) in general: no perception at a distance.

Philosophers have taken the same analogy between mind and body to be operative in regard to the second principle – as with mirrors and other images in the bodily realm, "intelligible" images are perceived. Such reasoning (in conjunction with the first principle), Arnauld argues, leads them to the theory of ideas: "If we sometimes see things which are not before our eyes, it is only by means of images which represent them to us. The same, then, must be true of the mind" (VFI, 192). Since the object itself is often not actually present to the eyes because it is too small, too distant, no longer existent, etc., and it is, consequently, only a representative image (e.g. a mirror reflection) of the object which (according to the second principle) is directly grasped, then, by analogy, the same must hold true of the mind in its perception or seeing of objects: what cannot be present to the mind is seen by means of a representative entity that is "intimately united" to the mind, and hence directly perceived by it.

Arnauld insists that the problem with this analogy, with this *compari-*

son de la vue corporelle avec la vue spirituelle, is that it rests on false assumptions. "It is the soul, and not the eyes, which see", and true perception does not take place according to the principles which some philosophers have supposed to operate in physical "seeing", in the mechanics of the optical apparatus. Arnauld's objection here is founded on the strict Cartesian dualism between mind and body, which rules out any such analogies:

They were not aware that this was a means not of clarifying, but rather of obscuring that which would have been very clear to them, if only they had been content to consider it in themselves. For since the mind and the body are two totally distinct and opposed natures, whose properties, consequently, cannot have anything in common, it is only confusing to try to explain the one by means of the other; and this is also one of the most general sources of our errors, that on thousands of occasions we apply the properties of the mind to bodies, and the properties of bodies to the mind. (VFI, 192).

One must not base one's reasoning about the mental act of perception on observations on, or beliefs about, the physiological processes which constitute bodily "seeing". Certainly the eyes play a role in true seeing; but perception should not be attributed to, or explained by analogy with, the eyes: it is a function of the mind.

Just as importantly, it is not even clear that these two principles (presence of object; perceiving representative images instead of objects) are applicable in the realm of optics, of physical or bodily "seeing"; and they certainly are not operative in the realm of perceiving.

Regarding the first principle, whereby the presence considered necessary is understood to be a *local* presence, Arnauld argues that this is just the opposite of what actually occurs in "seeing", in the physiological vision that takes place with the eye:

For although, in the popular way of speaking, it is said that the object must be present to our eyes in order for us to see it ... nonetheless, speaking strictly and philosophically, it is just the opposite. The object must be absent from the eyes, since it must be distant from them; and whatever is in the eye, or too close to the eye, cannot be seen. (VFI, 194)

With regard to true seeing or perceiving, it is obviously the case that we perceive objects distant from us. As Malebranche himself notes, we see the sun, the stars, etc. Indeed, it is just this fact which needs explaining (VFI, 215ff.). And the brain is certainly "present" to the mind (being the "principal seat" of the soul), yet it is not perceived by the mind.

Nor is the second principle applicable to either the eyes or the mind:

Likewise with the second condition, which concerns seeing certain representative entities which, being similar to objects, allow us to know them. [Malebranche] well knows that our eyes see nothing of the sort, nor does our mind through our eyes. He knows that when one sees oneself in the mirror, it is oneself that one sees, and not one's image. (VFI, 194)

This is an astute point. What one perceives when looking in a mirror, or at the reflection of an object in water, is the object mirrored or reflected. I perceive *myself* reflected in the mirror, the *sky* reflected in the water – not the mirror-image or the water-image themselves. Of course, one could just look at the image itself if one so wished – one could then be said to perceive the mirror-image or the water-image. But we are then dealing with a different act of perception: instead of the perception of *x* by means of the mirror, there now exists the perception of *y*, the mirror-image itself.

Arnauld has several other criticisms to make regarding the first principle. First, he notes that the principle "that our mind can know only objects which are present to our soul" is quite contrary to what is *si clair et si évident* (VFI, 213). Malebranche wrongly assumes, as a clear and evident principle, that the soul cannot perceive objects which are distant from itself:

Not only do I doubt this alleged principle, but I maintain that it is manifestly false, because it is manifestly evident that our soul can know an infinite number of things which are distant from the place where it is situated, and that it is able to do so because God has given it the power to do so ... I am certain that my soul has seen the sun, the stars and other works of God an infinite number of times. (VFI, 214)

The root of the problem lies not only in the false general analogy with bodily "seeing" noted above, but also in a related equivocation on the word 'presence' (VFI, 216). In the bodily realm, 'presence' is to be understood as "local presence", whereby for one body to act on another it must be locally present; that is, the two bodies must be contiguous and share a common boundary. With regard to mind, however, 'presence' is to be understood as "objective presence", and involves "being known or perceived" (Arnauld's understanding of this term is examined in Chapter 6). The error lies in not observing the distinction and in assuming that 'presence' is to be understood univocally with regard to both body and mind. Hence, Malebranche concludes that "bodies must be present to the soul in order to be known by it ... He thus regards local distance as an obstacle, which puts a body out of the condition of being able to be seen by our mind" (VFI, 216–17).

Arnauld insists that *local* presence is a notion appropriate with regard only to physical bodies, and completely irrelevant to perception and to minds in general; here, only *objective* presence is relevant (VFI, 217–18). Even Malebranche, Arnauld notes, recognizes this irrelevancy, and thus there appears to be an inconsistency in his position. Malebranche, Arnauld has discovered, would agree that even were the soul to travel to the stars, the sun, etc., "it would be making an entirely useless trip": according to Malebranche, one needs representative ideas to see even one's own body, to which the soul is immediately united (e.g. *Recherche*, III, ii, 7). Of what importance, then, is local presence for Malebranche? "Thus, it is in vain that he presents, as conditions which prevent our soul from seeing the sun by itself, the facts that the sun is remote from the soul and that the soul cannot leave the body to go travel in the sky; since present or distant, it is all the same to the soul" (VFI, 217). Thus, by his own reasoning, Malebranche is forced to agree with Arnauld that "local presence or local remoteness is irrelevant [*ne fait rien*] to a body's being able or not being able to be the object of our mind" (VFI, 218).

3 The second part of Arnauld's attack on *êtres représentatifs* is intended to show that such intermediary entities are superfluous, and that, consequently, they are not necessary to perception. Arnauld offers a number of demonstrations that "our mind *has no need* of certain representative entities, distinct from perceptions, in order to know material things". Indeed, it seems that the only way to prove that they are necessary is simply to assume so, and thus beg the question.

A. Malebranche states in one of his arguments that "everyone agrees that we do not perceive objects external to us by themselves [*par eux-mêmes*]" (*Recherche*, III, ii, 1. 1: OC I, 413; LO, 217). Arnauld notes that the expression *par eux-mêmes* is equivocal. If Malebranche means only that such objects do not cause in the mind the perceptions that one has of them, then Arnauld agrees: this is no more objectionable than saying that matter cannot move itself, since it does not give motion to itself. On the other hand, if Malebranche means *par eux-mêmes* to be contrasted with *par ces êtres représentatifs des objets distingués des perceptions* (and Arnauld feels that this is clearly Malebranche's meaning), then he has begged the question: "obviously, this is to assume that which is in question before having established it by any proof" (VFI, 212).

B. Arnauld feels that Malebranche further begs the question in what I referred to as his "argument from the possibility of error" (see Chapter 3). Malebranche claims that

for the mind to perceive an object, it is absolutely necessary for the idea [*idée*] of that object to be actually present to it – and about this there can be no doubt; but there need not be any external thing like that idea. For it often happens that we perceive things that do not exist, and that even have never existed – thus our mind often has real ideas of things that have never existed. (*Rech.*, III, 1. 1: OC I, 414; LO, 217)

Arnauld insists that if by *idée* Malebranche means *perception*, then the first proposition is trivially true: one cannot perceive an object without an act of perceiving. "How could our mind perceive something if it did not have ... the perception of it?" (VFI, 221). On the other hand, if, once again, *idée* means *être représentatif distingué de la perception*, then clearly *il suppose ce qui est en question*:

The proposition being conceived in these terms, not only is it possible to doubt it, but I absolutely deny the first part of it, since I do not see any need for this alleged "representative entity" in order to know any object, be it present or absent. Thus, to suppose that "it is impossible to doubt the necessity of this representative entity" is manifestly to assume that which is in question. (VFI, 221)

If there need not be an object beyond (*au dehors*) the *être représentatif*, why need there be one outside the perception itself? That is, why must there be an *être représentatif* in addition to the mental activity of perceiving? The "argument from error" cannot succeed without begging the question:

If it is not necessary for there to be some external thing similar to the "representative entity", then it is no more necessary for there to be some existing thing [i.e. an idea-object] external and similar to the perception which I have of the sun. Thus, just because I could conceive of the sun even if there were no sun at all in the universe, I am not obliged to make use of these "representative entities distinct from perceptions". (VFI, 221)

C. It is possible to provide a positive demonstration that there is no need for such *êtres représentatifs* in order to perceive material bodies. Arnauld's argument here (like the reference to "God's intentions" in 1 above) involves theological premises which he believes Malebranche himself accepts (VFI, 222–3). God would not have created our souls and placed them in bodies surrounded by other bodies without providing our souls with the ability to know and perceive those bodies. Since all of God's volitions are efficacious, and since he clearly wants us to perceive such bodies, it is certain that he gave our souls the faculty to perceive them. Now God does not perform by complex means (*des voies composées*) what can be performed by simple means (*des voies simples*). Thus:

Since God desired that our mind should know bodies, and that bodies should be known by our mind, it was undoubtedly simpler for him to render our mind capable of knowing bodies immediately, that is, without representative entities distinct from perceptions ... and bodies capable of being known immediately by our mind, rather than leaving the soul powerless to see them otherwise than by means of certain representative entities. (VFI, 222–3)

On Malebranche's terms, God has taken a complex and roundabout way of accomplishing what he might have done by simpler means; and this is inconsistent with *le grand principe* regarding God's *simplicité des voies* that even Malebranche accepts (VFI, 223). The "object theory of ideas" brand of representationalism demands two operations of the mind in the perception of a single object: first, the perception of the representative entity (P_1), and, second, the perception of the object (P_2), which is based on P_1.

If it is said that this first perception is nothing but the perception of the representative entity, then a second perception, which would be the perception of body A, will still be needed. For it is body A that I need to see, since it may be either useful or harmful to the preservation of my machine. (VFI, 223)

If one must finally arrive at the perception of the material body itself (P_2), why may not God, being infinitely perfect and always acting by *les voies les plus simples*, have provided for such a perception immediately and directly? To argue otherwise is to contradict God's infinite wisdom, omnipotence, and simplicity (VFI, 223–4):

Is this not to ascribe to God bizarre and groundless laws? Is it not to subject him to the vain imaginations of philosophers, when we oblige him, who always acts in the most simple ways, to take as strange a route as we could desire him to take, in order to execute his will to allow our soul to know material things? (VFI, 225)

D. Arnauld insists that there is no need for *êtres représentatifs* to explain how it is that we are able to perceive or know both the particular and the general properties of bodies and, more generally, to perform mathematical computations. "It is also clear what is to be understood when it is said that 'it is in the idea of each thing that one sees its properties'. And surely nothing is more useless for this than that representative entity distinct from perceptions which, it is claimed, our mind needs to conceive numbers" (VFI, 207). Malebranche's idea-objects are intended to represent external objects to the mind. By the direct and immediate perception of the idea, it is argued, one can determine the properties of the object. More general knowledge (e.g. geometrical truths) is obtained by means of the perception of general ideas (e.g. the idea of extension in general).

Arnauld argues, however, that such intermediary entities are unnecessary and useless for these purposes. One can perceive the properties of a given object (e.g. a particular man) by means of the perception of the object itself. It is then possible to reflect on this primary perception, together with another, different primary perception (e.g. the perception of a woman), in order to compare or contrast the two. This reflection itself constitutes a third act of perception which has as its object[s] the [two] primary act[s]. In this way one can arrive at the abstract idea of "human being", "two", "body", etc. But in no way do any representative entities distinct from acts of perception make an appearance here (VFI, 207ff.). The second-order act of reflective perception is the perception of "woman", "two", "body", or whatever else is abstracted from the primary perceptions. Similarly, I perceive twenty objects; I then reflect on that perception (which reflection is itself an act of perception) and arrive at a perception (idea) of twenty in general. By reflecting on this perception of the number twenty (again, an act of perception), I can discover any number of properties contained therein (e.g. that twenty is divisible by five).

I suggested in the last chapter that Arnauld's reading of Malebranche's theory of perception occasionally appears to misrepresent Malebranche's position. Although Malebranche does, for the most part, insist that external objects are perceived, albeit indirectly, Arnauld sometimes sees Malebranche as holding the position that all that is ever perceived are intelligible entities, idea-objects. Although these ideas may present us with information regarding the external world, the latter is never perceived, directly or indirectly. We have perceptual acquaintance only with *êtres représentatifs*.

The question now arises as to how this bears on Arnauld's critique of Malebranche. How much of Arnauld's criticism of Malebranche depends on this reading of the latter's theory?

Of the arguments presented in VFI, only the argument under 1 above (pp. 88–90) depends on reading Malebranche in this way. His points there are based on the claim that Malebranche has not provided for perceptual contact (direct or indirect) with the external world. His *reductio* of Malebranche's position, for example, rests on the fact that in Malebranche's theory the mind is perceptually cut off from the world, even though our perceptual acquaintance with this world is what that theory was intended to explain in the first place.

The rest of his criticisms, for the most part, deal with Malebranche's arguments for *êtres représentatifs*. None of these criticisms entail or require for their relevancy that Malebranche held ideas to be the only objects of perception. In fact, in these cases (especially 3.C above), Arnauld allows that Malebranche does provide for indirect perception of objects. Does this point to an inconsistency in Arnauld's interpretation of Malebranche? I think that Arnauld's response to this objection would be that it points rather to an inconsistency in the representationalist's position. The representationalist who holds an object theory of ideas claims to have provided for the indirect perception of external objects. In fact, Arnauld would insist, a close analysis of the representationalist's position reveals that this is, for him, an untenable claim. So when Arnauld is concerned with the representationalist's *arguments* for his position, for the existence and necessity of *êtres représentatifs*, he is willing to grant, for the moment, the representationalist's claim that what he is arguing for is the indirect perception of external objects. When, however, Arnauld turns to examining the representationalist's doctrine itself, and its ramifications, as he does in 1, he interprets it in the only way he feels it can be interpreted: if ideas, such as Malebranche has defined them, are the direct and immediate objects of perception, then he has precluded perceptual contact of any kind with the external world. Arnauld then bases his criticisms on this interpretation.

Thus, what I have been calling a "misrepresentation" on Arnauld's part is, in fact, a criticism of Malebranche's theory. Arnauld is saying that, in spite of Malebranche's claims to the contrary, the only possible way to read his doctrine of ideas is as one which holds ideas to be the *sole* objects of perception. In Arnauld's eyes, this is an unfortunate doctrine to be caught holding.

V
Arnauld's direct realism

It is clear from the foregoing that Arnauld holds at least the following position regarding the perception of external objects: it is not necessary, for an external object to be perceived, that a non-physical intermediary representing that object, an *être représentatif distingué de la perception*, be present to the mind and directly and immediately perceived by it. VFI is mainly polemical, and this might be called the negative thesis of the work. In other words, the debate regarding perception between Arnauld and Malebranche concerns the direct and immediate objects of perception.[1] Malebranche, as we have seen, maintains that these are "intelligible" entities, divine ideas, which represent the mathematical properties (and, when "colored" by sensation, indicate the qualitative properties) of material bodies. Arnauld denies the necessity of such mediating entities in perception. He, on the contrary, holds that material bodies are the direct and immediate objects of veridical external perception. This is the positive side of Arnauld's claim. The perceiving mind, by means of an act of perception, is put in direct perceptual contact with a physical body. Arnauld does, however, insist that such mental acts are themselves essentially representative. This second element of Arnauld's theory is discussed in the next chapter.

13 *Misinterpretations of Arnauld*

Arnauld's act theory of ideas, the foundation of his direct realism, has been subject to misunderstanding ever since the publication of VFI in 1683. In particular, Malebranche and others have not realized that Arnauld argues for ideas that are not mental *objects* of perception, but

[1]Of course, the nature of perception itself is not the main issue. Cf. 38: iiiff. See section 16 and the appendix.

rather *acts* of perceiving directed immediately towards external objects. Thus, they have fallen into seeing Arnauld not as a direct realist, but as a representationalist or indirect realist.[2]

As we saw in the previous chapter, Malebranche's characterization of what is at issue is more relevant and accurate than some commentators have been willing to allow, but I do not think that Malebranche is entirely clear on the position Arnauld is arguing for. For one, Malebranche does not seem to recognize the possibility that Arnauld might be identifying ideas with *acts* of perception. And in his summary of the debate, Malebranche concentrates on Arnauld's claim that perceptions, which are modifications of the mind, are representative; not on Arnauld's insistence that no *êtres représentatifs* mediate between the act and the external world.

> What is the issue at hand? M. Arnauld insists that the modalities of the soul are essentially representative of objects distinct from the soul; and I maintain that these modalities are nothing but sensations, which do not represent to the soul anything different from itself. (*Réponse*, V, i: OC VI, 50)

It is true that I have denied this proposition ["It is clear to whoever reflects on his mind, that all our perceptions are essentially representative"] perhaps five

---

[2] Certainly, not everyone has misunderstood Arnauld. Norman Kemp Smith, for example, notes that "the only thinker within the early Cartesian school who called in question the doctrine of representative perception was Arnauld ... he states in a most definite manner that there is no direct evidence of the existence of subjective states, acting as intermediaries between mind and matter" (*Studies in the Cartesian Philosophy*, pp. 115–16). More recent scholars have rightly acknowledged that Arnauld was opposing Malebranche's theologically-weighted representationalism not with a different kind of indirect realism stripped of the vision in God, but with a direct realism. Geneviève Rodis-Lewis notes that Arnauld "combat inlassablement les idées posées devant la pensée, comme des entités superflues, des fallacieux êtres représentatifs ... il refuse donc la dissociation de Malebranche entre l'idée et la perception" (*Nicolas Malebranche*, pp. 97–8). Daisie Radner, too, recognizes that Arnauld "seeks to do away with the dichotomy between direct and indirect objects of perception ... when the mind perceives a body, there are two things, the act of perceiving and the object perceived. The object perceived is the body" (*Malebranche*, p. 99). In the commentary on his translation of Malebranche's *Recherche*, Thomas M. Lennon contrasts the direct realism, or "presentationalism", of Arnauld with the representationalism of Malebranche. He stresses the fact that for Arnauld "material things are objects of direct perception", not indirect or mediate perception (*The Search after Truth*, pp. 794–802). See also Radner, "Representationalism in Arnauld's Act Theory of Perception", *Journal of the History of Philosophy*, 14 (1976), 96–8; Cook, "Arnauld's Alleged Representationalism"; Yolton, "Ideas and Knowledge in Seventeenth-Century Philosophy", and *Perceptual Acquaintance*; and McRae, "'Idea' as a Philosophical Term in the 17th Century".

hundred times. I have always declared to M. Arnauld that if it were true, he would be right and I would be wrong on the question of ideas ... the entire dispute between the two of us concerning ideas rests on this. (RLA: OC VIII, 902)

Malebranche moves easily from this characterization of the debate to the view that what Arnauld is proposing, as an alternative to Malebranche's vision in God, is the direct perception of such representative mental modes. In other words, Malebranche believes that Arnauld has simply moved the idea *qua être représentatif* into the mind, making it the modification thereof while it remains the direct and immediate object of perception. Malebranche insists that according to Arnauld

when we see a woman, it is the color, i.e. the mind's own modification, which is the immediate object of the mind; for it is really only color which distinguishes visible objects. Thus, the soul sees only itself, since the immediate object of the mind is an essentially representative modification which the soul sees. For it is certain that the material object is never the immediate object of the mind, since frequently this object does not actually exist, and never did exist, such as when we are sleeping or have a fever ... According to his view, the soul sees only itself. (*Réponse*, IX, xii: OC VI, 78).

In this and other passages, Malebranche rules out the possibility that Arnauld (or anyone else) might hold external objects to be the direct objects of perception. Nor does he consider the possibility that *une modalité essentiellement représentative* (i.e. an idea) might be an act, not an object, of the mind.[3] For Malebranche, when Arnauld insists that *perceptions* represent, he must mean that what is directly perceived is a representative modification of the mind, a mental idea-object. That this is Malebranche's reading of Arnauld is clear from his frequent reiteration of the claim that on Arnauld's theory of ideas one never perceives anything but one's own self (i.e. the modifications or properties of one's own mind):

M. Arnauld agrees ... that we have an idea of God, and he insists that this idea of God is nothing other than the soul's perception, which he understands to be an essentially representative modality. He insists that the soul never sees

---

[3] See Cook, *op. cit.*, p. 54.

God in Himself, or in the universal Reason ... but only in contemplating its own modality. (*Réponse*, XXIV, vi: OC VI, 170)[4]

More recently, there was a minor resurgence of interest in Arnauld in the 1920s, when a number of scholars examined Arnauld's theory of ideas with the hope of claiming him as a proponent of their own respective views on perception. The debate between A. O. Lovejoy, Morris Ginsberg, and Ralph Withington Church is interesting in that, although Lovejoy and Church argue that Arnauld is a representationalist and Ginsberg argues that he is a direct realist, all three ascribe to Arnauld a theory in which ideas are objects of perception; that is, they are all committed (Ginsberg in spite of himself) to attributing to Arnauld an indirect realism of some sort.[5]

Lovejoy argues that Arnauld "plainly and persistently" repudiated "the doctrine of direct knowledge of real things" in favor of "epistemological dualism" (representationalism).[6] In fact, Lovejoy explicitly follows Malebranche in insisting that it is Malebranche's specific theory of ideas, and not the notion of representative perception in general, that Arnauld is attacking:

Thus it was agreed by both disputants that the issue under discussion was not whether *êtres représentatifs* of *some* kind are involved in our apprehension of physical objects, but whether the *êtres représentatifs* which both believed to be indispensible were, as Malebranche held, *êtres représentatifs distingués des perceptions*.[7]

Lovejoy believes that by *êtres représentatifs distingués des perceptions* Arnauld meant, and was concerned with, only "objective logical entities or essences" external to the mind, e.g. divine ideas. However, Arnauld did (Lovejoy argues) allow for ideas as "representative subjective states", i.e. modifications of the mind. By 'modification of the mind', Lovejoy insists, Arnauld here meant "mental content" or "percept", *not* mental act or function.[8] Ideas taken in this sense are "a unique kind of

---

[4] Malebranche is not alone among early modern philosophers in misinterpreting Arnauld. Thomas Reid, quite conveniently, also sees Arnauld as holding an object theory of ideas and an indirect realist view of perception. See Nadler, "Reid, Arnauld and the Objects of Perception".

[5] I am much indebted here to Cook's discussion and analysis of this debate (*op. cit.*); and Lennon, "Philosophical Commentary" to *The Search after Truth*.

[6] Lovejoy, "Representative Ideas in Malebranche and Arnauld", p.457.

[7] *Ibid.*, p. 452.

[8] *Ibid.*, p. 453–4.

images", and are directly perceived instead of corporeal objects; the latter are still perceived, albeit indirectly. "The duality, then, which Arnauld must be here understood to deny is not the duality of mental percept and physical thing perceived; it is, once more, the specific duality asserted by Malebranche, that of *perceptions* and *êtres représentatifs distingués de nos perceptions*."[9] According to Lovejoy, the theory of mediate perception that Arnauld is criticizing is that which would introduce not a *tertium quid* but a *quartum quid*; he is criticizing the doctrine which would add to the real object, the perceptual act, and the idea or percept (which is a modification of the mind), a non-mental, immaterial, and non-sensuous essence. "An immediatism which should dispense with ideas and percepts altogether was not within Arnauld's intellectual horizon."[10] "I contend ... that he held to the familiar theory that we perceive physical objects, not directly, but through the intermediation of mental entities called ideas, which are representative of the objects."[11] This last statement is correct, but, as we shall see, not in the indirect realist sense in which Lovejoy intends it to be taken.

In his study of Malebranche, Church explicitly follows Lovejoy in arguing that the view "that Arnauld is a naif realist of any sort is an interpretation of his doctrine for which there is not ... any good evidence": "the question which both Arnauld and Malebranche are attempting to decide is not whether knowledge is unmediated and direct, but whether representative ideas, which they both agree are necessary to knowledge, are, or are not, entities separate from perception."[12] 'Separate from perception', in this context, means, as Lovejoy understood it, "independently real". Arnauld is thus arguing against *êtres représentatifs* which are independently-existing objects; he is *not*, on this reading, antagonistic to the view that, although inseparable from (not existing independently of) acts of perception, representative ideas serve as the direct and immediate objects thereof: "[Arnauld] asserts that ideas are the immediate objects of knowledge; he denies that it follows from this fact that ideas are independent of perception, and he adds that it is only such ideas as are alleged to be independently real that he rejects."[13] According to Church, "Arnauld ... is aiming his

[9] *Ibid.*, p. 455.
[10] *Ibid.*, p. 459.
[11] A. O. Lovejoy, "Reply to Professor Laird", *Mind*, 33 (1924), p.180.
[12] Church, *A Study in the Philosophy of Malebranche*, pp. 154–5,
[13] *Ibid.*, p. 151.

criticism at what he calls a 'palace of ideas', a realm of beings independent of both thought and matter, and not, as he says, against representative ideas which are inseparable from perception,"[14] He provides the following analysis of Arnauld's theory: When Arnauld stresses that act of perception and idea are one (see Section 14 below), he means that in any perceptual experience there is necessarily involved both a mental act or operation and its immediate, non-physical representative object. These two "components" of perception are inseparable (neither can exist independently of the other: every perception has its immediate object, which is the "objective reality" of the external thing perceived; representative ideas exist only insofar as they are perceived) yet distinguishable. A *perception* is thus a complex, consisting of an act of the mind and an idea. "Perception [for Arnauld] is essentially representative because it contains an idea, and this idea, never a body, is the immediate object of every act of perception."[15] Veridical perception is tripartite, consisting of the mental act, its immediate mental object, and the external object which is mediately and indirectly perceived. Arnauld is a representationalist because "not things themselves, but ideas of them, are the immediate objects of perception."[16]

In the introduction to his translation of Malebranche's *Entretiens sur la Métaphysique et sur la Religion*, Ginsberg notes that Arnauld argues for the possibility of direct perception of real, corporeal things. Interestingly enough, however, his reading of Arnauld's analysis of perception closely follows that of Lovejoy and Church, in that he insists that ideas and acts of perception, although inseparable, are distinguishable, with ideas serving as the immediate objects of perception. That is, he too ascribes to Arnauld an object theory of ideas:

Arnauld is, in fact, prepared to give an analysis of the nature of apprehension (*perception*, as he calls it) which will obviate the need of assuming *êtres représentatifs*. Every idea, he urges, though in itself a unitary whole, has yet two relations. In the first place, it is related to the soul which it modifies, i.e. it involves an act or process of the mind; in the second place, it is related to the thing known, insofar as it is "objectively", i.e. as a content of the mind, present

[14] *Ibid.*, p.161.
[15] *Ibid.*, p. 160.
[16] *Ibid.*, p. 152.

to the mind. Apprehension is always *the apprehension of a content*. The act of apprehending includes or contains *the content apprehended* [emphases added].[17]

Note that once again perception, "through in itself a unitary whole", is a compound: it involves both a mental act and a mental content towards which that act is immediately directed. The content is that which is "apprehended" by the act. "The act of apprehending and the content or idea *apprehended*, though distinguishable, are not separable, but are rather aspects of one and the same concrete fact" (emphasis added).[18] What Arnauld stresses, according to Ginsberg, is that one is not entitled to speak here of two different entities. But all this means is that "we are not ... entitled to hypostatise the idea ... and regard it as something which has *an existence prior to all perception* and which must act upon the mind, in order to be perceived by it ... it is absurd to interpret this notion of an 'intelligible' sun, or an idea of the sun, as being a real existing object, standing between the mind and the real external sun, and rendering a knowledge of the latter forever impossible" (emphasis added).[19] Ginsberg's "realist" interpretation of Arnauld is remarkably similar to the representationalist interpretation offered by Lovejoy and Church. In fact, there seems to be only a nominal difference between the two, with Ginsberg stressing the inseparability of act and idea, and Church (and, it seems, Lovejoy) stressing their distinguishability.[20] We will see below just where these commentators have gone wrong.

14 *Arnauld's direct realism*

There are two essential ingredients in Arnauld's direct realism. The first is his general rejection of the object theory of ideas; that is, of *êtres représentatifs distingués des perceptions*. There are no representative ideas standing between the mental act (the act of perception) and the external object towards which that act is directed. His arguments against such a *tertium quid* were examined in the previous chapter. The second element is his identification of representative idea (*idée*) and act

[17] Morris Ginsberg, *Malebranche's Dialogues on Metaphysics and Religion* (New York: Macmillan, 1923), p. 40.
[18] *Ibid.*, p. 41.
[19] *Ibid.*, p. 41.
[20] Cf. Cook, "Arnauld's Alleged Representationalism".

of perception (*perception*). What such an identification comes to, and how it constitutes a theory of perceptual direct realism, is the subject of this section.

The act theory of ideas

Arnauld's declared aim is to prove *géometriquement la fausseté des idées, prises pour des être représentatifs*, where the term *être représentatif* refers to a representative idea distinct from the act of perception. In order to appreciate fully Arnauld's theory of ideas, one must keep in mind the theory of ideas against which he is arguing. It is necessary to remember, that is, that Arnauld is not arguing against the existence of representative ideas *per se*, but only representative ideas considered distinct from the act of perception, i.e. idea-objects:

The only representative entities which I reject as superfluous are those which are imagined to be really distinct from ideas considered as perceptions. For I am far from rejecting all kinds of representative entities or modalities; since I maintain that it is clear, to whoever reflects on what goes on in the mind, that all our perceptions are essentially representative modalities. (VFI, 199)

This representative character of ideas will be looked at in greater detail in the next chapter. For the present, it is sufficient to note that such acts *do* represent external objects, and do so in a non-pictorial way; that is, they are *images*, but not pictures, of objects (VFI, 199). What I want to stress here, however, is Arnauld's contention that because ideas do represent, the *idea* of an external object is *identical* with the *perception* of that object. In his first three definitions, which serve as the "axioms" for his "geometric proof", Arnauld identifies the idea of an object with the *act* of thinking of, perceiving, or otherwise knowing that object:

1. I call soul or mind thinking substance.
2. Thinking, knowing and perceiving are all the same thing.
3. I also take the idea of an object and the perception of an object to be the same thing. I leave aside the question whether there are other things to which the name 'idea' might be given. But it is certain that there are ideas in this sense, and that these ideas are attributes or modifications of our soul. (VFI, 198)

The idea of an object is *not* the object of the act of perceiving; it is that act, the perception, itself.

Since he rejects *des êtres représentatifs distingués des perceptions*, that is, representative entities standing between the mind of the perceiver and the external object; and since he identifies the idea of an object with the act of perceiving that object, which act is a modification of the mind, Arnauld's ontology of perception is clear: in normal, veridical perceptual acquaintance with an external object, there exists only the perceiving mind (that is, the mind of the percipient modified only by its own activity) and the external object perceived. Nothing stands or mediates between them.

If Arnauld identifies the idea of an object with the act of perceiving the object, if they are one and the same entity, then why does he need two names, 'idea' and 'perception'? Because this single entity, the act of the perceiving mind, stands in two relations. One relation is to the mind of which the perceptual act is the activity, i.e. which it modifies; the other relation is to the object perceived:

I have said that I take the perception and the idea to be the same thing. Nevertheless, it must be remarked that this thing, although single, stands in two relations: one to the soul which it modifies, the other to the thing perceived, in so far as it exists objectively in the soul. The word *perception* more directly indicates the first relation; the word *idea*, the latter. (VFI, 198)

The *perception* of a square refers to the fact that the perceptual act is a modification or property of the mind, of a perceiving, thinking substance. The *idea* of the square refers to the fact that such an act is itself essentially related to an object by way of representing it (see Chapter 6). Arnauld stresses that it is important to keep in mind that we are dealing here *not* with two intimately related, even inseparable, entities, but with one single entity standing in two different relations:

There are not two different entities here, but one and the same modification of our soul, which involves essentially these two relations; since I cannot have a perception which is not, at the same time, my perceiving mind's perception [*la perception de mon esprit comme apercevant*] and the perception of something as perceived. (VFI, 198)

As noted in chapter 2, mind, for Arnauld, is active, not only in willing, judging, and doubting (as it is for Descartes), but also in understanding and perceiving. "To acknowledge that the soul is active with regard to one of its faculties, i.e. the will, is to acknowledge that it is active absolutely and by its nature" (VFI, 343). The activities of the mind thus include perceiving and knowing. Moreover, these activities are just modifications of the mind. Being a wholly active substance, any modification (property) of the mind must be an activity. For the mind to be active, then, is simply for it to give itself new modifications, which it can do at any moment not only with regard to willing, but also with regard to perceiving (VFI, 342). Thus, to perceive is for the mind to act, to perform an operation, and, thus, to give itself a new modification. [*L'esprit*] *a ... le pouvoir de se donner différents perceptions* (VFI, 343). The mind, for Arnauld, does not *receive* ideas; it is not passive with regard to its cognitive functions (as Arnauld felt Malebranche made it). It perceives, it acts. These acts, being modifications of the soul, are just the soul existing in such-and-such a manner. They are not entities existing independently of the mind, nor are they entities which the mind receives from without or towards which it is directed.

When Arnauld says that representative ideas are *la même chose* as these mental acts of perceiving, he is saying that these modifications of the mind are related both to the mind which they modify and to the objects which they represent. The terms 'idea' and 'perception' refer to one entity: the mental act of perceiving. The latter term denotes the ontological status of the idea-perception: it is a mode of a mental substance. The former term denotes the fact that it has external reference. They do not refer to two inseparable but distinct entities.

Can we clarify Arnauld's position? Consider, for example, the case of a boy whose father has a brother. Here we have a single entity (the boy) who stands in two relations – one to his father (and the causal relationship between the father and his son might be seen as analogous to the causal relationship that obtains, for Arnauld, between an active thinking substance and its thoughts and perceptions, although a son is not a mode of his father), and one to his father's brother. By virtue of the first relation the boy is called a 'son'. By virtue of the second relation he is called a 'nephew'. But there are not two different entities, a son and a nephew. Or consider an outstretched arm pointing to an object. The arm is related to the body of which it forms a part; but it is also related to the object towards which it is directed, much in the same way (as we shall see) as mental acts are, for Arnauld, related to the external objects towards which they are directed.

Insufficient attention to this point leads one into the confusions of

Lovejoy, Church, and Ginsberg. They misinterpret Arnauld's *identification* of mental act and idea as a statement of mere *inseparability* between act and content apprehended as parts of a single yet complex whole. Thus, they have fallen into the erroneous reading discussed above.

Lovejoy is closest to a proper understanding of Arnauld in this regard. He agrees that Arnauld maintains that *êtres représentatifs* are "identical with our perceptions as subjective states."[21] Lovejoy realizes that Arnauld is dealing here not with two entities, but with "a single modification of the mind which essentially has two relations." Where Lovejoy's interpretation goes wrong is in deciding what the status of this modification is. "Is the 'modification of the mind' denoted by this word [idea] and by its synonym 'perception', a mental act or function, or a mental content? perceiving or percept?"[22] As we saw above, Lovejoy opts for the mental content or percept. While he does recognize the strict identity between idea and perception, he takes the representative idea-perception to be a content perceived. Thus, he says that the "duality" Arnauld denies is not that between mental percept and physical thing, but between perception and *êtres représentatifs distingués de nos perceptions*.[23] But has not Lovejoy reintroduced the duality between perception as mental act and perception as separate representative entity? If the term 'idea-perception' refers to the matter or content apprehended by the mind, rather than to the act of perceiving or apprehending, does not Arnauld then require a process of apprehending on the part of the mind? How else could this "psychic content apprehended" be apprehended? In spite of himself, Lovejoy must hold that Arnauld posited both idea-perceptions *qua* content, and mental processes of apprehending this content; that is, that Arnauld posited *des idées distingués des perceptions*.

Church and Ginsberg, on the other hand, do not even realize that Arnauld's intention is to identify, in a very strict sense, the idea of an object with the mental act of perceiving that object. Church, as noted earlier, sees the idea-perception as a complex containing two inseparable, yet distinguishable, entities, one of which (the perception) is directed toward the other (the idea). For two things to be *une même*

---

[21] Lovejoy, "Representative Ideas in Malebranche and Arnauld", 453.
[22] *Ibid.*, pp. 453–5.
[23] *Ibid.*, p. 455.

chose is, on this reading, merely for them to be inseparable components of a unified, but complex, whole: "Perception has two components; and to the one of these that is a modification of the soul the term 'perception', taken strictly, belongs. The other one of these components ... is what the term 'idea' ought to signify."[24] Ginsberg's reading is the same: perception is a "unitary whole", a "concrete fact" composed of the act of apprehending and the content or idea *apprehended*. These constituents of perception, "though distinguishable, are not separable."[25] Like Church, Ginsberg fails to perceive Arnauld's intention. 'Idea' and 'perception' are two names for one and the same entity; not for two inseparable parts composing a complex whole, one of which parts apprehends, or is directed toward, the other. Nonetheless, there is a core of truth in Church's and Ginsberg's readings. As Arnauld states (VFI, 199), every perception can be considered *qua* mental act or *qua* representation (see Chapter 6). Thus, there *is* a sense in which it is possible to distinguish two aspects of any perception: namely, its reality as an act of perceiving and its representational content. But the content is *not* what is *apprehended* by the act, as Church and Ginsberg would have it.

Arnauld's identifiction of the idea of an object with the perception of it forms the basis of what can be called his "act theory of ideas". It remains to be seen how this ties in with a direct realist theory of perceptual acquaintance. Once again, it is helpful to examine Arnauld's theory of perception in the light of the theory he rejects.

For Malebranche, there are three things involved in the perception of an external object: the act of perceiving, the representative idea (which I speak of here as "colored" by sensation, as discussed in Chapter 3; technically, however, sensation adds a fourth element to the list), and the external body. There are, thus, two immediate relations involved, as there are in any version of a representative theory of perception: one relation between the mental act and the idea, and another between the idea and the object it represents. Each of these two relations is direct. A third relation, between the mental act and the external body, is indirect, mediated by the idea.

For Arnauld, there are only two things involved in the perception of an external object: the mental activity of perceiving, and the external

24 Church, *op. cit.*, p. 152.
25 Ginsberg, *op. cit.*, p. 41.

object perceived. There is, thus, only one relation, that between the act of the mind and the external object, and this relation is direct and immediate. External things are perceived directly, without the mediation of any third thing (or second relation) standing between the act and its external object. Since 'idea' and 'perception' refer to one and the same thing, to have an idea of an object is to have a perception of that object, i.e. to perceive that object, not some non-physical proxy. Several passages in VFI support such a direct realist reading of Arnauld:

> Since God desired that our mind should know bodies, and that bodies should be known by our mind, it was undoubtedly simpler for him to render our mind capable of knowing bodies immediately, that is, without representative entities distinct from perceptions ... and bodies capable of being known immediately by our mind, rather than leaving the soul powerless to see them otherwise than by means of certain representative entities. (VFI, 222)

Arnauld later stresses that God did, in fact, provide us with the ability "to perceive immediately" external bodies:

> If someone should ask ... why our soul is able to see material things (such as its own body and those which surround it), even though they are remote from it, it is much better to respond by saying that it is able to see them because such is its nature, and because God has given it the faculty of thinking. (VFI, 290–1)

Elsewhere, Arnauld has recourse to the efficacy of God's will in arguing for the direct and unmediated perception of external objects. The mind is able to see, and, in fact, does see, what God wants it to see. Having joined the mind to a body, God clearly wants the mind to be able to perceive this body, and not merely some *corps intelligible*. The same applies to the sun, the sky, etc. Thus, the mind *is* able to perceive, and does perceive, these external, physical bodies, and not intelligible representative proxies (VFI, 231).

In Section 13 above, I note that Lovejoy is, in a sense, correct in asserting that Arnauld holds "that we perceive physical objects, not directly, but through the intermediation of mental entities called ideas, which are representative of the objects." Lovejoy, in other words, rightly claims that Arnauld does maintain the distinction between immediate and mediate objects of perception, and that external objects are perceived mediately. Yet if the above exposition is correct, and

Arnauld holds that external objects are the direct and immediate objects of perception, that there is a direct and unmediated relation between the mental act of perceiving and the material body perceived, it would seem that Lovejoy's claim is, for Arnauld, an untenable one (except in some philosophically uninteresting everyday situation where one sees something indirectly because one sees its reflection in a mirror; or, in general, where one sees, hears, tastes, smells, etc. some material body indirectly by means of some other material body or proxy). There is, however, only a *prima facie* conflict here. And a close examintion of Arnauld's text shows that Lovejoy, though correct in his general claim, is mistaken in his representationalist interpretation of Arnauld's meaning on this point.

Arnauld did maintain that we do, indeed, perceive external things only mediately, i.e. by means of ideas. But the sense in which this is true is such that it turns out to be a trivial claim, and one which further supports a direct realist reading of Arnauld.

I here declare that if conceiving the sun, a square or a cubic number *immediately* is understood as opposed to conceiving them by means of ideas, such as I have defined them in the preceding chapter, i.e. by ideas which are not distinct from perceptions, then I agree that we never see them immediately; for it is clearer than day that we are only able to see, perceive or know them by means of the perceptions which we have of them ... If *not* knowing them immediately is understood to mean not being able to know them except by means of representative entities distinct from perceptions, then I insist that, in this sense, we can know material things not only mediately, but also immediately ... without there being any intermediary between our perceptions and the object [*sans qu'il y ait aucun milieu entre nos perceptions et l'objet*]. (VFI, 210)

Arnauld is emphatic here in maintaining that the mind's perception of external objects is, in the ordinary sense of the term, direct and immediate. Certainly it is true that one cannot perceive an object without a perception, without any perceptual activity on the part of the mind. Acts of perceiving mediate in the sense that they make known their objects. Thus, one cannot perceive an object without a perceiving of the object. Yet Arnauld is insisting here that this is a trivial claim. If all that is meant by *mediate* perception is perception of an object mediated by an act of perceiving (the "idea" in Arnauld's sense), then he is willing to grant that objects are mediately perceived. "How could our mind perceive something if there were no idea of it, that is to say, no perception of it ?" (VFI, 221). Likewise, a baseball cannot be thrown without a throwing of the baseball. But there is a great difference between claiming that perception is mediate in this trivial sense and claiming that perception is mediate in the sense that there is a *milieu entre nos perceptions et l'objet*. Since it is with this latter sense in mind that representationalists have claimed that we perceive objects only mediately, Arnauld's concession to "mediate" perception is only a verbal concession. In any non-trivial sense, the perception of external things is direct and unmediated.

Another way of putting Arnauld's point is that ideas *qua* perceptions (mental acts) are *means* of perceiving external objects. Ideas are not that which we perceive, but rather the perceivings by which we perceive physical things. Arnauld brings in a Scholastic distinction to make his point. He insists that an idea-perception is primarily *id quo intelligitur*; only by means of a second-order act of (reflective) perception (or by means of the *réflexion virtuelle* which accompanies every perception) is it *id quod intelligitur* (VFI, 246).[26] A representationalist might claim, as well, that ideas are *id quo intelligitur*: one is able to perceive external things only because (as Malebranche would say) their intelligible proxies are present to the mind. Yet the difference lies in the fact that, for the representationalist, the external object is perceived because some other thing (the means) is apprehended immediately. For Arnauld, the external object is perceived because an act of perception is directed towards it, has it as its immediate object.

There seems to be, however, an apparently sturdier basis for attributing to Arnauld an object theory of ideas and the accompanying non-trivial claim that external objects are perceived only mediately while ideas are the immediate objects of perception. All commentators who do interpret Arnauld in this way focus on Chapter VI of VFI to support their claims. Does he, in that chapter, waver at all from a direct realist account of perceptual acquaintance? He begins the chapter by insisting that he does not reject certain *façons de parler*, such as "we never see things immediately; it is their ideas which are the immediate object of our thought" (VFI, 203: this proposition will hereafter be referred to as *P*). The passage commentators have had

---

[26] See St Thomas, *Summa Theologia*, Part I, Q. 85, Art. 2: "The intelligible species is not what is actually understood (*id quod intelligitur*), but that by means of which (*id quo*) the intellect understands."

the most trouble reconciling with a direct realist reading of Arnauld is the following:

Since every perception is essentially representative of something, and is thus called an idea, a perception cannot be essentially reflective on itself without this idea (that is, the objective reality of the thing which the mind is said to perceive) being its immediate object. So if I am thinking of the sun, the objective reality of the sun, which is present to my mind, is the immediate object of this perception; and the possible or actual sun, which is outside of my mind, is its mediate object, so to speak. And thus, it is clear that, without having recourse to representative entities distinct from perceptions, it is quite true, in this sense, that it is our ideas which we immediately see and which are the immediate object of our thought, not only with regard to material things, but with regard to all things generally. (VFI, 204)

Most commentators on Arnauld stumble on this passage. Lovejoy, for example, insists that "I do not know that epistemological dualism could be more plainly expressed." Church, too, believes that Arnauld is firmly insisting on a representational view of perception.[27] Certainly, the passage seems to assert that in veridical perception external objects are, in a non-trivial sense, only indirectly and mediately perceived; representative ideas, on the other hand, are directly and immediately perceived, and it is by means of perceiving these latter that objects are perceived. It seems, in other words, either that Arnauld is caught in an inconsistency, or that the direct realist reading of him is wrong.

Yet, as Arnauld himself insists, the inconsistency is only *prima facie*. It would appear that one cannot *admettre pour vraies ces façons de parler* (that is, that one cannot accept *P*) without at the same time being obliged to admit *la philosophie des fausses idées* (VFI, 203): "It is hard to understand how these ways of speaking [*façons de parler*] can be true if, besides the objects which we know, there is not something in our mind that represents them" (VFI, 203). It is important to note that Arnauld constantly refers to *P* as a *façon de parler*. To accept *P* is not necessarily to accept the substantive theory of perception it would seem to involve; it is only to accept a way of speaking. One may, then, try to reconcile this way of speaking with whatever position on perception one may, in fact, hold. This can be done simply by interpreting *P* as one sees fit. This is exactly what Arnauld does.

I do not reject these ways of speaking. In fact, I believe that they are true, if they are understood properly ... But I deny that it follows from this that it is necessary to acknowledge that there are ideas other than those which I have defined ... which have nothing in common with representative entities distinct from perceptions. (VFI, 203–4)

Thomas Reid insists that Arnauld is here caught in "a weak attempt to reconcile two inconsistent doctrines ... Arnauld's notion of ideas ... seemed to be, in some sort, given up by himself in his attempting to reconcile it to the common doctrine concerning ideas".[28] But Arnauld is *not* trying here to reconcile two conflicting theories of perception. He *is* trying here to reconcile a mere *façon de parler* with is own act theory of ideas. Alternatively stated, he is trying to reconcile a phrase most often found accompanying a representative theory of perception with his own direct realism: "I do not need to acknowledge any ideas other than those which I have defined, which are not at all distinct from perceptions, in order to accept the truth of this way of speaking: we never see things immediately; it is their ideas which are the immediate object of our thought" (VFI, 206–7).

Two questions, then, need to be answered. First, why does Arnauld feel the need to admit *P*, to accept this *façon de parler*, in the first place? And second, how does he effect the reconciliation? How does he interpret *P* to fit his act theory of ideas and the direct realism it involves?

The first question seems difficult to answer in a definitive way. Cook suggests that accepting such a way of speaking is all a part of being "genuinely Cartesian":

Arnauld attempts to interpret, in a way consonant with his theory, the Cartesian dictum that we perceive ideas immediately and physical objects only mediately. Apparently, he cannot maintain this, but Arnauld is eager to show that this theory is genuinely Cartesian. Thus, he never questions the dictum; he sees the apparent clash between it and his theory as a difficulty that must be surmounted. His stance is that of a follower of Descartes who must interpret the truths of the master.[29]

---

[28] See Reid, *Philosophical Works*, vol. 1, p. 297.
[29] Cook, "Arnauld's Alleged Representationalism", p. 58.

Cook never justifies the claim that accepting *P* is part of being "genuinely Cartesian". It is not clear that such a thesis is true, much less that it could be maintained without begging the question and not admitting anyone to be a Cartesian who does not accept *P*. Nor does Cook support his contention that *P* is a "principle found in Descartes' philosophy".[30] Nevertheless, there is support for part of Cook's claim, namely that *Arnauld* felt that in order to be a faithful disciple of Descartes one had to subscribe to *P* (at least nominally, as a *façon de parler*). Immediately after offering his understanding of *P*, Arnauld insists that this interpretation is not *ad hoc*, but follows closely Descartes' own meaning: "Lest it be thought that I have invented all this in order to extricate myself from this difficulty, the author of the *Recherche* will find the same thing in the *Meditations* of M. Descartes" (VFI, 205). Like Descartes, Arnauld insists, he too is capable of admitting *P* and its distinction between immediate and mediate objects of perception without recourse to *êtres représentatifs distingués de ma pensée* (VFI, 205–6).

How, then, does Arnauld reconcile *P* with a direct realist theory of perception? The key lies in his account of "virtual reflection". Every perceptual act (taken broadly to mean not only acts of perception *per se*, but *any* thought activity) is a conscious act; that is, one accompanied by awareness. One cannot think of something without being aware that one is thinking of something. This position is stated very early in VFI. *La pensée que notre âme a de soi-même* is a constant feature of one's mental life, since "whatever it is that I am knowing, I know that I know it, by means of a certain virtual reflection [*réflexion virtuelle*] which accompanies all my thoughts ... I thus know myself while knowing other things. And, in effect, it is principally this which, it seems, distinguishes intelligent beings from those which are not intelligent – the former *sunt conscia sui, et suae operationis*, the latter are not" (VFI, 184–5). He elaborates in Chapter vi:

Our thought or perception is essentially reflective on itself, or, as it is said more aptly in Latin, *est sui conscia*. For I never think without knowing that I am

---

[30] *Ibid.*, p. 61. Such a claim might be supported by Descartes' definition of an idea as the object of "immediate awareness" (Second Replies: AT VII, 160; CSM II, 113). In his reply to the Third Set of Objections Descartes says that he uses 'idea' to stand for "whatever is immediately perceived by the mind" (*quod immediate a mente percipitur*) (AT VII, 181; CSM II, 127).

thinking. I never know a square without my knowing that I know it; I never see the sun, or, to put the matter beyond all doubt, I never seem to see the sun without my being certain that I seem to see it ... at the same time that I conceive [something], I know that I am conceiving it. (VFI, 204)

Arnauld accounts for this feature of mental life by insisting that every mental act is reflective on itself and, thus, accompanied by a self-awareness. Every perception, in addition to being the perception of some object, also has itself (an idea-perception) as its object. Thus, whenever one perceives, one is aware that one is perceiving.

Two brief remarks need to be made here before continuing. First, in Arnauld's mind this is a very traditional position to take. Elsewhere in the passage quoted from above (VFI, 204), Arnauld refers the reader to St Augustine's *De Trinitate* (X, 10), where Augustine discusses the knowledge that the mind necessarily has of itself. And clearly he saw it as the correct Cartesian position. He was not unaware of Descartes' definition of *cogitatio*: "I use this term [thought] to include everything that is within us in such a way that we are immediately aware of it" (Second Replies: AT VII, 160; CSM II, 113). In a letter to Mersenne (January 28, 1641) Descartes writes that "we have ideas not only of all that is in our intellect, but also of all that is in the will. For we cannot will anything without knowing that we will it, nor could we know this without an idea; but I do not claim that the idea is different from the action itself" (AT III, 295; Kenny, 93).

Second, this last phrase from Descartes' letter is extremely important for both Arnauld and Descartes. "Virtual reflection" does not, for Arnauld, involve a second perceptual act directed at the first. On the contrary, it is the *self*-awareness possessed by the act of perception itself. Self-reflection is an essential part of any mental act. The immediate awareness of a perception is not an experience distinct from having a perception. "It is certain that we cannot will anything without perceiving *by the same means (par mesme moyen)* that we are willing it ..." (*Passions de l'Ame*, I, xix: AT XI, 343; CSM I, 335 [translation modified]; emphasis added).

Arnauld distinguishes the "virtual reflection", or awareness, accompanying every perceptual act from "explicit" reflection, from a second-order act of perception directed towards the first and having it as its object: "Besides this reflection which can be called virtual, which is found in all our perceptions, there is another, more explicit reflection by which we examine our perception by means of another perception" (VFI, 204). "Virtual" reflection necessarily and involuntarily accompanies every perception. "Express" reflection is a deliberate act performed on one's perception, and has the latter as its intended object. Once again, the distinction is one which is found in Descartes. In addition to an awareness accompanying every thought, it is possible, by focusing one's attention on that thought, to obtain a reflective knowledge of it: "It must be noted that all things, the cognition of which is said to be placed in us by nature, are not thereby expressly known by us; but only are such that, without any sense experience, we can know them from the powers of our own mind" (*Epistola ad Voetium*: AT VIII-2, 166–7). I follow Robert McRae's gloss on this passage: "We have implicit knowledge of everything present to consciousness, and any part of this implicit knowledge can be rendered explicit by the direction of attention upon it."[31]

To return to Arnauld's argument, every perception is reflective upon itself and thus has itself as an object (in addition to having as its object the external thing of which it is a direct perception). That is, every perception of an external object also has as its object a perception of an external object – namely, itself. Now every perception of an external object, being essentially representative of its external object, is an "idea". Thus, every perception has an idea as its object – again, itself:

> Since *every perception* is essentially representative of something, and is thus called an idea, a perception cannot be essentially *reflective on itself* without this idea (that is, the objective reality of the thing which the mind is said to perceive) being its immediate object. So that ... the objective reality ... is the object *of this perception*. (VFI, 204; emphases added)

This brings out the important point that what is brought to awareness in virtual reflection is not simply that one is perceiving, but that one is perceiving such-and-such an object. I am aware not only that I am perceiving, but that I am perceiving *x*. This is the sense in which the second clause of P (*ce sont leurs idées qui sont l'objet immédiat de notre pensée*) is true. And we have seen that the first clause of P (*nous ne voyons point immédiatement les choses*) is, for Arnauld, trivially true. In fact,

---

[31] Robert McRae, "Descartes' Definition of Thought", in R. J. Butler, ed. *Cartesian Studies* (New York: Bobbs-Merrill, 1972), p. 67. See also Margaret Wilson, *Descartes* (London: Routledge and Kegan Paul), 160–65.

he argues for this in Chapter VI immeditely following his discussion of "virtual reflection". Thus, the sense in which Arnauld accepts *P* is clear.

Does *P* compromise Arnauld's direct realism? I do not see why it should, contrary to what Lovejoy and Church have to say on the passage. Arnauld's position is simply the following: every act of perception, by which we immediately and directly perceive an external object (or which allows for the *mediate* perception of such an object, in the trivial sense outlined above) is also immediately reflective upon itself. Thus, when directly perceiving an external thing, one is always aware that one is perceiving that thing. Arnauld's position may be represented as follows, where an arrow (→) indicates the relation 'immediately directed towards':

act of perception of *x* (idea of *x*)→ external object *x*

Arnauld later states that since the act of perception is essentially representative of the external object perceived (the feature of perception represented in the diagram by 'of *x*'), and thus *is* the object in the understanding *objectivement* or *intelligiblement* (see Chapter 6 below), his position can be understood as follows: "Although I immediately see this intelligible sun by means of the virtual reflection which I have of my perception, I do not leave it at that, but *this same perception*, in which I see this sun intelligibly, allows me to see [*me fait voir*], at the same time, the material sun which God has created" (VFI, 230; emphasis added). The same act of perception which reflects on (is aware of) itself is the means of perceiving immediately and directly an external body. As he puts it, a perception is both *id quo intelligitur* and *id quod intelligitur* (*elle soit aussi en quelque sort* id quod intelligitur *par la réflexion virtuelle qui lui est essentielle* [VFI, 246]).

It is possible, I think, to misread Arnauld's remarks on "virtual reflection" as supporting a theory of indirect realism, by interpreting the immediate self-awareness inherent in every perceptual act as a means of perceiving the external object. In other words, one is tempted to read Arnauld as saying that mediate perception (awareness) of the object comes about by means of immediate perception (awareness) of the perception itself. However, it should be clear from the foregoing that this is an incorrect reading. The immediate self-awareness in every perceptual act necessarily *accompanies*, or occurs along with, that perceptual act's direct and immediate apprehension of an external thing. But this awareness is *not* itself a means by which the thing is perceived, in the sense that an indirect realist might insist that awareness of a sense datum is a means by which the external object is perceived.

Michael J. Costa offers an interesting interpretation of Arnauld's meaning here. He suggests that we see *P* and the remarks on *réflexion virtuelle* as describing a criterial relation instead of a method- or means-relation: "Arnauld, indeed, holds that mediate awareness of the object of thought *requires* immediate awareness of the thought itself; but this is because immediate awareness is an *essential* or *criterial* property of thoughts for Arnauld, and not because immediate awareness is the method or means by which we achieve mediate awareness."[32] If 'mediate awareness of the object of thought' has the trivial sense discussed above, then I think Costa accurately captures Arnauld's meaning. When I see the sun, the reflective awareness that I am seeing the sun is not the means by which I see the sun. Rather, it is a property of my activity which qualifies it as a *seeing* of the sun. If this property were not present, then we would be dealing with something less than seeing proper (e.g. the "perception" accomplished by non-human beings or things, such as animals or electronic eyes).[33] As we saw above, Arnauld himself makes this implicit self-awareness that which distinguishes human thought and perception from the thought processes of non-intelligent beings (VFI, 184).[34]

---

[32] Michael J. Costa, "Arnauld, Ideas and Perception" (unpublished MS), pp. 11–12.

[33] *Ibid.*, p. 12.

[34] Costa's interpretation of *réflexion virtuelle*, however, is less than satisfying. He reduces it to "the capacity or potentiality of mental states to become the objects of explicit awareness of other mental states. A mental state has the feature of being reflexive only if it has the capacity to be the object of explicit awareness of another mental state" (*ibid.*, p. 10). His only basis for this reading is Arnauld's use of the term *virtuelle*. To be virtually or implicitly aware of a mental state is to have the capacity to become explicitly aware of it; it is not to be aware of it in any way. Clearly such a reading goes against the interpretation offered above, which holds that for Arnauld every perceptual act is, *in fact*, reflective on itself as well as capable of becoming the object of explicit awareness (*réflexion expresse*) for another mental act. Costa, in fact, notes that Arnauld might believe that his explanation "leaves something out, the 'feel' of immediate awareness, perhaps; but he admittedly could not further *describe* what is left out" (p. 11). Arnauld would insist that Costa's reading does, indeed, overlook an important phenomenological fact, as my quotations from VFI indicate.

Idea-perceptions and sensations

In Chapter 2, we saw that Arnauld gives a standard, though occasionalist, Cartesian account of sensations (*qualités sensibles*). Pains, color, heat and other sensations are simply mental correlates of matter in motion.[35] More particularly, on the occasion of certain motions in the brain (transmitted there mechanistically from the outer nerve-extremities by means of small fibers), God causes *perceptions* of color, sound, light, and pain: "It can hardly be doubted that it is God who gives us our perceptions of light, sounds and other sensible qualities, as well as of pain, hunger and thirst, although he does so on the occasion of what takes place in our sense organs or in the constitution of our body" (VFI, 349).

The colors and other sensible qualities we perceive are not actual properties of the external world, but have only a mental existence. There is nothing in the material world, comprised solely of extended matter in motion, even remotely similar to the sensations occurring in the mind. This is, of course, Descartes' position:

We know that the nature of our soul is such that different local motions are quite sufficient to produce all the sensations in the soul. What is more, we actually experience the various sensations as they are produced in the soul, and we do not find that anything reaches the brain from the external sense organs except for motions of this kind. In view of all this we have every reason to conclude that the properties in external objects to which we apply

---

Costa insists that from his reading "certain other of Arnauld's claims follow without further effort: If immediate awareness is merely a capacity, then it is nothing like seeing an image-like content of one's mental state. Also, the immediate awareness of a mental state, on this view, is nothing distinct from the having of that mental state" (p. 11). With regard to the first point, it is not clear how actual, as opposed to merely potential, immediate self-awareness on the part of a perceptual act implies "seeing an image-like content". The *réflexion*, virtual or explicit, is directed at the same object – the primary perceptual act. Arnauld constantly insists that this act, though representative, is not "image-like" in the sense of "pictorial". If explicit reflection is not seeing an "image-like content", then neither is virtual reflection. With regard to the second point, I have shown above that reading *réflexion virtuelle* as an actual self-awareness still does not commit one to positing anything more than the mental act itself, an act which also happens to be self-reflective. Thus, Costa's interpretation does not have any special explanatory advantage, and it does not square either with Arnauld's text, particularly the passages cited above, or with the phenomenological data Arnauld intends to capture. Compare Jean-Paul Sartre's discussion of self-consciousness in *The Transcendence of the Ego* (New York: Noonday Press, 1957), pp. 40–41, 45.

[35] Cf. *Principia* IV, 189: AT VIII-1, 315–16; CSM I, 279–80.

the terms light, color, smell, taste, sound, heat and cold – as well as the other tactile qualities and even what are called "substantial forms" – are, so far as we can see, simply various dispositions in those objects which make them able to set up various kinds of motions in our nerves which are required to produce all the various sensations in our soul ... Now I have given an account of the various sizes, shapes and motions which are to be found in all bodies; and apart from these the only things which we perceive by our senses as being located outside are light, color, smell, taste, sound and tactile qualities. And I have just demonstrated that these are nothing else in the objects – or at least we cannot apprehend them as being anything else – but certain dispositions depending on size, shape and motion. (*Principia*, IV, 198–9: AT VIII–1, 321; CSM I, 285–6)

For Descartes, our perceptions of extended bodies *qua* extended, that is our perceptions of the mathematical properties of physical bodies, do have a "true" relation to the world. Such perceptions are clear and distinct, and are reliable guides to the nature of the material world (Med. III: AT VII, 43; CSM II, 30). Sensations, on the other hand, are "obscure and confused" and "provide [the mind with] subject matter for error" (Fourth Replies: AT VII, 232; CSM II, 163. Med. III: AT VII, 44; CSM II, 30). They do not furnish true and reliable information about the material world.

For the most part, Arnauld follows Descartes closely here. He insists that sensations are, in an important sense, clear and distinct: they display a content to the mind, and can be distinguished from other perceptions. Considered in themselves, without any external reference, *all* ideas are true. "I know my sensations clearly and distinctly when I consider them only as modifications of my soul" (VFI, 318). It is only when one relates sensations to the world and considers them to be properties of material things that they are false. Contrary to Malebranche's view, it is wrong to oppose "seeing a thing by means of a clear idea" and "seeing it only by means of an internal sensation": "since pain, color and other similar things are known obscurely and confusedly only when we consider them, erroneously, as existing outside our soul, it follows that the ideas of these sensible qualities are obscure and confused only when they are related to bodies, as if they were modifications of them" (VFI, 317–18).

Although false and misleading, such a projection of sensible qualities onto the material bodies perceived is, nevertheless, a constant, even essential, feature of sense perception. Arnauld asks:

What is sensing a body? Let us consider the sense of sight, being that which we know the best. It is seeing the body as luminous or colored. Now how can we see a colored body, since color is not a modification of bodies, but of our mind? By applying to a body the sensation of color, which God gives us in order that we may discern the body more easily. Which are the bodies that we sense by the sense of sight? Those to which we apply the sensations of color or of light. (*Défense*, 38: 409)

This is Arnauld's clearest statement regarding the role of sensations in perception: *Notre esprit les applique aux corps sensibles*. The position is, as Arnauld indicates, a Cartesian one. In *Les Passions de l'Ame* (I, xxiii: "The perceptions we refer to objects outside us"), Descartes states:

When we see the light of a torch and hear the sound of a bell, the sound and the light are two different actions which, simply by producing two different movements in some of our nerves, and through them in our brain, give to the soul two different sensations. And we refer these sensations to the subjects which we suppose to be their causes in such a way that we think that we see the torch itself and hear the bell, and not that we have sensory perception merely of movements coming from these objects. (AT XI, 346; CSM I, 337)

Any adequate theory of direct realism should tell how sensation is related to perception, how a sense impression relates to a perceptual act. Arnauld does not provide much detail on this, but some main features of an account are discernible. Because Arnauld holds a direct realist theory of perception, sensations are not going to function as apprehended phenomenal objects (such is the role given to sense data by recent theorists). That is, they are not intermediary mental entities which we perceive or otherwise experience and from which we infer what is in the world. They are not objects the immediate awareness of which causally provokes, or otherwise provides a basis for, a mediate awareness of external objects. It is evident from the passage quoted above that sensations are incorporated into the *immediate* perception of external objects. They are, in effect, the basis of the sensuous character of that perception: I perceive a red, hot iron; a yellow, warm sun; a blue, cold piece of ice. Sensation is thus an integral part of external perception – it is what allows one to perceive an object *lumineux ou coloré*. Though only a modification of the mind occurring on the occasion of certain motions in the brain, the sensation (red, for example) is projected by the perceiver onto the perceived object which initiated the train of motions terminating in the brain. The sensation, then, "colors" the direct and immediate perception of the external object, making it the perception of a colored object, a hot object, a pleasant object, etc.

Arnauld's Cartesian account of sensation, and his acceptance of Descartes' picture of the physical world, indicate that he was far-removed from any simplistic form of naive realism. Sensible qualities are not parts of material bodies. They are mental phenomena which are projected onto perceived bodies. In this sense, normal veridical sense perception is misleading: it leads one to attribute to physical things properties which have only a mental existence.

15 *Descartes' theory of ideas*

Arnauld presents himself as a faithful follower and interpreter of Descartes. He proposes his act theory of ideas as the correct reading of Descartes' understanding of 'idea'. That Descartes was not a representationalist, as has been traditionally maintained, is well argued in the recent literature.[36] Proponents of such arguments usually need to take into account Descartes' complete *oeuvre*, particularly his work in physiology (*Les Passions de l'Ame, La Dioptrique, L'Homme*), and it would take me too far afield to go over that material here. I am inclined to agree with this view. Be that as it may, I approach the issue here solely from the perspective of Descartes' philosophical notion of 'idea'. Are ideas, for Descartes, *acts* of perception or *objects* of perception? Is Arnauld's understanding of 'idea' indeed a correct reading of Descartes? There is much evidence to support Arnauld's claim.

To summarize briefly Arnauld's act theory of ideas: in the normal veridical perception of an external object, there is only the mental activity of perceiving, and the external thing perceived; the act of

[36]For the argument that Descartes did not hold a representative theory of perception see Yolton, *Perceptual Acquaintance*, Chapter 1; Michael J. Costa, "What Cartesian Ideas Are Not", *Journal of the History of Philosophy*, 21 (1983), 537–50; Ronald Arbini, "Did Descartes Have a Philosophical Theory of Sense Perception?" *Journal of the History of Philosophy*, 21 (1983), 317–38; Thomas M. Lennon, "The Inherence Pattern and Descartes' Ideas", *Journal of the History of Philosophy*, 12 (1974), 43–52; O'Neil, *Epistemological Direct Realism in Descartes' Philosophy*; and Monte Cook, "Descartes' Alleged Representationalism", *History of Philosophy Quarterly*, 4 (1987), 179–85.

perception is essentially representative of the object of which it is a perception; the act is called a 'perception' in regard to its capacity as an activity of the mind, and an 'idea' in regard to its capacity as representing something outside the mind (see Chapter 6). Is there any indication that something like this was Descartes' view?

As Kenny and others point out,[37] Descartes' use of the term 'idea' is ambiguous and inconsistent. Sometimes it is used to refer to material images in the brain (Third Replies: AT VII, 181; CSM II, 127. *L'Homme*: AT XI, 174); at other times it seems to refer to immaterial images in the mind (Med. III: AT VII, 37; CSM II, 25). There are, however, a number of important contexts in which 'idea' is used to refer to perceptual *acts* that represent. Arnauld cites several passages which, he feels, support his claim that Descartes held an act theory of ideas. In VFI (204) he quotes the following from Descartes' reply to the Second Set of Objections:

II. *Idea.* I understand this term to mean the form of any given thought, immediate perception of which makes me aware of the thought.
III. *Objective reality of an idea.* By this I mean the being of the thing which is represented by an idea, in so far as this exists in the idea ... whatever we perceive as being in the objects of our ideas exists objectively in the ideas themselves. (AT VII, 160–61; CSM II, 113)

Descartes here identifies 'idea' with the form of a thought (*forma cogitationis*). Since perception falls under the category of thought for Descartes, an idea can be said to be the form of an act of perception. In fact, in his replies to the Third Set of Objections, Descartes states that "by an idea I mean whatever is the form of a given perception [*forma perceptionis*]" (AT VII, 188; CSM II, 132). Ideas are not the objects of thought or perception here, not a content apprehended by the mental activity of which it is the form. Descartes' definition of 'idea' here is open to a reading quite similar to the definition given by Arnauld.

On the one hand, there is the perceptual act, the thought or perception which is a modification of the mind. It is always the perception of a certain object, and is thus essentially representative of

[37] Anthony Kenny, "Descartes on Ideas", in Willis Doney, ed., *Descartes: A Collection of Critical Essays* (Notre Dame: University of Notre Dame Press, 1967), pp. 227–49. See also Costa, "What Cartesian Ideas Are Not"; Yolton, "John Locke and the Seventeenth-Century Logic of Ideas"; and Lennon, "The Inherence Pattern and Descartes' Ideas".

some entity, by definition III. What makes it a perception *of*, or representative of, an object is its having a particular form – the form of the object of which it is the perception (in just what sense this is so is discussed in my next chapter). This is the second relation in which Arnauld insists that every perceptual act essentially stands – to the object perceived. In this capacity – that is, with regard to the *form* of the perception which determines it to be the perception of one object rather than another – it is referred to as an "idea". By virtue of its form, every thought (perception) stands in an essential relation to an object (in addition to its relation to the mind of which it is a mode). Furthermore, since every perception has a particular form, any reflective awareness or "consciousness" (implicit or express) of a perception is an awareness of the form thereof.[38] This is the sense of the second phrase in definition II, and is the reading Arnauld gives it to emphasize his claim that one need not accept the object theory of ideas in order to accept *P*:

It appears, according to these two definitions, ... that what he calls an idea ... is nothing really distinct from our thought or perception, but that it is our thought itself, in so far as it objectively contains that which is in the object formally. And it appears that it is this idea which he claims to be the immediate object of our thought ... since thought knows itself, and I think of nothing *cujus non conscius sim*. And, consequently, he has no more need than I to have recourse to a representative entity distinct from my thought in order to acknowledge these propositions which, when correctly understood, are quite true: The ideas of things are what we immediately see, these ideas are the immediate object of our thought. (VFI, 205–6)

Arnauld also cites Descartes' discussion, in his letter to Clerselier (AT IX-1, 210; CSM II, 273), of the Third Meditation proof of God's existence. In this context, Descartes identifies having an *idea* of God with having a *perception* of him, and, more generally, the idea of an object with *la perception que nous avons d'un objet* (cited in VFI, 338–9). In the Third Meditation itself, Descartes again speaks of thoughts (*cogitationes*) having different forms (AT VIII, 37; CSM II, 25–6), and thus being different ideas. Here he uses 'thought' (*cogitatio*, an operation of the mind) as a synonym for 'idea'. Similarly, in *Discours* IV, "thoughts (*pensées*) ... of many other things outside me, like the heavens, the

---

[38] For a further discussion of this passage, see Lennon, *op. cit.*, pp. 46–8.

earth, light, heat, and numerous others are just *ideas* of such things (AT VI, 34; CSM I, 128).

The most telling piece of evidence lies in Descartes' preface to the *Meditations*: "There is an ambiguity here in the word 'idea'. 'Idea' can be taken materially, as an operation of the intellect [*operatio intellectus*], in which case it cannot be said to be more perfect than me. Alternatively, it can be taken objectively, as the thing represented by that operation" (AT VII, 8; CSM II, 7). Once again, here is a reference to the two relations in which any perceptual act stands: one to the mind of which it is the activity (since it is an *operatio intellectus*), and, thus, which it modifies; the other to the object which the act represents. Thus 'idea' refers to a single entity, the perceptual act. Such an act can be considered *materialiter*, as a modification of the mind. Or it can be considered *objective*, as representing something outside the mind. The last phrase in the passage quoted above might seem to refer to the object itself existing outside the mind. But if this is taken literally, clearly it cannot be Descartes' meaning. He certainly does not want to claim that an external object *per se* is an *idea*. 'Idea' does refer to the thing outside the mind, but only as that thing exists in the mind as an object of thought, that is, as it is represented by the perceptual act.[39] The same point is reiterated in *Meditation III*. Descartes says there that ideas can be considered either as modes of thought, as acts of the mind, in which case no difference or inequality can be recognized among them; or as imges (*imagines*, representations) of external things (Med. III: AT VII, 40; CSM II, 27–8). He is once again simply referring to the two features of an idea – as a property of the mind (being a mental act), and as representing something outside the mind.

In his reply to Arnauld's Fourth Set of Objections, Descartes insists that we can consider an idea either as an "operation of the intellect", *operatio intellectus*, in which case it is considered "materially"; or "as representing something" (*aliquid representant*), in which case it is considered "formally" (Fourth Replies: AT VII, 232; CSM II, 163). His meaning is that it is the operation of the mind which does the representing here, not some mental object towards which the act of mind is directed. Finally, in the letter to Mersenne quoted from above

---

[39] For discussions of this passage, see Costa, "What Cartesian Ideas Are Not", p. 540; and Monte Cook, "The Alleged Ambiguity of 'Idea' in Descartes' Philosophy", *Southwestern Journal of Philosophy*, 6 (1975), 87–103.

(January 28, 1641), Descartes states "I do not claim that the idea is different from the action itself" (AT III, 295; Kenny, 93).

Certainly, ambiguities remain in Descartes' use of the term 'idea', ambiguities which, as Kenny points out, cause confusion not only for the reader of Descartes, but also in Descartes' thought, particularly his epistemology. Certain passages from Meditation V, for example, appear hard to reconcile with the foregoing interpretation. Nonetheless, as the passages presented indicate, Descartes did, in more than an occasional manner, use 'idea' to refer to *acts* of perception or thought which represent external objects. He does, that is, have a conception of ideas which is, in important respects, similar to Arnauld's act theory.

16 *Issues and problems*

1 As we saw in Chapter 3, one of Malebranche's arguments for representationalism is based on the possibility of existential error in perception. Every perception must have some object which the mind immediately perceives; otherwise the perception would be of nothing, hence not a perception. Physical things cannot be the immediate objects of perception, because often we have a perception of a body which, in fact, does not exist. Such is the case in hallucination and other similar perceptual illusions. Since there must be some entity immediately perceived, this must be an intelligible (i.e. not-material) one. In this way, Malebranche feels he can account for perceptual error. In fact, it has often been claimed that an important advantage for representationalist theories is that they can account for hallucinations and the like, while the direct realist cannot. Such a claim is not necessarily true; nor does Arnauld think it is. Nonetheless, it is true that any theory of perception must be able to deal with all the perceptual facts and phenomena, and it counts against a theory if it cannot do so. Arnauld denies that he is any less able to account for perceptual error and hallucination with his direct realist act theory of ideas than Malebranche is with his idea-objects.

Like Malebranche, Arnauld realizes that there is no necessary relationship between the perception of an object and the existence of that object. Certainly it is possible to have a perception of the sun or a square when, in fact, there is no such object present to my senses (*quoiqu'il n'existât pas hors de mon esprit* [VFI, 202, 221; cf. also 198]). But

Arnauld insists that hallucinatory experiences do not demand *êtres représentatifs* for their explanation:

> How could our mind perceive something if it did not have the idea of it, that is to say, the perception of it? Furthermore, it is certain that the perceptions of many objects are actually in our mind, although these things do not actually exist outside us ... [I see] no need for this alleged "representative entity" in order to know any object, be it present or absent. (VFI, 221).

If it be granted, as Malebranche claims, that there need not necessarily be something "external" corresponding to (*semblable à*) the *être représentatif*, it is no more necessary, Arnauld insists, that there be an existing external object corresponding to the perception one may have of the sun (VFI, 221). In other words, with respect to the issue of explaining hallucinations, one theory is no better or worse than the other. Arnauld agrees that every perceptual act must have an object. But, he insists, Malebranche misinterprets this to mean that it must be immediately directed towards an actually-present entity (an idea-object). All it really means (as argued in my next chapter) is that every perception is intentional, is the "perception *of* some object"; that is, every perceptual act objectively contains or represents some entity: "[It is] impossible to think without thinking of something" (VFI, 184). But having the perception of an object does not guarantee the actual existence of the object perceived. Alternatively stated, to say that every perception must have an object is to say that every perception is the perception of some x. To be a perception of x is to be a perception that represents x; it is *not* necessarily to perceive an actually-existing x (*Défense*, 38:382, 391, 406). Whether the direct objects of veridical perception are always intelligible (non-physical) representative proxies, or external physical bodies, it is still possible that a particular perceptual experience is hallucinatory.

2 This, of course, is bound up with the issue of skepticism. The standard claim is that direct realism is epistemologically superior to representationalism, that representationalism necessarily leads to skepticism regarding knowledge of the existence and the nature of the external world. This was Reid's view of the matter: "Des Cartes' system of the human understanding, which I shall beg leave to call the ideal system, and which ... is now generally received, hath some original defect; that this skepticism is inlaid in it, and reared along with

it."[40] Some of Arnauld's criticisms of Malebranche, as we saw in Chapter 4, are based on concerns about skepticism. But a distinction needs to be drawn between skepticism with regard to *perception* of the external world and skepticism with regard to *knowledge* of or about the external world. So far, we have seen the way in which the former plays a role in Arnauld's critique. Arnauld insists that Malebranche's doctrine of ideas leads to a problematic theory of perception whereby the external world is never perceived. (Let us even grant Malebranche's claim that, on his theory, the external world *is* ultimately perceived, albeit indirectly.) The question is, what are the *epistemological* ramifications of Malebranche's doctrine of ideas?

The standard claim is that such a theory, with the mind cut off from any direct cognitive contact with physical objects, opens the way for skepticism regarding *knowledge* of the existence and the nature of the external world. If the mind is perceptually acquainted only with intelligible entities, how it is possible to know anything certain about either the existence of the external world or the properties of physical bodies? How can the representationalist be sure that we are not always hallucinating? Is Arnauld among those who object to representationalism because it has unsatisfying epistemological consequences?

Prima facie, Arnauld sometimes appears to believe that his direct realism is epistemologically superior to Malebranche's representationalism, that such skeptical possibilities do not arise when physical bodies are made the direct and immediate objects of perception. In several contexts he appears simply to beg the skeptical question, and insists that since the mind is capable of directly perceiving physical bodies, it does actually perceive them; and, what is more, that there is, in most cases, no reason to doubt that it perceives them (e.g. VFI, 202). In the absence of intervening non-physical representative proxies between perceiver and external world, the proponent of direct realism has tended to claim that certain skeptical problems that the representationalist must deal with simply do not arise for him.

Certain considerations, however, undermine such confidence on the part of the direct realist and suggest that direct realism is not epistemologically superior to representative theories of perception.[41]

---

[40] Reid, *Works*, vol. 1, p. 103 (*Inquiry*, I, vii).
[41] Cf. Cornman, *Perception, Common Sense and Science*, p. 370.

There are two senses in which the two theories are on a par regarding our knowledge of the external world. On the one hand, there is the question of the nature of external bodies. The direct realist certainly must be willing to admit the distinction between the way an object appears and the way it actually is. The only real difference between him and the representationalist on this issue concerns the ontology of the distinction, with the latter admitting a real entity, distinct from the physical object, truly bearing the apparent properties (e.g. a sense datum). Thus, the direct realist still has a gap to fill between "looks" and "is", and is therefore also presented with an epistemological problem: that of moving from the way an object appears to the actual properties of the object. Furthermore, bridging such a gap poses problems for the direct realist similar to those faced by the representationalist:

Just as the representationalist cannot establish *observationally* a correlation between sense-data of certain kinds and objects of certain kinds, because he cannot allow that objects may be observed independently of observing sense-data; equally the direct realist cannot establish *observationally* a correlation between the color something looks to have and the color it actually has, because he cannot allow that the color something has may be observed independently of observing the color it looks to have ... it appears that, despite the difference in ontology, the basic approach to the epistemic problem has to be the same in both cases.[42]

On the other hand, there is the problem of the existence of the external world. And again, on experiential grounds, the direct realist is no better off here than the representationalist. Certainly, the direct realist must admit that at least some claims to perceive directly an external physical object are false. How does one know on any particular occasion that the perceptual experience is not hallucinatory? This is a problem for the direct realist as well as for the representationalist. In fact, how can either establish that we are not always hallucinating? The direct realist claims that at least sometimes we are in immediate and direct perceptual contact with a physical world. But how can he justify this claim? In neither theory is there a phenomenological basis for determining whether a particular perceptual

[42] Frank Jackson, *Perception: A Representative Theory* (Cambridge: Cambridge University Press, 1977), pp. 148–9.

experience is veridical or hallucinatory. "The question for the direct realist, then, how do we know when we are directly perceiving a physical object, has the same force as the stock objection against representationalism."[43]

Though often appearing to have begged the skeptical question, Arnauld is, for the most part, aware that by espousing a direct realism he does not necessarily avoid the skeptical (or solve the epistemological) problems of perception, particularly that dealing with the existence of the external world. As we saw in the discussion of perceptual error above, Arnauld realizes (as he must), no less than Malebranche, that often we perceive things that are not really there. Hallucination is always a possibility, whether one is a direct realist or a representationalist; and the direct realist, no less than the representationalist, must deal with this problem. "If it is not necessary that there be something external similar to the representative entity, it is no more necessary that there be some existing external thing which is similar to the perception which I have of the sun" (VFI, 221). The claim that the mind is capable of directly and immediately perceiving external things must be distinguished from the claim that such a relation does, in fact, ever occur.

With regard to the issues of skepticism, Malebranche takes two positions. He claims that it is possible to have certain and true knowledge of the *nature* of the external world in so far as it is considered in terms of quantifiable geometric properties. Such knowledge is guaranteed by the necessary reliability of the immediate objects of perception: God's ideas of extended beings, or, alternatively, the infinite intelligible extension in God. Since God will have created the world in accordance with these divine archetypes, our direct perception of them is a reliable guide to the nature of the created world, if it exists. This latter qualification is important, for Malebranche insists that with regard to the *existence* of the external world no certain knowledge is possible. If the world exists, God created it freely by his own volition. There is thus no necessary relation between God and a created world. Therefore, it is not possible to demonstrate with "geometric rigor" the existence of an external material world, "for such evidence is found only in necessary relations [*les rapports nécessaires*]" (*Recherche*, Ecl. VI: OC III, 64; LO, 574). Though sensations

[43] Lennon, "Philosophical Commentary", *The Search after Truth*, p. 796.

offer *some* evidence in this matter (see Chapter 3), to *know* for certain that such a world exists one must know God's volition. Hence it is only by revelation or by faith that certainty is possible in this matter; certainty *cannot* be gained "with an evidence necessitating us to believe, as in the case of mathematical demonstrations. Surely only faith can persuade us that there really are bodies" (*Recherche*, Ecl. VI: OC III, 64; LO, 574).

Arnauld takes issue with Malebranche here (cf. VFI, Chapter XXVIII). Acknowledging that even a direct realist is obliged to prove that at least some of our perceptions are veridical and not hallucinatory, i.e. that an external world exists, Arnauld insists that such a proof is possible. Indeed, though one may want to believe such a proposition on faith alone, or on the basis of the testimony of the senses alone, it is only "by reasoning that I am entirely assured that there truly is a world, a sun and stars outside of my mind" (VFI, 199). In true Cartesian fashion, Arnauld's arguments for the existence of physical bodies rest, he claims, on the assumption that *Dieu ne peut être trompeur* (VFI, 359).[44] If this principle "we must accept as true that which cannot be considered false without forcing us to admit in God things completely contrary to the divine nature, such as being a deceiver" is used as a premise, taken in conjunction with sense experience, the existence of an external world is *très bien démontré* (VFI, 354).

In spite, then, of certain of Arnauld's arguments against Malebranche's doctrine of ideas, and in spite of some of his complaints against the ramifications of any representative theory of perception, the real issue here is not skepticism. Arnauld does not say that because of his theory of *êtres représentatifs* Malebranche would be incapable of demonstrating the existence of the external world even if he wanted to. In fact, what Arnauld takes issue with is Malebranche's insistence that a demonstration of the existence of the external world is not possible. In other words, Arnauld's reason for adopting a direct realist account of external perception, as opposed to a representationalist account, is *not* that direct realism, in itself, has more acceptable epistemological consequences than representationalism, in

---

[44] For example, Arnauld argues that God would be a deceiver should it be the case that he provides me with all the vivid sensations of light, color, sound, etc. (sensations which appear to me to to depend on the body), even though I have no body (Argument VIII, VFI, 358; cf. Descartes' arguments in Meditation VI).

particular with regard to our knowledge of the existence of the external world.

This raises the question of why Arnauld *was* so committed to a direct realist theory of perception, and why he argued so forcefully against *êtres représentatifs*. The issue of Arnauld's rejection of the representationalist account of perception must be clearly distinguished from his objections to Malebranche's theory of the vision in God, according to which the *êtres représentatifs* are divine ideas. As noted above, Arnauld's attack on Malebranche's claim that *on voit tout en Dieu* is part of his more general attack on Malebranche's system as a whole. VFI is an attempt to undermine the philosophical foundactions of Malebranche's theology. As Sainte-Beuve notes in regard to the vision in God, "in order to discredit Malebranche, Arnauld grabs him by the most vulnerable part of his theory, by the aspect which is most offensive to good sense and most unpopular".[45]

Furthermore, one might conjecture that Arnauld's Jansenist sentiments are offended by the placing of God and man in the kind of close, familiar and constant contact that Malebranche's theory involves. Lucien Goldmann, in his study of Jansenism, claims that the God of the Jansenists is a "hidden God", a silent and absent deity separated from humankind by an "infinite abyss."[46] He notes this, in particular, with respect to "those who carried Jansenism to its highest degree of coherence", namely the Pascal of the *Pensées* and Racine.[47] He cites Fragment 559 of the *Pensées* (Brunschvicg):

Had there never appeared any sign of God, then this eternal privation would be ambiguous, and could just as well be caused by the complete absence of any divine principle as by man's unworthiness to know it; but since God shows himself intermittently, but not always, then all ambiguity disappears. For if God has once appeared, then he must always exist. From which we are forced to conclude that God exists, and that men are unworthy of Him.[48]

Goldmann sees this as expressing the sentiment that God always exists, but rarely appears; that God can and may appear at every

---

[45] Sainte-Beuve, *Port Royal*, vol. 6, p. 198.
[46] Lucien Goldmann, *The Hidden God* (London: Routledge and Kegan Paul, 1964), p. 69.
[47] *Ibid.*, p. 55.
[48] *Ibid.*, p. 36.

moment of a person's life, although he never actually does so. What greater contrast can be imagined with Malebranche's constant and everyday communion between God and man? Goldmann classifies Arnauld among the "moderate" Jansenists,[49] and thus it would seem that for him no strict parallels can be drawn between Pascal's sentiments and those of Arnauld.[50] Nevertheless, Arnauld did subscribe to the Augustinian (and Jansenist) principle of efficacious grace:[51] the human will, although before the Fall capable of choosing between good and evil, is now capable only of evil unless aided by God. In his *Augustinus*, Jansenius states that humankind is totally dependent upon God's grace in order to choose good and act virtuously.[52] God is thus hidden from all except those to whom he has granted grace. The Augustinian God accepted by Arnauld is a God from whom you may be estranged for a long period of time, until, by God's grace, you are permitted to turn yourself towards him (witness St Augustine's *Confessions*!). He is a God who keeps you distant until he chooses to allow you to be present to him. Arnauld sees in Malebranche a theory which makes God the immediate and direct object of perception. If the *êtres représentatifs* which are required for direct perception are God's ideas, is this not tantamount to making God himself the directly-perceived object? And is this not to eradicate the distance between man and God, and to put them in immediate and everyday contact? "If he speaks sincerely and sticks to the principles of his philosophy of ideas, he cannot say that in seeing things in God we do not see God himself, but only his creatures ... In this new philosophy of ideas, when we see creatures in God, God himself is the immediate object of our mind" (VFI, 275–6). This necessary consequence of Malebranche's doctrine of ideas is unacceptable to Arnauld.

Arnauld's Jansenism seems to be behind another criticism of the vision in God several pages later. The reformist character of Jansenism involves a renunciation of worldly matters in favor of introspection and spiritual reflection, a "complete and unilateral refusal of the world and consequent appeal to God".[53] Malebranche's

---

[49] *Ibid.*, p. 55.

[50] See Sedgwick, *Jansenism in Seventeenth-Century France*, pp. 79–80, 100, *et passim*, for a discussion of Arnauld's relationship to Pascal.

[51] *Seconde Apologie de M. Jansenius Evesque d'Ipres*, Book II, Chapters xviiff.: *Oeuvres*, Vol. 17.

[52] Sedgwick, *op. cit.*, pp. 48–9.

[53] See Goldmann, *op. cit.*, pp. 52–3; and Sedgwick, *op. cit.*, pp. 35ff.

doctrine, on the other hand, elevates and "divinizes" the objects of everyday worldly and scientific concern, giving them added importance and a more urgent claim on our attention.

Is this a good way to induce us to separate ourselves from corporeal things and to turn inward? Is it the way to lower our esteem for purely human sciences? For not only are they spiritualized, but even, in some sense, divinized, since those who apply themselves to these disciplines are led to believe that the objects of the sciences are something much greater and more noble than they previously thought. (VFI, 286)

When we regard the sky, it is not a material star that is seen, but an intelligible one which is in God. Such a doctrine could only encourage the unchristian and blameworthy *curiosité vague et inquiète* which seeks to know and investigate sensible objects.

However, all this is concerned with Malebranche's theory of the vision in God, and not with his representationalism *per se*, with *êtres représentatifs distingués des perceptions*. Yet Arnauld argues against the latter position at length before even taking up the issue of the vision in God. Why does it matter to Arnauld the theologian whether the direct and immediate objects of normal, veridical perception are physical things or representative, non-physical ideas? We have seen that Arnauld does not believe that direct realism is necessarily epistemically superior to representationalism, and that his main objection to representationalism is not based on any unfortunate skeptical consequences peculiar to such a theory.[54] Arnauld understood that a direct realist is equally faced with the task of dealing successfully with certain epistemological problems, particularly that concerning the

---

[54] As I note above, some of Arnauld's arguments do seem to support the claim that skepticism was his concern. Even if this were true, however, it would simply push the question back a step: why should skepticism regarding the existence of the external world, a purely philosophical problem (as Hume would later say), matter to the devout theologian Arnauld? Many other Jansenists were happy to give up the search for truth and knowledge based on man's natural faculties alone (cf. Sedgwick, *op. cit.*, pp. 88ff.). Pascal, St Cyran and others were distrustful of philosophy and natural science (particularly of the Cartesian variety). Why should Arnauld care whether true and certain knowledge is possible in those fields? A sketch of an answer to this question might be as follows. First, as I show in Chapter 2, Arnauld saw skepticism as a real threat to religion; hence his concern to combat it. Second, no self-respecting Cartesian (such as Arnauld saw himself) could help attacking skepticism wherever he believed it to rear its ugly head.

existence of the external world. If skepticism is not the issue, then what is?

Any answer to the question would be conjectural, since Arnauld himself affords few clues as to just why it should matter so profoundly to him whether external objects are directly perceived. Nevertheless, some remarks are warranted. On the one hand, Arnauld feels that the view that external objects are not directly perceived is so counter-intuitive, and so contrary to common sense, that it affords him the best and easiest means of attacking Malebranche. If he can demolish Malebranche's representationalism, he will thereby have destroyed his theory of the vision in God. It is, in effect, an easily grasped handle by means of which Malebranche's whole edifice, theology and all, can be torn down. Arnauld's real concern is with Malebranche's views on God, grace, and other theological matters. The critique of Malebranche's representationalism thus becomes the philosophical linchpin in Arnauld's attack on his unacceptable theology. This is, I believe, the real motivation behind Arnauld's concern with perception. That it is, in his eyes, an easy and obvious place to begin is underscored by Arnauld's constant complaints of *si peu de vraisemblance, contraire de la raison*, his calls to *la conscience de tout le monde*, and his request that each of us should *consulter soi-même* in order to discover the truth about these matters. His reasons *for* direct realism would be, on this view, mostly negative: representationalism is so obviously false.

Two subsidiary philosophical motivations are pertinent here: Cartesianism and nominalism. The view that physical things are directly perceived without the mediation of *êtres représentatifs* is, for Arnauld, the Cartesian view of perception, and thus demands his fealty, he having already accepted Descartes' methodology and metaphysics (see Chapter 2). Moreover, he feels that it is his duty to correct Malebranche when he deviates from the "true" Cartesian way. As he writes in a letter to Malebranche on May 22, 1694 (the *Troisième lettre de Monsieur Arnauld au R. P. Malebranche* to which Malebranche responds in RLA), "I have always said that when you confine yourself to teaching and confirming the opinions of M. Descartes, you perform marvelously; but this is not the case when you deviate from him" (see Malebranche, OC IX, 1028). As for nominalism, Arnauld accepts its central tenet: "do not multiply beings unnecessarily [*ne pas multiplier les êtres sans nécessité, ainsi qu'on fait si souvent dans la philosophie ordinaire*]" (VFI,

182). Clearly, the object theory of ideas offends Arnauld's nominalist sentiments, particularly since the arguments advanced for the theory, for such *entités superflues*, are, he insists, all fallacious in one way or another. Why, then, posit such entities? Not only does there appear to be no valid reason for doing so, but they also seem to render impossible that which they are intended to explain in the first place (see Chapter 4). Moreover, as the reference to *la philosophie ordinaire* in the second phrase indicates, Malebranche's 'ideas' probably represent for Arnauld just that kind of redundant entity which Cartesians find so characteristic of Scholastic metaphysics, and which they are so concerned to eliminate in philosophical and scientific explanations.

Tied up with this nominalist element is the theological principle which in Chapter 4 was found to be behind some of Arnauld's objections to the view that external objects are not directly perceived: God always acts in the most simple and straightforward way (VFI, 222). For Arnauld, this means that God never performs by more complex means that which can be performed by the most simple means, a principle which he rightly insists is also used by Malebranche in arguing for his position on ideas (cf. *Recherche*, III, ii, 4). Thus, if we want to relate Arnauld's direct realism to some of his more pressing theological concerns, and provide at least some explanation for the fervor with which he attacks *êtres représentatifs*, the answer might lie in an impiety he perceives in a representationalist position such as Malebranche holds. Such a view, which not only claims that God took a roundabout means of allowing us to perceive the external world in which he placed us, but which also seems to imply that he has cut us off from seeing that world altogether, is unworthy of God, and attributes to God *des choses toutes à fait contraires à la nature divine* (VFI, 354). To pursue this approach further involves examining the debate over divine volition found in Malebranche's *Traité de la Nature et de la Grace*, Arnauld's *Réflexions*, and their later correspondence (see Appendix).

3 By identifying ideas with acts of perceiving, or, more generally, with mental acts (conceiving, thinking, etc.), Arnauld seems to have exposed himself to an important objection. If the idea of an object is nothing more than the *act* of perceiving or conceiving that object, how can it be said that ideas persist in the mind of the knower beyond the actual moment(s) when one is thinking them, i.e. actively perceiving, conceiving, etc.? If ideas are reduced to activities, then it would seem that they are only as permanent as the activity itself, and cease to exist

with the cessation of the activity. But certainly one would want to say that the idea of something remains in the mind long after the actual thinking of that thing; that I have an idea of my brother, for example, whether I am actually thinking of him or not. What happens to the idea of a thing when I have stopped perceiving or thinking of that thing? Must Arnauld say that it no longer exists?

Perhaps something like this problem led Leibniz and, on occasion, Descartes to identify the idea of an object with the *capacity* to think of that object. Ideas are thus reduced not to an activity of thinking or perceiving, but to a disposition or power to think or perceive. In his short paper "What Is An Idea?", Leibniz claims: "An idea consists not in some act, but in the faculty of thinking, and we are said to have an idea of a thing even if we do not think of it ... Idea therefore requires a certain 'near' faculty or ability to think about a thing."[55] Though it is by no means his consistent position, Descartes occasionally appears to identify an idea with a latent capacity to think of, or otherwise apprehend, a thing. For example, in a letter to Hyperaspistes (August, 1649), Descartes says that to have an idea of God is to have "an aptitude to perceive him explicitly [*aptitudinem ad ipsam explicite percipiendam*]" (AT III, 430; Kenny, 117).[56]

These are not the only objections to be raised against Arnauld. Malebranche devotes much time to trying to demonstrate the falsity of Arnauld's account of perception and the weakness of Arnauld's critique of his own theory. How, for example, can Arnauld account for general or universal ideas? Because ideas are identical with mental acts, and since any mental act is a particular and singular occurrence (that is, a particular modification of a particular mind at a certain moment in time), how can we have a general idea, i.e. a general mental act? We do indeed have, for example, an idea of a circle in general. But the soul, which is particular, cannot have a modification in general. Similar reasoning applies to our idea of infinity: since the mind is finite, "it is not possible that ... the idea which I have of infinity is a modification of my soul" (*Response:* OC VI, 58). In response, Arnauld

---

[55]"Quid sit Idea", *Die Philosophischen Schriften von Gottfried Wilhelm Leibniz*, Gerhardt, ed., vol. 7, p. 263; translation quoted from *Philosophical Papers and Letters*, Loemker, 207ff.

[56]For a discussion of this, see Kenny, "Descartes on Ideas", in Doney, ed., *Descartes*, p. 230; and Wilson, *Descartes*, p. 156.

asserts that singular perceptions can represent general beings (*Dissertation*, 40:90). He insists in the *Défense*, for example, that the singular thought or perception (*une modification singulière de mon esprit*) of a triangle in general, or of any abstract concept, represents that triangle or concept. In a letter to Malebranche (May 22, 1694), he states that a finite modification of our soul can represent an infinite thing (God): although finite *in essendo*, it is infinte *in representando* (OC IX, 1035–6). The generality lies in the *content* of the act, not in the act considered in its "material" aspect.

I will not take the time here to examine Malebranche's criticisms of Arnauld. A few are to the point, others are either irrelevant or based on misunderstandings of Arnauld's position.[57] The debate is often interesting, but tends to become tedious, and more personal than philosophical, as it drags on through the years. Let us turn, instead, to Arnauld's claim that acts of perception represent. It is important to examine what such a claim amounts to, and how this apparent "representationalism" can be incorporated into the direct realism which we have just seen to be Arnauld's considered account of perception.

---

[57]For discussion of Malebranche's response to Arnauld, see Rodis-Lewis, *Nicolas Malebranche*, Chapter 5; and Church, *A Study in the Philosophy of Malebranche*, Chapters 7–8.

V I
Intentionality and Arnauld's representationalism

Every act of perception is related to the mind of which it is an operation; considered in this capacity it is called a "perception". On the other hand, every perceptual act is also essentially related to an object, and is thus called an "idea". This second relation raises the issue of the intentionality of mental acts, perception in particular. In this chapter, we will look at Arnauld's discussion of the representative character which he claims is an essential feature of every perceptual act, and which is his way of accounting for the intentionality of such acts. Since Arnauld's approach to this problem centers on the notion of objective being (*esse objectivum*), we need also to examine this notion as it is present in the works of some later Scholastics (most importantly, Suarez, whose influence on Descartes in this matter is clear) and in Descartes.

17 *Intentionality*

There are two separate but related issues at stake in the debate between Arnauld and Malebranche over perception and the nature of ideas. On the one hand, there is the problem of direct realism vs. representationalism, as discussed in the preceding chapters. On the other hand, there is the problem of intentionality. It may be an historical, if not a philosophical, truth that one's answer to either issue determines one's solution to the other. This was certainly the case in this debate. Be that as it may, the issues are distinct.

Central to the notion of the intentionality of mental acts is the claim that every act of consciousness (or, to put it in seventeenth-century terms, every thought) is consciousness *of* (thought *of*) something. As Husserl notes, "every state of consciousness in general is in itself consciousness *of* something. The word 'intentionality' signifies nothing else than that universal and basic characteristic of all consciousness that it is consciousness *of* something, that, precisely as *cogito*, it bears within itself its own *cogitatum*."[1] Earlier, Brentano formulated this as the essential and defining characteristic of the mental: "Every mental phenomenon is characterized by ... reference to a content, direction toward an object ... In presentation something is presented, in judgement something is affirmed or denied, in love loved, in hate hated, in desire desired, and so on."[2] On this view, all mental phenomena are intentional, or object-directed. This does not necessarily imply that the object of thought or consciousness actually exists outside the consciousness. It means simply that there is no act of consciousness which is not directed toward, aiming at, or pointing to something. In other words, every mental act is characterized by *directedness toward an object*, whether or nor a corresponding "ordinary" object exists (in space and time).[3]

Both Arnauld and Malebranche accept intentionality as an essential feature of much of mental life, and as a fundamental assumption in their respective analyses of perception. As noted in Chapter 3, Malebranche claims that *il n'y a point de pensée qui n'ait son objet*. To perceive is to perceive something, since to perceive nothing, to perceive no thing, is not to perceive (*voir le néant, voir rien, c'est ne point voir* [cf. TL, I: OC VI, 202; RLA: OC VIII, 910]). Arnauld, too, insists that every thought is the thought of something, i.e. has an object: "Just as it is clear that I am thinking, it is also clear that I am thinking of something; that is, that I know and that I perceive something; for this is essential to thought" (VFI, 184). Arnauld and Malebranche disagree about how to solve the *problem* of intentionality, that is, how to characterize and account for this feature of thought. They both agree that it cannot be accounted for by claiming that every act of consciousness is in fact directed toward an actually-existing object of the ordinary type. Such a claim is clearly false. We often think of or imagine objects which are

---

[1] Edmund Husserl, *Cartesian Meditations*, Dorian Cairns, trans. (The Hague: Martinus Nijhoff, 1960), Section 14.

[2] Franz Brentano, *Psychology from an Empirical Standpoint*, Antos C. Rancurello, D. B. Terrell, and Linda L. McAlister, trans. (New York: Humanities Press, 1973), p. 88.

[3] Husserl differs from Brentano in not regarding intentionality as the *defining* characteristic of the mental. See his *Ideas Pertaining to a Pure Phenomenology and to a Phenomenological Philosophy*, F. Kersten, trans. (The Hague: Martinus Nijhoff, 1982), Sections 36, 85.

fictitious; and we often perceive things that do not in fact exist (e.g. in hallucinations or dreams).

Traditionally, there are two general ways of accounting for the intentionality of mental acts, for the fact that perception, for example, is always the perception of some object. One approach is to argue that every mental act is in fact directed at some object which is actually present to it. I call this the *object approach* to intentionality.[4] In the terms of the object approach, intentionality is an ordinary sort of relation between two entities: the perceiver (thinker, lover, etc.) and an intended object of some peculiar ontological sort.[5] Since a mental act can be intentional although no corresponding ordinary (external) object exists in the world, such an intended object has an ontological status different from that of ordinary objects in the world. (Object-approach theories differ on the ontological status, or kind of existence, to be accorded such immediately-intended objects – mental, "ideal", "unreal", etc.) A mental act is intentional (object-directed), on this theory, because it is actually directed or aimed at some object really present to it.[6]

Malebranche offers such an object theory to account for the intentionality of perception. In his arguments for his theory of ideas, Malebranche supposes that if to perceive is to perceive something, then there is always some entity towards which the perception is immediately directed. Since we often perceive things which do not, in fact, exist in the external world, the objects which fill the role of immediately-intended objects cannot be ordinary physical objects. Thus, when Malebranche claims that there is no thought that does not have an object (RLA: OC VIII, 910) he means that there is always an object of a special ontological type (an idea) to which the thinking subject is immediately related. The intentionality (*directedness toward an object*) of perception is thus preserved without implying that there is always a corresponding external object.[7]

---

[4] I am indebted here to the discussion by David Woodruff Smith and Ronald McIntyre, *Husserl and Intentionality* (Dordrecht: D. Reidel, 1982), pp. 40ff.

[5] An "ordinary-type" relation can hold only between two existing objects. For example, Smith can be taller than the postman or to the left of the clock if the postman and the clock are existing entities. See Smith and McIntyre, *op. cit.*, pp. 41–2.

[6] Smith and McIntyre, *op. cit.*, p. 42.

[7] For an analysis of Brentano's object theory of intentionality, see Smith and McIntyre, *op. cit.*, Chapter 2; and Dagfinn Føllesdal, "Brentano and Husserl on Intentional Objects and Perception", in *Husserl, Intentionality, and Cognitive Science*, ed. Hubert L. Dreyfus (Cambridge: MIT Press, 1982), pp. 31–42.

The second approach to intentionality (and the one taken by Arnauld) I call the *content approach*. It involves the rejection of the claim that the object-directedness of the act is explained by means of some really-present object toward which the act is directed. According to this view, intentionality is not an ordinary-type relation (which demands the real existence of the *relata*) between subject and object. Rather, the intentionality of a mental act is accounted for by the structure or content of the act itself, by some feature(s) intrinsic to the operation of the mind. Acts are not aimed at a content, but possess a content within themselves. That is, unlike the *object* approach, the *content* approach holds that intentionality is based on a non-relational property of the act, not on some real ordinary relation in which the act stands to some present object. In many cases, what the mind is directed toward is a real external object. In other cases, there will be no such object existing outside of the mind. But the real external object towards which the act is directed (when there is one) does not *account for* the act's *directedness toward an object*. Otherwise, in cases where no external object exists, the directedness of the act would not be preserved.

Because the content approach to the intentionality of mental acts is that which Arnauld adopts, the particular details are covered below. In general, however, any content theory involves at least the following features:[8]

1 The content of an act is to be distingushed from the act's object. The perception of a chair, for example, involves not only the intended external object which is the chair, but also a content which inheres in the act itself.

2 The content of an act is alone what confers intentionality on the act: it is precisely in virtue of having a content that the act points beyond itself toward something (its object). And what object an act points to, what it is directed towards, is a function of that act's content. An act intends this particular object, and not another, because this is the object *prescribed* by the act's content.

3 The intentionality, or directedness, of the act is indifferent to the existence of non-existence of the object intended by the act. This follows from the fact that the directedness is a function of the act's content, of a non-relational intrinsic feature of the act. It also

---

[8] See Smith and McIntyre, *op. cit.*, pp. 106ff.

represents an important difference between the *content* and the *object* approaches: the object approach requires the real presence of an immediately-intended object.

A good example of the content approach to intentionality is Husserl's concept of *noema* or *noematic Sinn*. The noematic sense of an act of consciousness (*noesis*) is that in virtue of which the act relates to an object ("consciousness relates in and through this Sinn to its object"). This sense is something inherent *in* the act itself; it is not something perceived or otherwise apprehended by the act. It is the act's meaning, and gives the act a *directedness toward an object*.[9] Arnauld also offers a content theory of intentionality, whereby what makes a perception the "perception of this object" is something intrinsic to the perceptual act itself.

18 *Objective being in Suarez and Descartes*

Central to Arnauld's account of intentionality is the notion of objective being (*esse objectivum*). The concept is not new with Arnauld, but has its immediate source in late Scholastic philosophy, and its ancestral roots as far back as Aristotle. It figures prominently in medieval analyses of divine cognition and, later, in Cartesian analyses of human knowledge. Rather than offer a full survey of the development of *esse objectivum*, including its sources and transformations throughout medieval philosophy (a survey which has been undertaken in part several times, from different approaches),[10] I will restrict

---

[9] Such is the interpretation of Husserl given by Smith and McIntyre, *op. cit.*, and Dagfinn Føllesdal, "Husserl's Notion of Noema", in Dreyfus, *op. cit.*, pp. 73–80. See Husserl's *Ideas*, Sections 36, 88, 89, 90. In Section 90 Husserl insists that "like perception, every intentive mental process – just this makes up the fundamental part of intentionality – has its 'intentional object', i.e. its objective sense. Or in other words: to have sense or 'to intend something' is the fundamental characteristic of all consciousness which, therefore, is not just any mental living whatsoever, but is rather a mental living having sense, which is 'noetic'" (p. 217). In Section 88, this "sense" is something inhering in the act: "In every case the noematic correlate, which is called 'sense' here ... is to be taken precisely as it inheres 'immanently' in the mental process of perceiving, of judging, of liking, and so forth; that is, just as it is offered to us when we inquire purely into this mental process itself" (p. 214). Aron Gurwitsch offers a different reading of Husserl in his "Husserl's Theory of the Intentionality of Consciousness", in Dreyfus, *op. cit.*, pp. 59–71.

[10] Roland Dalbiez, "Les sources scolastiques de la théorie Cartésienne de l'être objectif", *Revue d'histoire de la philosophie*, 3 (1929), 464–72; T. J. Cronin, *Objective Being in*

my discussion to that notion as it appears in the work of the late Scholastic Spanish Jesuit, Francisco Suarez (1548–1617), and in Arnauld's philosophical mentor, Descartes. Next to Augustine, it is Descartes who has the greatest impact on the development of Arnauld's philosophical persuasions, to the extent that Arnauld can be called an orthodox Cartesian (see Chapter 2). Hence, it is not surprising to find Arnauld appropriating Descartes' methodological and conceptual apparatus in his approach to certain philosophical problems. In particular, Arnauld's understanding of 'objective being' is thoroughly Cartesian and, as he insists, faithful to Descartes' use of the notion.[11] Moreover, Descartes' own understanding of 'objective being' was probably influenced by that of Suarez. Certainly, his Jesuit professors at La Flèche were influenced by the ideas of one of the major thinkers of their order. And they could not, in their lessons in philosophy, ignore the debates between Suarez and Gabriel Vasquez (1549–1604), Suarez's successor to the chair of theology at Rome.[12] In

---

Descartes and Suarez, Analecta Gregoriana, Vol. 154 (Rome: Gregorian University Press, 1966); Calvin Normore, "Meaning and Objective Being: Descartes and his Sources", in *Essays in Descartes' Meditations*, ed. A. O. Rorty (Berkeley: University of California Press, 1986), pp. 223–42; Brian O'Neil, *Epistemological Direct Realism in Descartes' Philosophy* (Albuquerque: University of New Mexico Press, 1974), 70–97.

[11] I speak here of the *Cartesian* understanding of 'objective being'. But how original is Descartes' understanding and use of the term? Does he simply appropriate a Scholastic way of speaking, giving the term a new meaning and usage; or is his use and understanding of 'objective being' the same as, or close to, that of his Scholastic predecessors? Some have argued that his use of the notion is original, in spite of the fact that he obviously borrowed from the Scholastic conception: see Cronin, *op. cit.*, pp. 3–6, and Appendix III; and Gilson, *Etudes sur le rôle de la pensée médiévale dans la formation du système Cartésien*, p. 204. Dalbiez, on the other hand (*opt. cit.*, pp. 470–71), seems to see less originality on Descartes' part in this matter. He contends that Descartes borrows both the terminology and the "sense" of the doctrine from the Scholastic tradition. See also Norman J. Wells, "Objective Being: Descartes and his Sources", *The Modern Schoolman*, 45 (1967), pp. 49–61.

[12] Cf. Dalbiez, *op. cit.*, p. 470: "Il est bien évident que les Jésuites, professeurs à la Flèche, devaient s'inspirer des théories adoptées par les célébrités de leur ordre [Suarez et Vasquez] ... Que son professeur de philosophie ait été partisan de Suarez ou de Vasquez, il ne pouvait négliger d'exposer une controverse qui divisait deux des plus célèbres docteurs de la Compagnie. D'ailleurs, tout le monde accorde que Descartes a emprunté aux scolastiques l'expression d'esse objectivum; comme il est bien évident qu'il n'a pu reprendre cette expression sans tenir compte de son sens, il nous paraît légitime d'admettre que la théorie Cartésienne de l'être objectif plonge ses racines en terre scolastique." Thus, while Dalbiez sees a remote predecessor of Cartesian 'objective being' in Duns Scotus (in particular, because Descartes might possibly have come into contact with Scotus by means of Cajetan's commentary), he insists that the

the discussions between Suarez and Vasquez, and in other Scholastic sources Descartes knew, the notions of *conceptus objectivus* (and its distinction from *conceptus formalis*) and *esse objectivum* are prominent. Historians of early modern philosophy generally agree that Descartes derives his notion of the objective reality of ideas from this notion of the *conceptus objectivus* (objective conceiving).[13] In fact, in the *Meditations* Descartes refers to earlier thinkers as the source for at least the terminology of the distinction between 'formal' and 'objective' reality.[14] Descartes read Suarez and knew him well. He acknowledges his indebtedness to Suarez on the issue of materially false ideas, an issue not unconnected with that of the objective reality of ideas (cf. Second Replies: AT VII, 235; CSM II, 164). Thus, to understand better the Cartesian theory of objective being as Arnauld adopts it, one must look at its immediate Scholastic sources.

In the tradition preceding Suarez, the term 'objective being' is used to denote a mode of being distinct from both actual existence and non-being: a being in the mind as something known. Duns Scotus, for example, insists that although a thing may not actually exist, it is still able to have being or reality in the understanding, an *esse intelligibile* or *esse cognitum*, which is nevertheless not nothing (*non est nihil*), nor a mere being of reason (*ens rationis*):[15]

Indeed, this is demonstrated by Plato, who first introduced the term 'idea'; for he asserted that beyond the sensible world, there is an intelligible world in the divine mind; and he called this intelligible world in the divine mind the idea of the sensible world ... however the intelligible world is nothing but the external world as it exits objectively in being known in the divine mind.

---

more proximate and influential source was Suarez. Cronin also favors Suarez, although he rightly acknowledges that the roots of the doctrine extend through Scotus back to Avicenna (see his *Objective Being in Descartes and Suarez*, pp. 31 ff., and Appendix II). Normore, on the other hand, prefers to minimize Suarez's role here. He believes that "dialectical" road to Descartes' position begins directly with Duns Scotus and his student William of Alnwick, and moves by means of the debate between William of Ockham and Walter Chatton, towards 1340, when "all the ingredients of the Cartesian theory of formal and objective reality ... are in place" ("Meaning and Objective Being", pp. 231-5).

[13] See Cronin, *op. cit.*, pp. 31ff.
[14] Only in the French edition, AT IX-1, 32. See also n. 11 above.
[15] Duns Scotus, *Questiones in Primum Librum Sententiorum*, Distinction 36: *Opera Omnia*, 18 vols. (Paris: Vives, 1893), vol. 10, pp. 575, 577-8, 584. (Cf. Cronin, *op. cit.*, pp. 187 ff.)

[Hoc etiam probatur per Platonem, qui primo introduxit nomen ideae; posuit enim mundum sensibilem extra et mundum intelligibilem in mente divina; et mundum intelligibilem in mente divina vocavit ideam mundi sensibilis ... mundus autem intelligibilis non est nisi mundus extra, ut est objective in esse cognito in mente divina.][16]

Although not actual existence, this intelligible being "is not entirely nothing, but is a kind of being [*non est omnino nihil, sed aliquod ens*]". Elsewhere, Scotus refers to it as an *esse diminutum* and *esse secundum quid*, in order both to contrast it with *esse reale* and to underscore the point that although the object possessing *esse intelligibile* or *esse cognitum* does not actually exist, it still possesses more reality than nothing, than non-being.[17] To have *esse cognitum* is "to exist only in knowing, just as the thing known is said to exist in knowing [*tantum [esse] in cognoscente, sicut cognitum dicitur esse in cognoscente*]."[18] It is a being in the understanding:

Being in the mind is different from all being outside the mind. Thus, if something has a lesser being in the mind, in no way does it follow that it therefore has actual existence.

[Esse in anima aliud est ab omni esse extra animam, et ideo de nullo ente sequitur: si habet esse diminutum in anima, quod propter hoc habeat esse simpliciter.][19]

This *esse intelligibile* or *esse cognitum* (in particular, the being proper to ideas in the divine understanding) Scotus also calls *esse obiectivum*.[20]

Ockham, in his early view, introduces the notion of *esse cognitum* or *esse obiectivum* to account for the fact that one can think about non-existent entities, especially universals.[21] Objective existence in the mind is thus presented as a mode of being distinct from, and

---

[16] *Ibid.*, D. 35, n. 12.
[17] *Ibid.*, D. 35, n. 20, p. 558.
[18] *Ibid.*, D. 36, n. 14, p. 583.
[19] *Ibid.*, D. 36, n. 14, p. 584.
[20] Cf. *Ibid.*, D. 36, n. 10. p. 578.
[21] William Ockham, *Ordinatio*, D. 2, Q. 8: *Opera Philosophica et Theologica*, 9 vols. (St Bonaventure, New York: Franciscan Institute, University of St Bonaventure, 1970), Opera Theologica II, pp. 266–92. Ockham later abandoned his objective-existence theory as a solution to the problem of universals. See Marilyn McCord Adams, "Ockham's Nominalism and Unreal Entities", *Philosophical Review*, 86 (1976), 144–76.

independent of, actual existence: one can think about entities which do not actually exist since they nevertheless possess *esse obiectivum*, or a being in the mind:

> Therefore, it can be said that a universal is not something real that actually exists, either in the mind or outside the mind, but that it has only an objective being in the mind, and is a kind of image which, in its objective being, has a being similar to that which the thing outside the mind has in its actual existence ... Furthermore, fictions have a being in the mind, but they do not have actual existence, since then they would be real things, and thus a chimera and a goat-stag and other similar things would be real things. Therefore, there are some things which have only an objective being ... thus, their being consists in being known.

> [Ideo potest aliter dici probabiliter quod universale non est aliquod reale habens esse subiectivum, nec in anima nec extra animam, sed tantum habet esse obiectivum in anima, et est quoddam fictum habens esse tale in esse obiectivo quale habet res extra in esse subiectivo ... Praeterea, figmenta habent esse in anima et non subiectivum, quia tunc essent verae res, et ita chimera et hircocervus et huiusmodi essent vera res, igitur sunt aliqua quae tantum habent esse obiectivum ... ita quod eorum esse est eorum cognosci.][22]

The distinction here is between *esse subiectivum*, whereby something is a *vera res et realis* (either in the mind or outside of it), and *esse obiectivum*, or a being solely in the mind (*in anima*). The latter "being in the mind" is not an *esse subiectivum*, not a being as something "real" in the mind (such is the being possessed by its operations and properties [*intellectio enim, et universaliter omne accidens informans animan, est vera qualitas* ...]), but as something known or thought.

Suarez makes this same distinction between actual existence, or *esse formalis*, and another mode of being which, while not actual being, is nonetheless not non-being. Moreover, like Scotus and Ockham, Suarez sees this mode of being as a being in the understanding, that is, a being in the mind as something known. In Disputatio XXXI of his *Disputationes Metaphysicae* he considers the being of the essences of creatures before they (the creatures) have been actually created by God (*Quid sit essentia creaturae, priusquam a Deo producatur*) and the related issue of the being of the eternal truths. He concludes, first, that before creatures are created by God and receive from him real existence, the

[22]*Ibid.*, pp. 271–3.

essences of created things, or the creatures themselves, do not have an actual or existential being, that is, a real being intrinsic to them outside of God. He insists that

the essence of a creature or the creature itself, before it is created by God, has in itself no true and real being; and in this sense (i.e. the being of existence) the essence is not something, but is entirely nothing ... the essences of creatures, even if they are known eternally by God, are nothing, and have no true and real being before they receive it through the free efficacy of God ... this being known is not some real being intrinsic to them.

[essentiam creaturae, seu creaturam de se, et priusquam a Deo fiat, nullam habere in se verum esse reale, et in hoc sensu, praeciso esse existentiae, essentiam nonesse rem aliquam, sed omnino esse nihil ... essentiae creaturarum, etiamsi a Deo sit cognitiae ab aeterno, nihil sunt, nullumque verum esse reale habent, antequam per liberam Dei efficientiam illud recipiant ... hoc esse cognitum non esse in illis aliquod esse reale intrinsecum ipsis.] (31.2.1)[23]

Before it has received a real being intrinsic to itself (*esse in actu*) by means of the creative act of God, a creature is really nothing more than an essence in the divine understanding. But neither does this essence itself possess any *verum esse reale* or *esse reale intrinsecum*, since it is not an actual being but only a possible being that is known by God (*a Deo sint cognitiae*).

On the other hand, uncreated essences do have a degree of reality as essences in the mind of God, and the question is: what kind of being is this being of an essence if it is not *esse reale intrinsecum*? Suarez claims that uncreated creatures as essences in the mind of God have a potential or possible being, an *esse potentiale* or *esse objectivum*, which, although not actual and real being, is nonetheless not wholly non-being, unlike fictions and beings of reason (*entes rationis*). They are *capable of real existence*, of being produced by God:

This is what distinguishes the essences of creatures from fictitious and impossible entities, such as a chimera; and in this sense, creatures are said to have real essences, even if they do not exist.

[In hoc enim distinguuntur essentiae creaturarum a rebus fictitiis et

---

[23] All references to Suarez are to his *Disputationes Metaphysicae*, 2 vols. (Hildesheim: George Olms, 1965), by *disputatio, sectio,* and paragraph.

impossibilibus ut chymera, et hoc sensu dicuntur creaturae habere reales essentias, etiamsi non existant.] (31.2.2)

A creature *qua* essence is a potential or possible being, not an actual being. Nor can it become actual (instantiated or realized) through any power intrinsic to itself, but only through God, just as the totality of created being is contained potentially in God before it is created by him:

And thus, such an essence, before it is created, is called real – not because it has the proper and true reality which it would have in itself if it actually existed, but because it can become real by receiving true being from its cause ... The being which belongs to essences before the divine activity of creation is only a *potential or objective being*.

[Atque hoc etiam modo dicitur talis essentia, antequam fiat, realis, non propria ac vera realitate quam in se actu habeat, sed quia fieri potest realis, recipiendo veram entitatem a sua causa ... esse, quod appellant essentiae ante effectionem, seu creationem divinam, solum est *esse potentiale objectivum*.] (31.2.2, emphasis added)

Thus, this *esse potentiale* or *esse objectivum* is to be distinguished from both real existence and non-being. Prior to the creative act of God, the essence of a creature has no real and true being intrinsic to itself (since it is not actual but only possible being). On the other hand, it is not simply nothing, or nothing real. The being of an essence is, in a sense, a "real" being because the essence is something known in the mind of God, is an object of *divina scientia*. This is possible because, unlike an *ens rationis*, the essence is not something created, not a mental fiction, but has an objectivity which makes it binding on God. The independence of essences from the will of God, hence also the independence of the eternal truths based on them, guarantees their necessity (see 31.12.40).

Suarez notes that 'real being' can have two senses. First, it can be contrasted with a being fabricated by the intellect, a fiction or being of reason (*ens fabricatum ab intellectu, quod proprie est ens rationis*). Second, it can be taken to mean actual existence (*existens actu*). Suarez insists that essences have real being in the first sense, but not in the second sense (*essentia creaturae est ens reale primo modo, scilicet in potentia, non vero posteriori modo, et in actu, quod est proprie esse ens reale* [32.2.10]). The difference between an essence in the divine understanding and a mere fiction or *ens rationis* is that the essence is uncreated and is real in the sense that it is a potentially actual being, capable of real being in the strict (second) sense:

The possible essence of a creature is an object of divine knowledge; it is not a being fabricated by the intellect, but a truly possibile being capable of real existence. Thus, it is not a being of reason, but, in some sense, is considered a real entity ... the essence of a creature is, in some sense, a real essence.

[Essentiam possibilem creaturae objectivam divinae scientiae, non esse ens confictum ab intellectu, sed esse ens revera possible et capax realis existentiae ideoque non esse ens rationis, sed sub ente reali aliquo modo comprehendi ... essentiam creaturae [est] aliquo modo essentiam realem ...] (31.2.10)

Sometimes Suarez does speak as though that which does not have real *existence* is entirely nothing: "It must be admitted that the being of an essence is entirely nothing [*fatendum est entitatem essentiae omnino nihil est*]":

That which does not exist is simply and entirely nothing ... what is simply and entirely nothing cannot, in any way, be something having true being ... Therefore, an essence cannot have any true being really distinct from the being of the creator.

[Illud, quod nihil habet existentiae, esse simpliciter et omnino nihil ... quod est simpliciter et omnino nihil, non potest vera et realiter esse aliquid in aliqua ratione veri entis ... ergo essentia [non] manere potest sub aliquo vero esse reali distincto ab esse creatoris.] (31.2.4–5)

Some commentators have taken this, and other passages, to mean that the objective mode of being is, for Suarez, *omnino nihil*.[24] But what Suarez is concerned with here are those who would accord to essences a real and absolute existence in themselves really distinct from the mind of God. He is siding here with Scotus in his attack against those who accorded essences a real being in the strict sense; in particular, against Henry of Ghent, who claimed that, in addition to their being in the divine intellect with an *esse essentiae*, essences also possess an *esse existentia*. It is not true, Suarez insists, that for Scotus *esse cognitum* is a

---

[24]For a discussion of Suarez on the being of essences, *esse objectivum*, see Wells, "Objective Being", and Cronin, *Objective Being in Descartes and Suarez*.

"real being distinct from the being of God [*esse reale distinctum ab esse Dei*]", for Scotus clearly declares that "this being known ... is not some real being intrinsic to creatures [*hoc esse cognitum ... non esse in [creaturis] aliquod esse reale intrinsecum ipsis*]" (32.2.1). Thus, what Suarez has in mind in the paragraph quoted above, where he says that *esse objectivum* is *omnino nihil*, is a sense of *omnino nihil* which is to be contrasted with *esse reale intrinsecum*, but not with possessing an *esse diminutum* (to borrow Scotus's phrase). *Esse objectivum, esse potentiale,* is *omnino nihil* in contrast with *esse reale intrinsecum*, but not in contrast with possessing an *esse diminutum*. Essences are *not* real if by 'real' is meant possessing a being in and of themselves outside of God's mind (since they are only possible, and not actual, beings). They *are* real, or do have some degree of being, since (as regards their content) they are uncreated and binding on God, and hence in this respect are not dependent on him. This allows them to be objects of *divina scientia*. But that does not imply that they exist apart from God, outside his mind. They exist only within the divine understanding as objects known. Again, to borrow Scotus's phrase, essences have a "cognitive being", a being as being known.

The same can be said, according to Suarez, about the eternal truths, which are wholly founded on these essences. Such truths are indifferent to actual existence (hence their necessity and eternality). But they do exist objectively in the divine mind, being the objects of God's knowledge. Indeed, to say that they have objective being *is* simply to say that they are known, that they have being in the understanding:

rom time eternal, there has been no truth to these propositions except in so ar as they existed objectively in the divine mind, since they did not actually or eally exist in themselves ... For the proposition 'man is a rational animal' to e true knowledge that God has known eternally, the essence of man did not eed to have from eternity some real and actual being, since 'is' here does not ignify real and actual being, but only an intrinsic connection between the erms of the proposition. Moreover, this connection is not grounded in actual eing, but in potential being.

Ab aeterno non fuisse veritatem in illis propositionibus, nisi quatenus erant bjective in mente divina, quia subjective seu realiter non erant in se ... Ut utem vera esset scientia qua Deus ab aeterno cognovit, hominem esse animal ationale, non oportuit essentiam hominis habere ex aeternitate aliquod esse eal in actu, quia illud esse non significat actuale esse et reale, sed solam connexionam intrinsicam talium extremorum; haec autem connexio non fundatur in actuali esse, sed in potentiali.] (31.2.8)

Suarez thus posits a mode of being, *esse possible, esse objectivum, esse potentiale*, which is the being proper to essences (and, thus, to eternal truths) in the divine understanding. It is not real being in the sense of actual (or "intrinsic") existence (that is, *esse possibile* is not *esse reale actuale* [32.2.11]). But neither is it wholly nothing. Such essences are nothing only in the sense that they possess no actual being. But they are nonetheless potential or possible beings, independent of God's will, and thus are "real" beings. For Suarez, to exist objectively (or potentially) is to exist in the understanding as something known. It is a being in the mind (*in anima*), the kind of being possessed by something in the understanding as it is known (in this case he is concerned with essences in the divine understanding which form the basis for God's knowledge). "The essences of creatures only have either a being in their cause, or an objective being in the mind [*Essentia creaturarum tantum habent vel esse in causa, vel objective in intellectu*]" (31.2.11). Essences, before they are created *in actu* (that is, before they are realized as actually-existing creatures), are present (as possible beings) in the divine understanding as objects known. Since they are uncreated, hence independent of God in regard to their content (being a rational animal is eternally an essential property of mankind, irrespective of God's will) they have a certain degree of reality: not a real being in themselves, but an objective being in the mind. "They do not exist in themselves; they exist only objectively in the mind [*Non [sunt] in se, sed objective tantum in intellectu*]" (31.2.10).

Descartes works within the Scholastic tradition in his use of the term *esse objectivum* or *esse objective* to refer to existence in the mind *qua* object thought. But he modifies the medieval doctrine in certain important and controversial respects. Descartes rejects Suarez's views on the relationship between the eternal truths and God, taking also the *content* of those truths to be dependent on God.[25] Thus, unlike Suarez, he does not believe that the doctrine of objective being works the same way with the human mind and the divine mind. For

[25] For Descartes' views on the creation of the eternal truths, see his letters to Mersenne of April 15 and May 27, 1630 (AT I, 135; AT I, 151) and a letter to Mesland on May 2, 1644 (AT IV, 110). See also the Sixth Replies: AT VII, 435f.; CSM II, 293–4.

Descartes, there is a difference between the way in which God knows eternal truths and the way in which we know eternal truths.[26] And although Descartes is influenced by Suarez in the matter of *esse objectivum* with regard to the human mind, he nevertheless departs from the Jesuit's view by insisting that the objective reality of an idea (i.e. objective existence in the mind) is itself something that requires an efficient cause.

The doctrine of objective being plays a central role in Descartes' *Meditations*. It functions as the fulcrum on which Descartes is able to move from his ideas to the existence of something distinct from and outside himself *qua* thinking substance. Descartes' argument for God's existence in the Third Mediation is much discussed in the scholarly literature. Rather than examining it in detail here, we will turn to it only as the *locus classicus* for any understanding of the *Cartesian* notion of objective being.

Like his Scholastic predecessors, Descartes distinguishes between actual existence in the world and a kind of being in the mind which is not actual being but, nonetheless, is not nothing. He calls actual being "formal" being or reality (*esse formale*), and being in the mind "objective" being. Formal being characterizes ordinary physical objects in space and time, as well mental substance and its actual modifications (ideas, i.e. mental acts, possess a degree of formal reality); in short, anything that has actual being (finite or infinite, spiritual or physical). Objective being, on the other hand, is a mode of being in the understanding (*in intellectu*); not, however, as a real constituent part or property of the mind (that is, not "formally", as the mind's operations exist in it), but "in the way in which objects are normally there" (*esse in intellectu eo modo quo objecta in illo esse solent* [First Replies: AT VII, 102; CSM II, 74]). Objects are normally in the understanding not formally, but by means of ideas of them (*res est objective in intellectu per ideam* [Med. III: AT VII, 41]). To put it differently, something is objectively in the understanding when it is understood, thought about, known, etc., i.e. when it is the object of some cognitive act. Thus, when I think about the sun, the sun thereby has objective existence in my mind, a cognitive presence therein, in addition to the "formal" existence it already possesses external to and independently of my thinking. In reply to Caterus's

---

[26] For an extensive discussion of this issue, see Jean-Luc Marion, *Sur la théologie blanche de Descartes* (Paris: PUF, 1981).

question, in the First Set of Objections, "What is it to exist objectively in the understanding?", Descartes states that

'Objective being in the intellect' ... will signify the object's being in the intellect in the way in which its objects are normally there. By this I mean that the idea of the sun is the sun itself existing in the intellect – not of course formally existing, as it does in the heavens, but objectively existing, i.e. in the way in which objects are normally in the intellect. Now this mode of being is of course much less perfect than that possessed by things which exist outside the intellect; but, as I did explain, it is not therefore simply nothing. (First Replies: AT VII, 102; CSM II, 75)

As this last phrase indicates, objective existence is to be distinguished not only from formal or actual existence, but also from non-being or mere *esse rationale*. Descartes' response to Caterus is intended to establish that the objective being of an object, its being in the understanding, is at least sufficiently real as to require a cause.[27] That is, it makes sense to ask for a causal explanation why something is conceived or thought about (*nihil enim aliud hic quaeritur quam quae sit causa quare concipitur* [First Replies: AT VII, 103; CSM II, 75]). Descartes' whole project in Meditation III rests on this point:

He [Caterus] says, first of all, that when a thing exists in the intellect by means of an idea, it is not an actual entity, that is, it is not a being located outside the intellect; and this is quite true. Next he goes on to say that "it is not something fictitious or a conceptual entity but something real which is distinctly conceived"; here he concedes everything which I have assumed. But he then adds "since it is merely conceived and is not actual" – i.e. since it is merely an idea, and not a thing located outside the intellect – "although it can be conceived it cannot in any way be caused." This is to say that it does not require a cause enabling it to exist outside the intellect. This I accept; but it surely needs a cause enabling it to be conceived, which is the sole point at issue. (First Replies: AT VII, 103; CSM II, 75).

Objective existence is, once again, a mode of being between actual (formal) existence and either non-being or being a mere *ens rationis*. It is a real being in the mind or understanding as something known, a cognitive presence. When we have an idea of an external object, certain properties of the object (those picked out by the idea) which it

[27] This is where Descartes departs from Suarez, and from Scholastic doctrine in general – thus Caterus's confusion. See Gilson, *Etudes*, p. 204, n. 3.

possesses "formally" are thereby "objectively" in the mind (cf. Second Replies: AT VII, 161; CSM II, 114: *quaecumque percipimus tanquam in idearum objectis, ea sunt in ipsis ideis objective*).

The issue of objective being can also be approached from the inside out, that is working solely from the ideas themselves in the mind. In fact, at the point in the Third Meditation where Descartes brings up the issue of objective being, this is the only option open to him. Thus, on the one hand, when some object is objectively in the mind, it is present there by means of an idea of it. From the mind's point of view, this means that such an idea contains objectively (but not formally) that object. Another way of putting this is to say that the idea *is* the object as it exists objectively in the mind. (Note that *objects* have objective existence in the mind, ideas do not (except in so far as they are the object of a further act of thought); ideas have *objective reality*. The distinction is a fine one, but important.)

Descartes distinguishes between ideas taken in their formal aspect as modes of thinking substances, and ideas taken objectively as representing this or that thing. Taken formally or materially as a "work of the mind", as pure mental activity, all ideas are the same, being simply modes of thought. Where they differ is in regard to their respective objective realities: one idea is the idea of x, another of y, etc. (alternatively, one idea objectively contains x, another y, etc.): "In so far as the ideas are considered simply as modes of thought, there is no recognizable inequality among them: they all appear to come from within me in the same fashion. But in so far as different ideas are considered as images which represent different things, it is clear that they differ widely" (Med. III: AT VII, 40; CSM II, 27-8; cf. also *Principia*, I, 17). The distinction, Descartes notes, is similar to that between considering a painting in its formal aspect as a pattern of paint applied to a canvas, and considering it as a representation depicting such-and-such a subject (Letter to Regius, June, 1642: AT III, 567). When ideas are considered from the point of view of their objective reality, what is being considered is their representational content. By 'representational content' I mean that in virtue of which ideas are, as Descartes says, *tanquam rerum imagines* (Med. III: AT VII, 37); that is, ideas *qua* images exhibit or present (*exhibent* [AT VII, 40]) an object to the mind by means of a content (although not themselves serving as the objects of the mind). The objective reality of an idea *is* its representational content. In the Preface to the *Meditations*, after noting that 'idea' can be taken formally as an act of the understanding, Descartes insists that when 'idea' is taken "objectively" it is taken as "the thing represented by that operation" (AT VII, 8; CSM II, 7).

In Suarez we find the same distinction between the "formal conceiving" and the "objective conceiving". The *conceptus formalis* is the mental act of conceiving *per se*, that which does the representing:

The act itself, or (which is the same thing) the means by which the mind conceives some thing or general notion, is called the *formal conceiving*. It is called a conceiving, because it is a kind of offspring of the mind; it is called formal either because it is the extreme form of the mind, or because it formally represents to the mind the thing known, or because it is, in fact, the intrinsic and formal determination of a mental conception, which differentiates it from the objective conceiving.

[Conceptus formalis dicitur ipse, seu (quod idem est) verbum quo intellectus rem aliquam seu communem rationem concipit; qui dicitur conceptus, quia est veluti proles mentis; formalis autem appellatur, vel quia est ultima forma mentis, vel quia formaliter repraesentat menti rem cognitum, vel quia revera est intrinsicus et formalis terminus conceptionis mentalis, in quo differt a conceptu objectivo.] (2.1.1)

The *conceptus formalis* (the act of conceiving) is always singular and individual, since it is "a thing produced by the mind, inhering in it [*res producta per intellectum, eique inhaerens*]" (2.1.1). The *conceptus objectivus*, on the other hand, is the thing made known or represented by the act (by the *conceptus formalis*):

That thing ... which is expressly and immediately known or represented by the formal conceiving is called the *objective conceiving*. For example, when we conceive a man, that act which we produce in the mind in order to conceive the man is called the formal conceiving. But the man known and represented by that act is called the objective conceiving ... It is called objective because it is the conceiving not as the form intrinsically determining the conception, but as the object and material with which the formal conception is concerned and towards which the mind's eye is directly inclined.

[Conceptus objectivus dicitur res illa ... quae proprie et immediate per conceptum formalem cognoscitur seu repraesentatur; ut, verbi gratia, cum hominem concipimus, ille actus, quem in mente efficimus ad concipiendum hominem, vocatur conceptus formalis; homo autem cognitus et repraesentatus illo actu dicitur conceptus objectivus ... dicitur objectivus, quia non et conceptus ut forma intrinsice terminans conceptionem, sed ut objectivum est materia circa quam versatur formalis conceptio, et ad quem mentis acies directe tendit.] (2.1.1)

The *conceptus objectivus* is the act of conceiving considered not as an intrinsic and formal property of the mind, but as the object represented by that act. (Likewise, Descartes insists that when 'idea' is taken objectively [*objective*], it is considered "as the thing represented by that operation [*pro re per istam operationem representata*]" [Preface to *Meditations*: AT VII, 8]). It is the *conceptus ut objectivum*, whether that object exists formally or not.

The formal conceiving is always a true and positive thing, and in creatures is a property inhering in the mind. The objective conceiving is not always a true and positive thing, for we occasionally conceive privations, and other things, which are called beings of reason, since they only have objective being in the intellect.

[[Conceptus] formalis semper est vera et positiva res et in creaturis qualitas menti inhaerens; objectivus vero non semper est vera res positiva; concipimus enim interdum privationes, et alia, quae vocantur entia rationis, quia solum habent esse objective in intellectu.] (2.1.1)

The *conceptus objectivus*, what is conceived, need not be something singular and individual, but rather is often universal or general (*saepe vero est res universalis vel confusa et communis, ut est homo, substantia, et simila* (2.1.1).[28]

To return to Descartes, every idea (every act of thought), by virtue of its objective reality, displays a certain content to the mind. And it is by virtue of this representational content that one idea differs from another. More important, it is by virtue of objective reality or representational content that one idea is the idea of one object, while another idea is the idea of another object. That is, objective reality confers intentionality on the idea-act. The object present objectively in the idea is the idea-act's (intentional) object. My idea of the sun is the "idea *of* the sun" because it has a particular objective reality; that is, the sun exists objectively in my idea, is represented by the idea. And since objective reality is the same thing as the representational content of the idea, it is clear that Descartes holds a "content theory" of inten-

[28]For a fuller discussion, see Cronin, *Objective Being in Descartes and Suarez*, Chapter 3.

tionality. What makes an idea-act the idea of this particular object is something inhering in or intrinsic to the idea-act itself – its representational content/objective reality, whatever it "displays" or "exhibits" to the mind.[29]

Most Cartesian scholars agree that for Descartes an idea's objective reality is identical with its representational content. Gueroult, for example, identifies objective reality with "the content of [an idea] having representational character."[30] And he rightly recognizes that such a content, hence an idea's objective reality, is something that can be read off the idea, i.e. is accessible to a purely immanent and phenomenological examination: "what constitutes an idea ... is the character it possesses that an internal observation reveals, to be manifest to our consciousness as the picture of something external, even if, in fact, nothing of this kind corresponds to it."[31] Indeed, it is absolutely essential to Descartes' project that the objective reality of an idea can be read off the idea itself. Otherwise, the proof of God's existence, which is founded on an introspective examination of the objective reality of the idea of God, is undermined.[32]

Margaret Wilson, on the other hand, believes that the representative character of Cartesian ideas must be distinguished from their objective reality. This argument follows from her claim that materially false ideas (sensations) have representational content (that is, they are, like all ideas, *rerum tanquam imagines*) but (unlike clear and distinct ideas) do not have objective reality. They are "as if of a thing" without

---

[29] It might be objected that by insisting that an idea's objective reality demands a cause which may differ from the cause of its formal reality (such is the case, e.g., with the idea of God), Descartes distinguishes the content from the act so much that he, in fact, reifies the content, and thus comes closer to an object approach. For discussions of different readings of the role of objective reality in Descartes, especially regarding his tendency to reify it, see O'Neil, *Epistemological Direct Realism*, pp. 81ff.; and Brenda Judge, "Thoughts – and their Contents", *American Philosophical Quarterly*, 20 (1983), 365–74. For a brief discussion of the problem of the relationship between an act-idea and its content, see Richard A. Watson's review of John Yolton's *Perceptual Acquaintance*, in *Journal of the History of Philosophy*, 23 (1985), 433–7.

[30] Martial Gueroult, *Descartes' Philosophy Interpreted According to the Order of Reasons*, Roger Ariew, trans., 2 vols. (Minneapolis: University of Minnesota Press, 1984), vol. 1, p. 138. See also Laporte, *Le Rationalisme de Descartes*, p. 80; and Yolton, *Perceptual Acquaintance*, Chapter 1.

[31] Gueroult, *op. cit.*, p. 151.

[32] Gilson identifies *la réalité objective* with *la réalité du contenu représentatif de la chose* (Etudes, p. 204, n. 3).

really being "of a thing" (they do not represent anything real), and this is why they afford us material for error:

The claim that an idea is "of a thing (*res*)" must be distinguished from the claim that it has representational character ... the fact that an idea has representational character – that it presents itself as if exhibiting something to the mind, or making something cognitively accessible – leads us to suppose that it does make something real cognitively accessible to us.[33]

All ideas, Wilson argues, have representational character, and are *rerum tanquam imagines*. Some ideas *really* represent (that is, what they exibit to the mind as a real and possible being *is* a real and possible being), and these ideas have objective reality. Objective reality thus becomes a relation that obtains only if what is representationally contained in the idea is indeed a real and possible being.

But such a distinction between objective reality and representational content cannot be correct. To her credit, Wilson recognizes that such a distinction would be disastrous for the Cartesian project, since "it entails that the objective reality of an idea is *not* something the idea wears on its face."[34] Just as importantly, it goes against Descartes' language and argumentation. For example, he insists in the Third Meditation that to be in an idea objectively is to be there "by representation" (*par représentation* [added in the French edition, AT IX-1, 33]). He speaks here of objective reality as something within the idea, and not as some relational property which the idea extrinsically possesses just in case the object it presents representationally is a real and positive being. In his reply to Carterus, Descartes likens the objective reality of the idea of God to the "objective artifice" (*artificium objectivum*) of the idea of a machine, and he calls this "objective artifice" something that the idea displays or contains (*contineat*) (First Replies: AT VII, 103–4; HR II, 11; CSM II, 75).

Wilson's mistake, I believe, is to assume that for Descartes all ideas or thoughts, clear and distinct or not, are *tanquam rerum imagines* in the same manner and to the same degree; that is, that all ideas present something to the mind as if it were a "real and positive thing". Some ideas, she believes, continue to do so even though there is no such real and positive (i.e. possible) thing (such is the case with the idea of cold),

[33] Wilson, *Descartes*, pp. 108–9.
[34] *Ibid.*, p. 112.

and these Descartes calls "materially false", being liable to mislead us in our judgements. Because Wilson sees materially false ideas and clear and distinct ideas as alike in presenting something to the mind as a positive thing (i.e. alike in terms of the quality of their representational content), she is compelled to identify some property possessed by clear and distinct ideas and lacking from materially false ideas in order that they might be distinguished. She calls this property 'to be "of a thing (*res*)"', 'to *really* represent', or 'to possess objective reality'.

But in fact what distinguishes materially false ideas from clear and distinct ideas is the sense in which they are *tanquam rerum imagines*, that is, the quality of their representational content. It must be borne in mind that the "falsity" of which ideas *per se* are capable is entirely different from the kind of falsity that belongs to judgements. Judgements are true or false according to their success or failure in corresponding with things outside of the mind. This is falsity proper (what Descartes calls "formal falsity"); but it is not what Descartes means when he says that, in a certain sense, ideas are capable of *falsitas* (Med. III: AT VII, 43-4; CSM II, 30). In fact, he insists that ideas are incapable of falsity in the proper sense (*falsae proprie esse non possunt* [Med. III: AT VII, 37; CSM II, 26]). Materially false ideas are *false* in the sense that, unlike clear and distinct ideas, they do not present something to the mind as if it were a real and positive being, since in fact their representational content is so obscure that one cannot tell whether what they are presenting is something positive and real or not:

But as for all the rest, including light and colours, sounds, smells, tastes, heat and cold and the other tactile qualities, I think of these only in a very confused and obscure way, to the extent that I do not even know whether they are true or false, that is, whether the ideas I have of them are ideas of real things or of non-things. (Med. III: AT VII, 43; CSM II, 30).

From my idea of cold alone, I cannot determine whether cold is a privation or a real and positive thing. In contrast with a clear and distinct idea, the evidence here is just not good enough (i.e. clear enough) for making an informed judgment. Such an idea, although still possessing some minimal degree of representational content, fails to represent in an adequate fashion. As Norman Wells points out, "Descartes is obviously struck by the failure of these ideas truly to represent and to represent truly a *res*, a true object, or a non *res*, a false object ... Such is their representation, or the lack thereof, that we cannot distinguish a non *res* from a *res* in the order of objects, as we can readily do with clear and distinct ideas wherein the truth and falsity of objects is manifest ... Due to the alleged deficiency of our sensory ideas, in spectator-like fashion, we cannot decide judgementally what their objects are."[35] In his reply to Arnauld's Fourth Objections, Descartes reaffirms the position he took in the *Meditations*: "my only reason for calling the idea [of cold] materially false is that, owing to the fact that it is obscure and confused, I am unable to judge whether or not what it displays [*exhibet*] to me is something positive which exists outside of my sensation. And hence I may be led to judge that it is something positive though in fact it may merely be an absence" (Fourth Replies: AT VII, 234; CSM II, 164 [translation modified]).[36] Although sensations, like clear and distinct ideas, possess a representational content, they are (unlike clear and distinct ideas) deficient in their capacity as representations, and hence are not *tanquam rerum imagines* in the same degree or as adequately as are clear and distinct ideas.

Thus, materially false ideas do not differ from clear and distinct ideas in having a similar kind of representational content but no objective reality. Rather, the difference lies in the nature of the content of materially false ideas: "the reality which they display to me is so extremely slight that I cannot even distinguish the thing represented from a non-thing" (Med. III: AT VII, 44; CSM II, 30 [translation modified]). In other words, their objective reality, being deficient, is such that it does not necessitate positing a real and positive cause of the idea outside of the mind (Med. III: AT VII, 42, 44; CSM II, 29, 30: *Quibus profecto non est necesse ut aliquem authorem a me diversum assignem*).

19 *Arnauld's account of the intentionality of perception*

Both Malebranche and Arnauld subscribe to the thesis of

---

[35]Norman J. Wells, "Material Falsity in Descartes, Arnauld, and Suarez", *Journal of the History of Philosophy*, 22 (1984), pp. 36–7.

[36]While Wells sees a continuity on the issue of material falsity between the *Meditations* and his reply to Arnauld, Wilson believes that Descartes' reply represents a "significant departure" from his approach in the *Meditations* (Wilson, *Descartes*, p. 115).

intentionality: that every perception is the perception *of* some object. Malebranche insists that there is no perception that is not the perception of something (*voir rien, c'est ne point voir*). As we have seen, he takes this to mean that every act of perception is essentially related to its direct and immediate object. To say that the act has an object is to say that there is necessarily some object really present toward which it is immediately directed. (Since such a necessary relationship clearly does not obtain between perceptual acts and objects in the world, Malebranche introduces ideal objects.) Malebranche, in other words, offers an object theory of intentionality. In Chapter II of VFI, Arnauld insists that every thought (*chaque pensée*) is essentially the thought *of* something, that every mental act has its object:

Just as it is clear that I am thinking, so it is clear that I am thinking of something, that is, that I know and perceive something; for this is essential to thought. And thus, since I cannot have any thought or knowledge without an object known, I can no more ask myself the reason why I am thinking of something than why I am thinking at all, since it is impossible to think without thinking of something. But I can very well ask why I am thinking of one thing rather than another. (VFI, 184)

This covers all mental activity, such as perception, judgement, memory, imagination, etc. In fact, Arnauld insists that intentionality is the defining mark of the mental in general – it characterizes not only cognitive activities but also such things as pleasures and sensations.

The mind remains substantially the same over any given period of time. During that period it is modified in various ways: it thinks, perceives, remembers, judges, etc., much as a piece of wax, while remaining substantially the same, assumes different forms or shapes (*Défense*, 38:383). Each of these modifications (mental acts) is thus, first of all, related to the mind (the thinking substance) of which it is a mode: "it cannot be doubted ... that all our perceptions, such as the perception of a number or a square, are modifications of our soul" (*Défense*, 38:383). However, every mental act, every modification of a finite thinking substance, also has its object. "One cannot think without thinking of something; to think of nothing is not to think at all; that is, there is no thought which does not have its object" (*Défense*, 38:383). In other words, every perception, every thought, in addition to being essentially related to the mind of which it is the activity, is also essentially related to some object. And it is in respect of their objects that one perception differs from another:

> I have said that I take perception and idea to be one and the same. Nonetheless, it must be remarked that this thing, although single, stands in two relations: one to the soul which it modifies, the other to the thing perceived ... and the word 'perception' more directly indicates the first relation; the word 'idea', the latter relation. (VFI, 198)

> Every thought stands essentially in two relations: one to the soul which it modifies, or of which it is a mode ... the other to the thing which it has as its object. And thus, when I think of a square, my soul is modified by this thought, and the square is the object of this modification of my soul, which is the thought of a square. (*Défense*, 38:383–4)

The problem, however, is this: just how does one account for this second relation, for the claim that every perception is the perception *of* some object? How does Arnauld explain this relatedness (directedness) to an object which is characteristic of any mental act? Arnauld rejects Malebranche's theory. He does not account for the perceptual act's object-directedness by positing an actual, ordinary-type relation between the act and some immediately-present object. First, he insists such a position leads to the obviously false conclusion that every perception, indeed every thought, is the perception or thought of some actually-existing object: the one which is so present (cf. VFI, 221). Second, it is simply contrary to the phenomenological data. If one takes the time to inspect carefully what takes place in the mind on the occasion of an act of perception, one will not find the *être représentatif distingué de la perception* which Malebranche claims is necessary for perception (cf. VFI, 212–213). What does account for the intentionality of the act, according to Arnauld, is something about the act itself, something intrinsic to it which makes it the perception of this object rather than another (*je puis bien me demander pourquoi je pense à une chose plutôt qu'à une autre*).

What gives any mental act its intentionality, what makes any perception the "perception *of* some object", is the fact that, as Arnauld claims, such an act *represents* an object. In fact, every perceptual act is essentially representative. Every perception represents some object, and hence is "the perception *of* that object" (*Les perceptions que notre âme a des objets, sont essentiellement représentatives de ces objets* [*Défense*, 38: 381]). Thus, in response to Malebranche, Arnauld claims that "I am far from rejecting all kinds of representative entities or modalities, since I maintain that it is clear to whoever reflects on what goes on in his mind, that all our perceptions are essentially representative modalities" (VFI, 199). Malebranche claims that every mental act is directed towards a representative entity (an idea). Arnauld, on the other hand, claims that every mental act *is* a representative entity, *is* an idea (*'perception' et 'idée' sont la même chose*). Thus, in addition to its relation to the mind of which it is the activity, every act is also related to some object in virtue of its representative character. My perception of the sun is, considered in itself, a "perception *of* the sun" (i.e. is intentionally related to the sun) because it represents the sun. The perception possesses a certain representational content or structure, without being directed towards this content (except insofar as it reflects upon itself). Act-ideas *have* a content, but they are not directed towards this content. On this point my interpretation differs from that of Ginsberg, who insists that "the act of apprehending includes or contains *the content apprehended* [emphasis added]" (see p. 107 above).

In other words, there is something about the act itself which makes it the perceiving of one object rather than another, and which differentiates it from other acts. Every act, by virtue of its own intrinsic representative nature, is the perception of some specified object, whether or not the object actually exists. Indeed, Arnauld insists that the intentionality of a perceptual act cannot be accounted for in any other way. That is, a perception of x would not be a "perception *of* x" if it were not representative of x (*Défense*, 38:391). Elsewhere, he states that to be the perception of x is to be representative of x (*Défense*, 38:383). For the most part, in addition to taking it to be an evident phenomenological datum, Arnauld seems to take the representative character of mental acts to be a self-evident, even "analytic" truth. He claims in the *Défense* that "being greater than its part is clearly included in the notion of the whole; but it is *equally* clear that included in the notion of the perceptions which our soul has of objects is the fact that they are essentially representative of these objects" (38:382; cf. also *Dissertation*, 40:84). Occasionally, he offers an argument of sorts: how else could we perceive or think of or otherwise know an object if our acts of perceiving, thinking, etc. did not represent them to us? (*Défense*, 38:406). Because of their representative function, these acts make their objects present to the mind (*c'est assurément nos perceptions [seules] qui nous rendent les choses présentes à notre esprit* [*Défense*, 38:587]). The kind of presence made possible by a representative perception is not a local presence, but an *objective* presence.

It is clear from the foregoing that Arnauld holds a content theory of the intentionality of perception. Perceptual acts are object-directed, or bear an "essential relation to an object", by virtue of some feature of the act itself. In his debate with Pierre Bayle, Arnauld insists that it is wrong to think that an act's relation to an object is not due to something intrinsic to the act itself, wrong to think that

the relation which different modifications of our soul (thoughts, loves, desires, pleasures) have to their objects is nothing essential to each, and does not enter into its constitution [*entité physique*], but that it is merely an extrinsic denomination which is accessory and accidental to the perception, and of which the perception can be stripped while remaining what it is in its basic constitution; such that the perception which I have of a spider can become the perception of an elephant without undergoing any change in its consitution or reality. (*Dissertation*, 40:61)

That feature of the act which is responsible for its intentionality is its representational content. This content is not something extrinsic to the act and, as it were, coming from outside, but rather constitutes a part of its being (*entre dans* [*son*] *entité* [*Dissertation*, 40:64]). The content of the perceptual act inheres in it, but not in the way in which coins inhere in a purse (*Dissertation*, 40:61). Although the coins may be removed from the purse without changing the purse in any essential respect, the perceptual act *is* a representation of a particular object, and hence the representational content of the act cannot be separated from it without changing that act in its essential nature (as the perception *of* such and such an object). "The perception of a circle, of a square or of a number is nothing other than the formal representation of a circle, a square or a number" (*Dissertation*, 40:62). The content is that aspect of the act which characterizes the act as just that particular act and no other. One might say that the content is the essential *structure* (or, to use Descartes' term, *form*) of the act, making it the act that it is. The content is thus realized, expressed, or manifested ontologically in the act. Arnauld's position might be represented as follows:[37]

---

[37] I am indebted to Richard A. Watson for this schematic suggestion.

This act   represents   this object

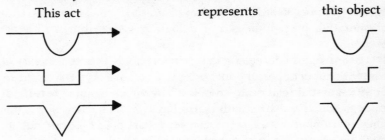

Thus, unlike Ginsberg, who views the act and its content as two distinguishable yet inseparable parts of a complex whole, one part (the act) directed towards the other (the content), I see the act and its content as more intimately related, with the content structuring the act and giving it its identity. On Ginsberg's interpretation, on the contrary, it would seem that one can substitute one content for another without any change in the act *per se* (although the complex as a whole would be changed). Yet for Arnauld, to change the content is to change the act. To change the content of a perception p from x to y is to change p (an act: "the perception of x") into q (a different act: "the perception of y").

This content of the act, inhering in it, prescribes an object for the act, determines its objective reference, making it the "perception *of* such-and-such an object". A perceptual act which represents the sun (i.e. which has a particular representational content) thereby bears within itself a directedness toward the sun. Such a directedness is not due to any ordinary-type relation obtaining between the act and either the sun itself or some other really-present object (e.g. a Malebranchian idea of the sun). As Arnauld insists, very often there is no real object present, immanent or otherwise (such is the case, for example, in imagination and hallucination). The intentional relation between the act and an object does not demand the real existence of the object prescribed (in this it differs from "ordinary-type" relations). An act can have "directedness" toward an object even though no such object exists.

We saw in the last chapter that where Malebranche sees two relations obtaining in a case of veridical perception, one between the act and the idea and another between the idea and the external physical object, Arnauld sees only one relation: between the act and the object. Arnauld thereby combines two notions which, for Male-branche, are distinct. Malebranche posits both an intentional relation, or relation of directedness (between the act and the idea), *and* a representative relation (between the idea and the external object): the act intends the idea, the idea represents the object. For Arnauld, the representative relation *is* the intentional relation (or, more strictly speaking, the former *accounts* for the latter). The representative function of the act *is* what confers intentionality or object-directedness upon the act. Because a perception represents an object it intends that object, or is the "perception *of* that object".[38]

Central to Arnauld's position on the representative character of mental acts is the notion of objective being. As in Descartes, this notion plays an important role in Arnauld's theory of ideas and inten-tionality. As was the case with the tradition examined above, which includes Descartes, objective being is, for Arnauld, a mode of being distinct from both actual existence (formal being) and non-being. It is a being in the mind, not formally, but in the way objects are wont to be there: as something known or understood.

To exist objectively in the mind is not only to be the object that is the terminus of my thought, but it is to be in my mind intelligibly, in the way in which objects are normally there. And the idea of the sun is the sun insofar as it exists in my mind, not formally, as it exists in the sky, but objectively, that is in the manner in which objects exist in our thought, which is a much more imperfect manner of being than that by which the sun really exists. Nonetheless, it cannot be said that it is nothing and that it does not need a cause. (VFI, 200).

Arnauld is toeing the Cartesian line here. In fact, he explicitly acknowledges Descartes as his authority on the matter of objective vs. formal being (VFI, 205).

Arnauld objects to Malebranche that local presence to the mind, which would imply a formal presence therein, is irrelevant to cognition. What is relevant to cognition is objective presence: "An object is present to our mind when our mind perceives it and knows it" (VFI, 198). Objective being is thus a being known. To be present objectively to the mind is not to be present there as some kind of immanent mental object, but simply to be known (*être connu*) by the

---

[38] Cf. Radner, "Representationalism in Arnauld'a Act Theory of Perception", p. 97.

mind; or, more particularly, to be the object of some cognitive act: "I say that a thing exists objectively in my mind when I conceive it. When I conceive the sun, a square or a sound, the sun, the square or this sound exists objectively in my mind, whether or not is also exists outside my mind" (VFI, 198). To be the object of a cognitive act is, for Arnauld, to be represented in that act. Thus, an object is objectively present to the mind when it is represented by some cognitive act (e.g. a perception) and, hence, is the (intentional) object of that act. Arnauld therefore identifies *être objectivement dans notre esprit* with *être representé par une idée ou perception* (VFI, 199). The perception of a square, insofar as its represents the square, *is* the square as it is objectively present to the mind:

> To say of the perception of a square that it is that by which I perceive a square, that it is that by which a square is objectively present to my mind, that it is that which represents a square, or that it is a modification of my soul which is representative of a square – all of these ways of speaking signify the same thing, although with different words (*Défense*, 38:384).

For something to be known, to be the object of a cognitive act, is for it to exist objectively in the mind; all of which is the same as saying that it is represented by some act of thought, some mode of thinking substance.

Considered with regard to the idea-perception, to say that an act represents an object is to say that it objectively contains that object, or, as Descartes says, possesses a particular objective reality (cf. VFI, 198). For Arnauld, as for Descartes, the objective reality of an idea is its representational content. The idea "displays" a certain objective reality to the intellect (cf. Fourth Objections: AT VII, 207; CSM II, 145: *menti nostrae exhibet*). Hence, objective being is tied up with the issue of intentionality: to be perception *of* an object x is to represent x/objectively contain x. The objective reality/representational content of a perception is that feature intrinsic to the act which gives it directedness toward an object, i.e. that particular object which exists objectively in the act-idea (is represented by the act). Moreover, objective reality/representational content individuates acts. Considered materially (formally), all acts are identical as modes of thinking substances. They differ in respect of their objective reality/representational content, in virtue of which one is the perception of x, another the perception of y, etc. (cf. *Dissertation*, 40:61ff.).

Arnauld is rather vague on just what he means by 'representation' and, more particularly, what it is about the content of a perceptual act which makes it a representation of some object. Given his adherence to Cartesian metaphysics and mind/body dualism, the relation between idea-perception and object is *not* one of similarity or resemblance. Being the orthodox Cartesian that he is, he finds it inconceivable that anything mental could resemble something material. Idea-perceptions, which are modes of active, unextended thought, cannot resemble inert, unthinking extension.[39] Arnauld also rejects the possibility that an idea represents an object pictorially, in the way in which paintings or other material images represent their originals:

When it is claimed that our ideas and perceptions (which I take to be the same thing) represent to us the things which we conceive, and are the images [*images*] of them, it is in an entirely different sense from that in which paintings are said to represent their originals and to be the images of them. (VFI, 199; cf. also 338).

Nor is an idea-perception like a mirror. "A comparison with mirrors cannot help us understand what takes place in our mind" (*Défense*, 38:390). Thus, while an idea is still an *image* of its object, this is in a unique, non-pictorial sense. The way in which a perception, or any thought, represents is completely *sui generis*, and like no other way of representing. Least of all, given its *mental* character, can it be clarified by means of analogy with *material* representations such as mirrors and pictures. "This manner of existing objectively in the mind is so peculiar to mind and to thought, as being that which, in particular, constitutes their nature, that is vain to look for anything even remotely similar in that which is not mind or thought" (VFI, 199).

In fact, the way in which thought represents is primary. All other kinds of representation (pictures, words, etc.) represent only in a secondary sense, in relation to thought:

These words [to represent, representative, representation] apply properly and primarily only to the perceptions of the mind, which are formal representations of their objects. It is only in relation to our perceptions that other things, such as paintings, images, words or written characters, are said to "represent", or are called "representations". (*Défense*, 38:584)

[39] This is Foucher's point against Malebranche. See Watson, *The Downfall of Cartesianism*, pp. 89ff.

A portrait of Louis XIV, for example, is only a representation (in the secondary sense) of its subject because it calls up in the viewer a mental (primary) representation, that is, the idea-perception of Louis XIV. The same applies to words and signs: "they can only be significative or representative in relation to our perceptions, which they call up" (*Défense*, 38:585). In fact, Arnauld turns this point into a critique of Malebranche's position. How could the *être représentatif distingué de la perception*, which Malebranche claims is necessary for perception, be a representation of the sun, for example, unless it called up in the perceiver's mind a perception which represents the sun in the primary sense of 'represent' and which confers a representative function upon the Malebranchian idea in the same, secondary sense as a painting is transformed into a representation by the spectator?

It might be said that it is not my perception which represents the sun to me when I think of the sun; it is a representative entity distinct from my perception, intimately united to my soul, which is the "archetypal idea of the sun". But can this alleged "archetype of the sun" represent the sun to me otherwise than as a portrait of the king represents the king to me? I do not see that it can be otherwise. It will, thus, call up in my mind the perception of the sun, without which it would not be possible for the sun to be represented to me by its representative entity ... (*Défense*, 38:586)

The *être représentatif* thus becomes, at best, superfluous; at worst, an impediment to the perception of the sun itself.

Thus, it appears that the way in which an idea represents, for Arnauld, is not reducible to, or explicable in terms of, any other mode of representing (e.g. pictorial, symbolic, etc.). Ideas function differently from material images (e.g. a painting), in that there is no resemblance between idea and object; and differently from signs and words, in that there is not simply an arbitrary conventional relationship of denotation, but the idea represents some particular object in virtue of features intrinsic to it. It is a primitive indefinable relation between the idea and the object it makes known. As Arnauld insists in the first line of the Port-Royal Logic, "the word 'idea' is among those which are so clear that they cannot be explained by others, because there are none more clear and simple".[40]

Is Arnauld's direct realism compromised by his "representation-

---

[40] For the orthodox Cartesian position on this issue, see Watson, *ibid.*, pp. 93ff.

alism"? I do not think so. It should be clear by now that the content of the act, that which makes it a representation, is not something aprehended, except in reflection. On the contrary, the representational content is that which allows for the immediate and direct apprehending of the external object. "How could we perceive, either immediately or mediately, [external objects, such as material things,] if our perceptions cannot represent them to us?" (*Défense*, 38:406). To exist objectively in the mind, to be represented by an idea-perception, is, on Arnauld's view, simply to be known or perceived: "This presence of an object in our mind, being none other than an objective presence, is nothing other than the mind's perception of the object ..." (VFI, 216; cf. also 213). Thus, it is that which is represented by the act which is perceived, not the representation itself. The representative idea-perception is primarily *id quo intelligitur*, not *id quod intelligitur* (cf. VFI, 246).

The question remains as to how Arnauld's approach to the intentionality of perception fits with his more general, and (to him) more important, concerns. In the last chapter, Arnauld's direct realism was placed in the larger context of his debate with Malebranche, particularly regarding theological issues. Arnauld's attack on Malebranche's representationalism is an attack on what he sees as both the philosophical linchpin and the weak point of Malebranche's whole system. By taking apart Malebranche's account of perception, particularly his theory of the vision in God, Arnauld believes he can thereby undermine the theology which he finds so unacceptable.

It is clear that Arnauld's content theory of intentionality also serves him well in his more general campaign against Malebranche. First, it supports his attack on Malebranche's representationalism. Given Arnauld's position, one need not introduce *êtres représentatifs* to explain the intentionality of perception, as Malebranche does. Intentionality is accounted for by means of the representational content of mental acts, *not* by means of really-present objects of a peculiar ontological sort. One of Malebranche's central arguments for his representationalism is thereby nullified (see Chapter 3). Second, Arnauld's content theory of intentionality ties in with and supports his critique of Malebranche's views on the nature of pleasure and human good or happiness. In his *Réflexions philosophiques et théologiques sur le nouveau système de la nature et de la grace*, Arnauld objects to Malebranche's claim that pleasure is a good in itself and truly renders happy whoever is enjoying it.[41] Arnauld is particularly bothered by the implication that this is true of the pleasures of the sense (*les plaisirs des sens*). These, he insists, are not true goods, or goods in themselves, but only *means* of preserving the body by indicating those objects which are to be pursued as contributing to its well-being and those which are to be shunned as harmful to it. Malebranche's identification of pleasure with happiness, with *le bonheur de l'homme*, is, according to Arnauld, repulsive, and leads to the blasphemous conclusion that sensuous pleasure is a true good. If such pleasure in itself is capable of making one happy, it will become the object of our love and desire.

If sensuous pleasure is what makes us happy, then it is desirable in itself, and, consequently, it is permissible to pursue pleasure [*volupté*] for pleasure's sake. Now to pursue pleasure for pleasure's sake is called by St Augustine *libido sentiendi*, and by St John the Apostle *concupiscentia carnis*, concupiscence of the flesh. Thus, if it is permissible to pursue pleasure for pleasure's sake, then concupiscence of the flesh, *libido sentiendi*, is not wicked, and it is not in us an effect of sin. Now this cannot be maintained without ruining one of the principal proofs of original sin. (*Réflexions*, 39:367–8)

Part of Arnauld's attack is to discriminate between spiritual pleasures and bodily (or sensuous) pleasures, and then claim that only spiritual pleasures are capable of being *notre vraie bien*; bodily pleasures are to be scorned: "Pleasures which cannot make us happy must be scorned; for since only the goods of the mind (spiritual goods) can be our true good, these pleasures of the senses, which are related only to our body, cannot be our true good" (*Réflexions*, 39:381).

Pierre Bayle, who rallied to Malebranche's defense after Arnauld's initial attack, held that all pleasures, considered in and of themselves, are alike. There is no recognizable intrinsic difference among them when they are examined as mental events without reference to their occasional causes. Hence, any distinction between purely spiritual pleasures and purely sensuous pleasures (both of which are mental phenomena) cannot be made on the basis of the nature of the pleasures themselves, but rather only on the basis of their causes. Bayle calls the labels 'spiritual' and 'physical', in regard to kinds of

---

[41] For Malebranche's view, see *Traité de la Nature et de la Grace*, II, xxix: "Il est certain que le plaisir rend heureux celui qui en jouit, du moins dans le tems qu'il en jouit" (OC V, 96).

pleasures, "extrinsic denominations", whereby the qualities of the respective causes are attributed to their effects in the mind.[42] Thus, the pleasure one feels upon eating a luxurious meal differs only "extrinsically" or nominally from the pleasure attending pious meditation. If one transposes the objects which are the occasional causes of such pleasures, so that a gourmet feast is attached to the pleasure that originally attended meditation, and vice versa, the pleasure that was formerly spiritual will now be a sensuous pleasure, and the pleasure that was formerly a bodily pleasure will now be a spiritual one. And yet no *intrinsic* change in the pleasures themselves will have occurred.[43]

The basis for Bayle's position, as Arnauld recognized and Bayle admitted, is the assumption that pleasure and pain do not bear in themselves any essential reference to an object or state of affairs. That is, they lack intentionality. If the pleasure attending eating cannot, when considered in itself without reference to its external cause, be distinguished from the pleasure attending pious meditation, then neither contains in itself a "directedness" toward a particular object, since such directedness *would* allow one to discriminate between that pleasure which intrinsically refers to the contemplation of God and that which refers to roast chicken.

Again, Arnauld insists that intentionality or directedness must be accounted for by something intrinsic to the mental event itself. In response to Bayle, he insists that pleasures, pains and feelings such as love, joy, and anger must be included with thoughts, perceptions, and desires as mental phenomena which are essentially related to some object (*Dissertation*, 40:60). This relation to an object is not something *extrinsique et accessoire* to the pleasure itself, as Bayle would have it, but is intrinsic to it, entering into the "being" (*entité*) of the mental event. Arnauld insists that it is absurd to imagine that the "relation to an object" which is possessed by the different modifications of the soul (thoughts, loves, desires, pleasures) is not something essential to each, and does not enter into its "physical" reality (*entité physique*), but is only an extrinsic denomination which is accessory and accidental to them (*Dissertation*, 40:61). On the contrary, as with other thoughts, there is something about each particular pleasure or pain itself which gives it an objective reference and differentiates it from other pleasures or

---

[42] Pierre Bayle, *Nouvelles de la République des Lettres*, December, 1685, in *Oeuvres Diverses*, Elisabeth Labrousse, ed., 4 vols. (Hildesheim: Georg Olms, 1964), vol. 1, p. 454.
[43] *Ibid.*, p. 455.

pains: it has objective reality/representational content. In this way, some pleasures are, in a non-extrinsic sense, corporeal, others are spiritual, depending upon the objects toward which they are intentionally (instrinsically) related (*Dissertation*, 40:60).

Arnauld thus claims that *all* mental phenomena (cognitive and volitional activities, as well as events such as pain, pleasure, and the like) have intentionality. Bayle responds with an acknowledgement that perceptions, thoughts, and similar activities do have "an essential relation to an object", but he denies that this is also the case with sensations: "The soul is capable of a sensation of cold without relating it to a foot, or a hand", or any other subject for that matter.[44]

Arnauld's position on intentionality, by supporting the distinction he wishes to make between purely spiritual pleasures and bodily pleasures, facilitates his attack on Malebranche's views on pleasure and happiness. We see, thereby, how what today would be considered a purely "philosophical" problem has, in the seventeenth century, moral and theological ramifications.

---

[44] *Dictionnaire Historique et Critique* (Rotherdam: Renier Leers, 1967), vol. 1, pp. 1048–9.

Appendix: The theological debate

Perception is not, of course, the main issue between Arnauld and Malebranche. Both thinkers were extremely devout individuals who were concerned more with the demands of positive theology than with speculative philosophy (though this may be more true of Arnauld than of Malebranche). Most of Arnauld's life was devoted to propagating Jansenist doctrine and encouraging reform within the Church, and to defending Port-Royal against vicious attacks by Jesuits and others. And Malebranche, as a member of the congregation of the Oratory, was committed first and foremost to a religious vocation, though he obviously had a penchant for metaphysics. Moreover, we have seen how Arnauld's critique of *êtres représentatifs* serves him mainly as a means of indirectly undermining Malebranche's theology by attacking the philosophical foundations which he finds so vulnerable (Section 16). If he can show how Malebranche's position on a general and abstract philosophical matter such as perception and human knowledge is false and inconsistent, then the way for his theological attack on Malebranche's position on grace and divine volition is made that much easier. We likewise saw how Arnauld's account of intentionality facilitates his critique of Malebranche's views on pleasure and happiness (Section 19). As he notes in a letter to Du Vaucel (June 18, 1663), VFI is only a preliminary, "a mere bagatelle, but it is useful for teaching the author of the new system regarding Grace that he ought not to have so much confidence in his meditations."

Is it possible, however, to draw a more direct and positive connection between the philosophical debate over ideas and the broader, and (to Arnauld) more important, theological debate? What does the critique in VFI, with its attendant direct realism, have in common with the general project represented by the *Réflexions philosophiques et théologiques sur le nouveau système de la nature et de la grace?*

The real issue between Arnauld and Malebranche regards providence and grace, and particularly the nature of divine volition. Malebranche himself tells us that a major part of his aim in the *Traité de la Nature et de la Grace* is to provide an alternative to the Jansenist theory of grace, which he finds to be full of *des sentimens dangereuses*: "What the Mssrs. of Port-Royal have written concerning grace is utter nonsense [*galimathias*] and completely incomprehensible" (*Résponse* I, vi: OC VI, 13ff.). Interestingly enough, Arnauld at first found nothing problematic with the *Recherche*. In fact, he initially praised it as a fine, if somewhat unorthodox, example of Cartesian philosophizing,[1] though it is likely that he did not have the opportunity to read it as closely as he would after the appearance of the *Traité* in 1680.[2] When he did get around to reading the *Traité*, and then reread in its light the *Recherche*, it became clear to him that both works contained unacceptable views on God's role in both the order of nature and the order of grace. It was then that he conceived the project of refuting the entire Malebranchian system, philosophy (especially epistemology) and theology together.

Briefly stated, the question is: what is providence and how does it govern the natural and human worlds? Malebranche insists that God acts only by a general will. There is a system of general laws chosen by God because of their goodness, simplicity, and wisdom. These laws are responsible for all the good and evil in the world – all its beings, relations, and operations. Everything in nature that God produces, everything in the visible world, thus come about by his *volontés générales*. Likewise, God acts in grace not by particular volitions, but by a general law which, in intent, encompasses all human beings. God wants everyone to be saved. But clearly not everyone is, in fact, saved; some are damned. Malebranche explains this by insisting that Jesus Christ mediates between God's general grace (his *volonté générale*) and

---

[1] See Père Y. André, *Vie de Malebranche* (Paris, 1886), p. 20; and Bouillier, *Histoire de la philosophie Cartésienne*, vol. 2, pp. 170–71.

[2] Arnauld did not read the manuscript, as Malebranche had hoped, in time for publication (they were still good friends at the time, and Malebranche wanted his comments). When Arnauld did see a copy as it was being published at Elzeviers', he tried (unsuccessfully) to halt the printing. For a good discussion of these events in their relationship, see Robinet's introduction to OC V, pp. xxiiff. See also André, *op. cit.*, pp. 72–98.

the grace actually received by individuals. The desires in Christ's soul serve as the "occasional cause" for the actual distribution of grace. The consequence (which is, of course, unacceptable to Arnauld's Jansenism) is that God's grace, as contained in a general will, is not efficacious in itself (*efficace par elle-même* [see *Traité*, III, xxi: OC V, 133]). Moreover, it may happen, as Malebranche puts it, that often *la grace tombe inutilement* and fails to overcome the concupiscence of the sinner (*Traité*, III, 25: OC V, 134). This, Malebranche claims, is Augustine's grace, not *Augustinus's* grace.[3]

Arnauld sees this account as a threat to the true Catholic system of providence. His critique of Malebranche, as found in the *Dissertation sur les miracles de l'Ancienne Loi (Oeuvres*, vol. 6), the *Réflexions*, and a voluminous correspondence, is centered on the claim that in both the order of nature and the order of grace God acts by particular volitions (*des volontés particulières*), and not as a *cause universelle* in the sense in which Malebranche understands this term. To be sure, there are general laws established by God. But it is necessary to distinguish between God acting in accordance with general laws and the *volontés particulières* by means of which he acts. Contrary to what he sees as Malebranche's view of God acting only in regard to general matters, Arnauld insists that God concerns himself *immediately* with all things (*Réflexions*, Book I), and that his providence *directly* embraces everyone, and everything that happens. Malebranche, he believes, ultimately takes responsibility away from God and places it in his creation: it is not really his will that such-and-such an event happen; rather, physical events or human volitions (and, in the order of grace, Christ's desires) are the occasional causes that determine the general and (with respect to particulars) indeterminate will of God (*Réflexions*, I, xiv). Not only is such a view not found in our idea of a perfect being, but it is unworthy (*indigne*) of God's goodness (*bonté*) and detracts from his omnipotence and liberty.[4]

We saw in Chapter 3 and elsewhere that it is not clear that Malebranche and Arnauld always understand each other's position on the nature of ideas. The same is true of this debate on providence, where Arnauld's theological passions may be getting in the way of a careful and accurate analysis of Malebranche's views (he was in a

---

[3] See also *Traité*, I, xlii–xliv: OC V, 49–52.

[4] For an interesting discussion of these issues, see Bayle's review of the *Réflexions*, in *Nouvelles de la République des Lettres*, August 1685: *Oeuvres Diverses*, vol. 1, pp. 346ff. Bayle, as we saw in Chapter 6, takes Malebranche's side.

hurry to get his critique out, and it appeared in 1685, less than a year after VFI). But it *is* clear that Malebranche explicitly and unequivocally allows for the possibility that God's grace, contained in a *volonté générale*, is not in itself efficacious and does occasionally fall on *des coeurs endurcis* ... [*et*] *corrompu*[*s*] (*Traité*, I, xliv: OC V, 51) without any effect. And Arnauld cannot accept this – he is committed to a rigorously efficacious grace. If Malebranche's principles lead him to deny such efficacy, then those principles are to be rejected as *fausses et dangereuses*.

These, then, are some of the more general and crucial theological issues at stake in the Arnauld–Malebranche debate. How do they relate to the debate on ideas? What binds together the maily philosophical issues of perception and cognition, dealt with in VFI and the *Recherche*, with those problems treated in Malebranche's *Traité* and Arnauld's *Réflexions*? I can here only make several suggestions, since neither thinker really tells us what that connection might be.

At one level, both debates (ideas and knowledge; providence) are really questions of orthodoxy. That is, they are both concerned with agreement with the views of the early Church fathers, especially Saint Augustine. In each stage of the controversy, Arnauld and Malebranche each put forth their respective position as the one to be found in the writings of Augustine and the one supported by Scripture. This is true with regard to the role of ideas, and the relationship between the human mind and the divine mind, in cognition; and it is true with regard to grace. Malebranche, for example, responding to Arnauld's charge in the *Défense* that "nothing is more contrary to St Augustine" than Malebranche's theory of ideas and intelligible extension, insists in TL (Letter I) that Chatpers VII and XXI of his *Réponse* clearly prove that "Mr. Arnauld is no more a faithful interpreter of Saint Augustine on the matter of ideas than on the matter of Grace" (TL, I, xii: OC VI, 238).[5] Thus, the controversy as a whole is between two Augustinians competing in their faithfulness to their mentor, in their conformity to the Saint's epistemology, metaphysics, and theology.

[5] There are too many instances to cite on this point. For Malebranche, see *Réponse*, VII (OC VI, 66-7), on ideas; and TL, II (OC VI, 291) and *Traité*, I, vi (OC V, 20-21), on grace. For Arnauld, see *Défense*, Chapters VII–IX ("Fausse conformité de l'Auteur avec S. Augustin . . ."), on ideas; and throughout the *Réfelexions* and later correspondence, on grace. Malebranche writes, for example: "Ce que dit ici Mr. Arnauld, 'que la grace efficace par elle-même est le fondement de la prédestination gratuit', est encore plus visiblement contraire au sentiment de S. Augustin" (TL, II: OC VI, 291).

To Arnauld, at least, both debates can also be seen as parts of a conflict over how best to dignify and do justice to the true conception of God. Which views fit together into the most worthy and accurate picture of His goodness, perfection, and wisdom – Arnauld's direct realism and his theory of efficacious grace, or Malebranche's *êtres représentatifs* and his account of God's *volontés générales*? Arnauld, as we have seen, argues for both his theory of ideas and his view of efficacious grace on the basis that each is more consistent with our idea of a perfect and benevolent God than the corresponding aspects of Malebranche's system are. For example, his theory of ideas and perception does not have God acting in roundabout and complex ways to accomplish that which might be done more simply and efficiently (Section 16). And his theory of grace has God immediately affecting the affairs of the world he created, and not merely responding to secondary, occasional causes. Thus, Arnauld's position in each of the two debates is, in his mind, not only the correct Augustinian position, but also the more pious and the one which most dignifies God.

Note, incidentally, that in each debate Arnauld opts for what he sees as the more direct and immediate, hence more simple, relationship: direct realism, i.e. perception without the "help" of any intermediary entities; and God acting by particular and efficacious volitions, without the mediation of secondary causes.

Finally, it is clear that Arnauld (in keeping with the Jansenist renunciation of worldly values and encouragement of introspection) sees his position in each debate as the one which best fosters individual piety and minimizes human pride, and which leads us to turn inward, away from everyday concerns in the material world and towards our soul and the contemplation of God. We saw that his critique of Malebranche's *êtres représentatifs* explicitly uses this kind of argument (Section 16), and accuses Malebranche of "divinizing" the objects of everyday concern. And the theory of efficacious grace is, for Arnauld, a theory which places responsibility for salvation solely in the hands of God and nullifies the role played therein by human volition and desire. What better way to discourage pride and inspire humility before God? Arnauld reads Malebranche, on the other hand, as allowing human volitions to be secondary causes occasioning the operations of God's general will. In Arnauld's eyes, Malebranche thus encourages pride through a belief that one's own activities are effective for securing true happiness, and comes dangerously close to the Pelagian and Molinist heresies. In this regard, Arnauld's pious and austere Jansenism appears to be a general force motivating his attacks on both Malebranche's theory of ideas and his theory of providence.

Bibliography

Primary texts

Arnauld, Antoine, *Oeuvres de Messire Antoine Arnauld*, 43 vols. (Paris: Sigismond D'Arnay, 1775).

— *Des vraies et des fausses idées* (Cologne: Nicolas Schouten, 1683).

Bayle, Pierre, *Dictionnaire Historique et Critique* (Rotterdam: Renier Leers, 1697).

— *Oeuvres Diverses*, Elisabeth Labrousse, ed., 4 vols. (Hildesheim: Georg Olms, 1964).

Berkeley, George, *The Works of George Berkeley*, A. A. Luce and T. E. Jessop, eds., 9 vols. (London: Nelson 1948–57).

Brentano, Franz, *Psychology from an Empirical Standpoint*, Antos C. Rancurello, D. B. Terrell, and Linda L. McAlister, trans. (New York: Humanities Press, 1973).

Descartes, René, *Oeuvres de Descartes*, Charles Adam and Paul Tannery, eds., 11 vols. (Paris: J. Vrin, 1974–83).

— *The Philosophical Writings of Descartes*, John Cottingham, Robert Stoothoff, and Dugald Murdoch, trans., 2 vols. (Cambridge: Cambridge University Press, 1985).

— *Philosophical Letters*, Anthony Kenny, trans. (Minneapolis: University of Minnesota Press, 1981).

Duns Scotus, John, *Opera Omnia*, 18 vols. (Paris: Vives, 1893).

Du Vaucel, Louis-Paul, "Observations sur la philosophie de Descartes", in Dijksterhuis, ed., *Descartes et le Cartésienisme Hollandais*, pp. 113–30.

Foucher, Simon, *Critique de la Recherche de la vérité* (Paris: Martin Coustelier, 1675).

Husserl, Edmund, *Cartesian Meditations*, Dorian Cairns, trans. (The Hague: Martinus Nijhoff, 1960).

— *Ideas Pertaining to a Pure Phenomenology and to a Phenomenological Philosophy*, F. Kersten, trans. (The Hague: Martinus Nijhoff, 1982).

Leibniz, Gottfried Wilhelm, *Die Philosophischen Schriften von Gottfried Wilhelm Leibniz*, C. J. Gerhardt, ed., 7 vols. (Hildesheim: Georg Olms, 1960–1962).

— *Philosophical Papers and Letters*, Leroy E. Loemker, ed. (Dordrecht: D. Reidel, 1969).

— *Discourse on Metaphysics/Correspondence with Arnauld/Monadology*, George R.

Montgomery, trans. (LaSalle: Open Court, 1980).

Locke, John, *The Works of John Locke*, 10 vols. (London: Tegg, 1823).

Malebranche, Nicholas, *Dialogues on Metaphysics and Religion*, Morris Ginsberg, trans. (New York: Macmillan, 1923).

— *Oeuvres Complètes*, André Robinet, ed., 20 vols. (Paris: J. Vrin, 1959–66).

— *The Search after Truth*, Thomas M. Lennon and Paul J. Olscamp, trans. (Columbus: Ohio State University Press, 1980).

— *Dialogues on Metaphysics*, Willis Doney, trans. (New York: Abaris Books, 1980).

Ockham, William, *Opera Philosophica et Theologica*, 9 vols. (St Bonaventure, New York: Franciscan Institute, University of St Bonaventure, 1970).

Régis, Pierre-Sylvain, *Cours entier de Philosophie, ou Système Général selon les principes de M. Descartes*, 3 vols. (Amsterdam: Huguetan, 1691).

— *Réponse aux Réflexions Critiques de M. Du Hamel sur le système cartésien de la philosophie de M. Régis* (Paris: Jean Cusson, 1692).

Reid, Thomas, *The Philosophical Works of Thomas Reid*, William Hamilton, ed., 2 vols. (Edinburgh: James Thin, 1896).

— *Inquiries and Essays*, Keith Lehrer and Ronald E. Beanblossom, eds. (Indiana: Bobbs-Merril, 1975).

Suarez, Francisco, *Disputationes Metaphysicae*, 2 vols. (Hildesheim: George Olms, 1965).

Secondary works

Aaron, Richard I., *John Locke*, 2nd ed. (Oxford: Oxford University Press, 1955).

Adams, Marilyn McCord, "Ockham's Nominalism and Unreal Entities", *Philosophical Review*, 86 (1976), 144–76.

Alquié, Ferdinand, *Le Cartésianisme de Malebranche* (Paris: J. Vrin, 1974).

André, Père Y., *Vie de Malebranche* (Paris, 1886).

Arbini, Ronald, "Did Descartes Have a Philosophical Theory of Sense Perception?", *Journal of the History of Philosophy*, 21 (1983), 317–38.

Armogathe, J.-R., *Theologica Cartesiana: L'explication physique de l'Eucharistie chez Descartes et Dom Desgabets*, International Archives of the History of Ideas, No. 84 (The Hague: Martinus Nijhoff, 1977).

Armstrong, D. M., *Perception and the Physical World* (London: Routledge and Kegan Paul, 1961).

— "Immediate Perception", in *The Nature of Mind and Other Essays*, pp. 119–31 (Ithaca: Cornell University Press, 1981).

Ayers, Michael, "Are Locke's 'Ideas' Images, Intentional Objects, or Natural Signs?", *Locke Newsletter*, 17 (1986), 3–36.

Bennett, Jonathan, *Locke, Berkeley, Hume: Central Themes* (Oxford: Oxford University Press, 1971).

Bouillier, Françisque, *Histoire de la philosophie Cartésienne*, 3rd ed., 2 vols. (Paris: Delagrave, 1868).

Bracken, Harry, "Berkely and Malebranche on Ideas", *The Modern Schoolman*, 41

(1963), 1–15.

Brunetière, Ferdinand, *Etudes critiques sur l'histoire de la littérature française*, 4 vols. (Paris: Hachette, 1904).

Butler, P. J., ed., *Cartesian Studies* (New York: Bobbs-Merrill, 1972).

Chisholm, Roderick, *Perceiving: A Philosophical Study* (Ithaca: Cornell University Press, 1957).

Church, Ralph W., *A Study in the Philosophy of Malebranche* (London: George Allen and Unwin, 1931).

Clark, Romane L., "Considerations for a Logic of Naive Realism", in Machamer and Turnbull, eds., *Studies in Perception*, pp. 525–6.

Cooke, Monte, "Arnauld's Alleged Representationalism", *Journal of the History of Philosophy*, 12 (1974), 53–64.

— "The Alleged Ambiguity of 'Idea' in Descartes' Philosophy", *Southwestern Journal of Philosophy*, 6 (1975), 87–103.

— "Descartes' Alleged Representationalism", *History of Philosophy Quarterly*, 4 (1987), 179–95.

Cornman, James, *Perception, Common Sense and Science* (New Haven: Yale University Press, 1975).

Costa, Michael J., "What Cartesian Ideas are Not", *Journal of the History of Philosophy*, 21 (1983), 537–50.

— "Arnauld, Ideas, and Perception", unpublished manuscript.

Cousin, Victor, "De la persécution du Cartésianisme en France", *Fragments Philosophiques*, in *Oeuvres*, 3 vols. (Brussels: Société Belge de Librairie, 1841), vol. 2, pp. 181–91.

Cronin, Timothy, J., *Objective Being in Descartes and Suarez*, Analecta Gregoriana, vol. 154 (Rome: Gregorian University Press, 1966).

Curley, Edwin, "Recent Work on 17th Century Philosophy", *American Philosophical Quarterly*, 11 (1974), 235–55.

Dalbiez, Roland, "Les sources scolastiques de la théorie Cartésienne de l'être objectif", *Revue d'histoire de la philosophie*, 3 (1929), 464–72.

Dijksterhuis, E. J., ed., *Descartes et le Cartésianisme Holllandais* (Paris: PUF, 1950).

Dominicy, Marc, *La naissance de la grammaire moderne* (Brussels: Pierre Mardaga, 1985).

Doney, Willis, ed., *Descartes: A Collection of Critical Essays* (Notre Dame: University of Notre Dame Press, 1967).

Dreyfus, Hubert, L., ed., *Husserl, Intentionality, and Cognitive Science* (Cambridge: MIT Press, 1982).

Føllesdal, Dagfinn, "Brentano and Husserl on Intentional Objects and Perception", in Dreyfus, ed., *Husserl*, pp. 31–42.

— "Husserl's Notion of *Noema*", in Dreyfus, ed., *Husserl*, pp. 73–80.

Fontaine, Nicholas, *Mémoires pour servir à l'histoire de Port-Royal*, 2 vols. (Cologne, 1738).

Fumerton, Richard, *Metaphysical and Epistemological Problems of Perception* (Lincoln: University of Nebraska Press, 1985).

Goanach, J. M., *La théorie des idées dans la philosophie de Malebranche* (Brest, 1908).

Garcia-Gomez, Sara F., *The Problem of Objective Knowledge in Descartes, Malebranche, and Arnauld* (Ph.D.diss., New School for Social Research, 1979).

Gilson, Etienne, *Etudes sur le rôle de la pensée médiévale dans la formation du système Cartésien* (Paris: J. Vrin, 1930).

Goldmann, Lucien, *The Hidden God* (London: Routledge and Kegan Paul, 1964).

Gouhier, Henri, *Cartésianisme et Augustinisme au XVIIe siècle* (Paris: J. Vrin, 1978).

— *La Pensée Religieuse de Descartes*, 2nd ed. (Paris: J. Vrin, 1970).

Grene, Marjorie, *Descartes* (Minneapolis: University of Minnesota Press, 1985).

Gueroult, Martial, *Descartes' Philosophy Interpreted According to the Order of Reasons*, Roger Ariew, trans., 2 vols. (Minneapolis: University of Minnesota Press, 1984).

— *Malebranche*, 3 vols. (Paris: Aubier, 1955).

Gurwitsch, Aron, "Husserl's Theory of the Intentionality of Consciousness", in Dreyfus, ed., *Husserl*, pp. 59–71.

Hicks, G. Dawes, "Sense Perception and Thought", *Proceedings of the Aristotelian Society*, 6 (1905–6), 271–346.

Hirst, R. J., *The Problems of Perception* (London: George Allen and Unwin, 1959).

Hooker, Michael, ed., *Descartes: Critical and Interpretive Essays* (Baltimore: Johns Hopkins University Press, 1978).

Imlay, Robert A., "Arnauld on Descartes' Essence: A Misunderstanding", *Studia Leibnitiana*, 11 (1979), 134–45.

Jackson, Frank, *Perception: A Representative Theory* (Cambridge: Cambridge University Press, 1977).

Judge, Brenda, "Thoughts – and their Contents", *American Philosophical Quarterly*, 20 (1983), 365–74.

Kenny, Anthony, "Descartes on Ideas", in Doney, ed., *Descartes*, pp. 277–49.

Kremer, Elmer J., *Malebranche and Arnauld: The Controversy Over the Nature of Ideas* (Ph.D. diss., Yale University, 1961).

Laird, John, *A Study in Realism* (Cambridge: Cambridge University Press, 1920).

— "The Legend of Arnauld's Realism", *Mind*, 33 (1924), 176–79.

Laporte, Jean, *Le Rationalisme de Descartes* (Paris: PUF, 1945).

Lennon, Thomas M., "The Inherence Pattern and Descartes' Ideas", *Journal of the History of Philosophy*, 12 (1974), 43–52.

— "Jansenism and the Crise Pyrrhonienne", *Journal of the History of Ideas*, 38 (1977), 297–306.

— "Philosophical Commentary", in Malebranche, *The Search after Truth*, pp. 755–848.

— "Representationalism, Judgement, and Perception of Distance: Further to Yolton and McRae", *Dialogue*, 19 (1980), 151–62.

— with J. M. Nicholas and J. W. Davis, eds., *Problems of Cartesianism* (Kingston and Montreal: McGill-Queen's University Press, 1982).

Loeb, Louis, E., *From Descartes to Hume* (Ithaca: Cornell University Press, 1981).

Lovejoy, A. O., "Representative Ideas in Malebranche and Arnauld", *Mind*, 32

(1923), 449–61.

— "Reply to Professor Laird", *Mind*, 33 (1924), 180–81.

— *The Revolt Against Dualism* (LaSalle: Open Court, 1930).

Machamer, Peter K. and Robert G. Turnbull, eds., *Studies in Perception* (Columbus: Ohio State University Press, 1978).

McRae, Robert, "'Idea' as a Philosophical Term in the 17th Century", *Journal of the History of Ideas*, 26 (1965), 175–84.

— "Descartes' Definition of Thought", in Butler, ed., *Cartesian Studies*, pp. 55–70.

Marion, Jean-Luc, *Sur la théologie blanche de Descartes* (Paris: PUF, 1981).

Mattern, Ruth, "Descartes' Correspondence with Elizabeth: Concerning Both the Union and Distinction of Mind and Body", in Hooker, ed., *Descartes*, pp. 212–22.

Matthews, H. E., "Locke, Malebranche, and the Representative Theory", in Tipton, ed., *Locke*, pp. 55–61.

Miel, Jan, "Pascal, Port-Royal and Cartesian Linguistics", *Journal of the History of Ideas*, 30 (1969), 261–71.

Moreau, Joseph, "Le réalisme de Malebranche et la fonction de l'idée", *Revue de Métaphysique et de Morale*, 56 (1946), 97–141.

Nadler, Steven, "Arnauld, Descartes, and Transubstantiation: Reconciling Cartesian Metaphysics and Real Presence", *Journal of the History of Ideas*, 59 (1988), 229–46.

— "Ideas and Perception in Malebranche", *Studies in Early Modern Philosophy* (forthcoming).

— "Reid, Arnauld and the Objects of Perception", *History of Philosophy Quarterly*, 3 (1986), 165–74.

— "Cartesianism and Port-Royal", The *Monist*, 71 (1988).

— "Scientific Certainty and the Creation of the Eternal Truths: A Problem in Descartes", *The Southern Journal of Philosophy*, 25 (1987), 175–92.

— review of Yoltan, *Perceptual Acquaintance*, in *Synthese* (forthcoming).

Normore, Calvin, "Meaning and Objective Being: Descartes and his Sources", in A. O. Rorty, ed., *Essays*, pp. 223–42.

O'Neil, Brian E., *Epistemological Direct Realism in Descartes' Philosophy* (Albuquerque: University of New Mexico Press, 1974).

Perkins, Moreland, *Sensing the World* (Indianapolis: Hackett, 1983).

Pitcher, George, *A Theory of Perception* (Princeton: Princeton University Press, 1971).

Popkin, Richard H., *The History of Skepticism from Erasmus to Spinoza* (Berkeley: University of California Press, 1979).

Price, H. H., *Perception* (London: Methuen, 1932).

Radner, Daisie, "Is there a problem of Cartesian Interaction?", *Journal of the History of Philosophy*, 23 (1985), 35–49.

— *Malebranche: A Study of a Cartesian System* (Amsterdam: Van Gorcum, 1978).

— "Representationalism in Arnauld's Act Theory of Perception", *Journal of the*

History of Philosophy, 14 (1976), 96–8.

Richardson, R. C., "The 'Scandal' of Cartesian Interactionism", *Mind*, 91 (1982), 20–37.

Robinet, André, *Malebranche et Leibniz: Relations personelles* (Paris: J. Vrin, 1955).

— *Système et existence dans l'oeuvre de Malebranche* (Paris: J. Vrin, 1965).

Rodis-Lewis, Geneviève, "Augustinisme et Cartésianisme à Port-Royal", in Dijksterhuis, ed., *Descartes et le Cartésienisme Hollandais*, pp. 131–82.

— "Augustinisme et Cartésianisme", *Augustinus Magister*, 2 (1954), 1087–1104.

— "L'Arrière-plan Platonicien de débat sur les idées: de Descartes à Leibniz", in *Permanence de la Philosophie: Mélanges offerts à J. Moreau* (Neuchâtel: La Baconnière, 1977), pp. 221–41.

— *Nicholas Malebranche* (Paris: PUF, 1963).

Rorty, Amélie O., ed., *Essays on Descartes' Meditations* (Berkeley: University of California Press, 1986).

Rorty, Richard, *Philosophy and the Mirror of Nature* (Princeton: Princeton University Press, 1979).

Sainte-Beuve, Charles Augustin, *Port-Royal*, 7 vols. (Paris: La Connaissance, 1928).

Sartre, Jean-Paul, *The Transcendence of the Ego* (New York: Noonday Press, 1957).

Schulthess, Daniel, "Antoine Arnauld et Thomas Reid, défenseurs des certitudes perceptives communes et critiques des entités représentatives", *Revue Internationale de Philosophie*, 40 (1986), 276–91.

Sedgwick, Alexander, *Jansenism in Seventeenth-Century France* (Charlottesville: University Press of Virginia, 1977).

Sidgwick, Henry, "The Philosophy of Common Sense", *Mind*, 4 (1985), 145–58.

Smith, David Woodruff and Ronald McIntyre, *Husserl and Intentionality* (Dordrecht: D. Reidel, 1982).

Smith, Norman Kemp, *Studies in the Cartesian Philsophy* (New York: Russell and Russel, 1902).

Stewart, M. A., "Locke's Mental Atomism and the Classification of Ideas", *The Locke Newsletter*, 10 (1979), 53–82; and 11 (1980), 25–75.

Strong, C. A., "Is Perception Direct or Representative?", *Mind*, 40 (1931), 217–36.

Tipton, I. C., ed., *Locke on Human Understanding* (Oxford: Oxford University Press, 1977).

Turner, J. E., *A Theory of Direct Realism* (New York: Macmillan, 1925).

Watson, Richard A., *The Downfall of Cartesianism* (The Hague: Martinus Nijhoff, 1966).

— "Transubstantiation among the Cartesians", in Lennon *et al.*, *Problems of Cartesianism*, pp. 127–48.

— review of Yolton, *Perceptual Acquaintance*, in *Journal of the History of Philosophy*, 23 (1985), 433–37.

Wells, Norman, J., "Material Falsity in Descartes, Arnauld, and Suarez", *Journal of the History of Philosophy,* 22 (1984), 25–50.

— "Objective Being: Descartes and his Sources", *The Modern Schoolman,* 45 (1967), 49–61.

Williams, Bernard, *Descartes: The Project of Pure Enquiry* (London: Penguin, 1978).

Wilson, Margaret D., *Descartes* (London: Routledge and Kegan Paul, 1978).

Yolton, John, "Ideas and Knowledge in Seventeenth-Century Philosophy", *Journal of the History of Philosophy,* 13 (1975), 145–66.

— "John Locke and the Seventeenth-Century Logic of Ideas", *Journal of the History of Ideas,* 16 (1955), 431–52.

— *Perceptual Acquaintance from Descartes to Reid,* (Minneapolis: University of Minnesota Press, 1984).

Zimmerman, C., "Arnauld's Kritik der Ideenlehre Malebranches", *Philosophisches Jahrbuch,* 24 (1911), 3–47.

Index

analysis, 39–40
Aquinas, Thomas, 3 n. 1, 19 n. 9, 31
    n. 25, 77 n. 16, 115 n. 26
Aristotle, 3 n. 1, 20, 147
Arnauld, Antoine (père), 16
Arnauld, Jacqueline (Mère
    Angélique), 16
Augustine, 14–15, 26, 29, 32, 40, 45,
    119, 137, 148, 181, 182–3
authority, 26–7, 29

Bayle, Pierre, 1, 2, 169, 176–8
Berkeley, George, 8, 12
body, see matter
Bossuet, Jacques, 14 n. 1
Brahe, Tycho, 28
Brentano, Franz, 144

Caterus, Johannes, 22–3, 157–8
causation, 51–2, 56–9, 71, 157, 158
Church, Ralph W., 104, 105–6, 107,
    111–12, 116
content, 37–8, 82–3, 107, 111–12,
    142, 146–7, 159–65, 168–75,
    177–8; see also idea, objective
    reality of
Cook, Monte, 82–8, 117–18
Copernicus, Nicolas, 28
Cordemoy, Géraud de, 15
Costa, Michael J., 122–3

Daniel, Pierre, 18 n. 6
De la Forge, Louis, 15
De Sacy, Le Maistre, 18,19, 21

Descartes, René,
    and Port-Royal, 20–1
    and the "way of ideas", 7–10
    as representationalist, 8, 85, 126
    immediate vs. mediate perception,
        118–19, 139
    on ideas, 126–30, 141, 159–65
    on objective being, 156–65
    on sensation, 123–5
    and passim
Desgabets, Dom Robert, 7, 24
direct realism, 6, 11–13, 90, 101–2,
    104–7, 107–26, 130, 131–6, 138,
    139, 140, 174–5, 183
dualism, see mind
Duns Scotus, John, 148 n. 12, 149–
    50, 154
Du Vaucel, Louis-Paul, 15 n. 3, 19,
    31–2

eminent being, 51–2
essences, 151–6
eternal truths, 155–6
existence
    of external world, 133–6
    of God, see God
extension, 53–4; see also matter

faith, 20, 26–7, 29–34, 135
Fontaine, Nicolas, 18, 19
formal being (formal reality), 51,
    149, 151, 157, 158, 171
Foucher, Simon, 52, 173 n. 39

Galilei, Galileo, 28
Gassendi, Pierre, 1, 29, 34
Ginsberg, Morris, 104, 106-7, 111-12, 168, 170
God
　and essences, 151-6
　as cause, 22-3, 57-9, 180-2
　as substance, 41
　ideas in, 5, 64, 72; *see also* Malebranche
　idea of, 183
　proofs for existence, 22, 23, 24, 162
　volitions of, 180-2
Goldmann, Lucien, 136-7
grace, 16, 137, 180-3

hallucination, 68, 72, 130-1
Hobbes, Thomas, 1
Hume, David, 8
Husserl, Edmund, 143-4
Huyghens, Christian, 28

idea
　and knowledge, 64-5, 134
　as act, 5-6, 84-8, 96, 102-3, 108-22, 126-30, 140-1, 169-70
　as disposition, 5, 141
　as image, 108, 127, 159, 162-5, 173
　as mode of mind, 82-8, 102-3, 109-10, 129, 141-2, 159, 166
　as object, 4-5, 60, 68-78, 80-1, 84-8, 103, 104-7, 108, 112
　clear and distinct, 36-8, 162-5
　objective reality of, 129, 149, 159-65, 172
　representative function of, 37-8, 62-5, 82-3, 102, 108, 129, 142, 159-60, 167-75
　see also material falsity; mental acts; perception
images, 91-4; *see also* idea
indirect realism, *see* representationalism
inference, 11-12, 76
intentionality, 68, 131, 143-7, 161, 165-78
　content theory, 146-7, 161-2, 167-78
　object theory, 145-7, 166

Jansenism, 16-21, 136-8, 179, 180, 183-4
Jansenius, Cornelius, 16-17, 137
Jesuits, 16, 20
Jurieu, Pierre, 18 n. 6

knowledge, 2-6, 28, 64-5, 132-6

Lancelot, Claude, 18
laws (of grace, of nature), 180-2
Le Grand, Antoine, 57
Leibniz, Gottfried Wilhelm, 1, 2, 5-6, 141
Le Maistre, Antoine, 18
Locke, John, 2, 4, 6, 8-9, 10, 65, 74, 77, 85
Lovejoy, Arthur O., 104-5, 107, 111, 113-14, 116

Malebranche, Nicholas
　and Cartesianism, 10, 15, 59
　natural judgement, 62-3
　on grace and providence, 180-1
　on ideas, 60-78, 80-1, *and passim*
　on intelligible extension, 66-8
　on intentionality, 68, 144-5, 165-6
　on perception, 60, 66-78, *and passim*
　on sensation, 60-4
　representationalism, 72-3, 75-8, *and passim*
　vision in God, 136-8, 139 *and passim*
material falsity, 37, 149, 162-5
matter, 31-2, 47-50
mechanism, 36, 48, 50

mental acts, 83–8, 106–7, 110–13, 115, 127, 129, 140–1, 145–6, 157, 166–71; *see also* idea
Mersenne, Marin, 1, 21–2, 25 n. 17
mind, 2–5, 9–11, 22, 24, 25, 45–7, 86–8, 108, 109–10, 144, 166, 178; *see also* soul
and body
  dualism, 22, 30, 36, 44–59, 70–1, 93, 173
  interaction, 51–2, 56–9
  union of, 51, 53–6
naive realism, 12 n. 25, 126
Newton, Isaac, 1
Nicole, Pierre, 18, 21, 27 n. 19
nominalism, 139–40

objective being, 95, 147–65, 171–2
occasionalism, 57–9, 123
Ockham, William, 150–1

Pascal, Blaise, 18–19, 21, 136, 137 n. 50, 138 n. 54
perception
  causal theory, 60, 73, 76
  clear and distinct, 23, 36–8, 65–6, 162–5
  direct vs. indirect, 11–13, 75–8, 99, 105–6
  immediate vs. mediate, 11–13, 75–8, 105–6, 113–22
  see also direct realism; idea; representationalism
philosophy, 18–21, 39
  and logic, 28–9
  and theology, 27–34
Plato, 149
pleasure, 175–8
Port-Royal, 16–21, 179
possible being, 152–6
presence to the mind, 70–2, 90–5, 171–2; *see also* objective being
Pyrrhonism, *see* skepticism

qualities, primary and secondary, 47–8, 65

Racine, Jean, 136
reason, 18–21, 28–34
  vs. faith, 20, 24, 26–8, 33–4
reflection
  express, 119–20
  virtual, 118–22
Régis, Pierre-Sylvain, 1, 9, 10, 15
Reid, Thomas, 7–10, 104 n. 4, 116 n. 27, 117, 131–2
relations
  intentional, *see* intentionality
  ordinary, 145, 146
representation, 167–75; *see also* content; idea
representationalism, 6, 8, 11–13, 68, 73, 75–8, 81, 88, 97, 99–100, 102–7, 112, 115, 116, 121–2, 126, 130, 131–6, 138, 139, 140, 175
revelation, 135
Rohault, Jacques, 1, 7, 15, 57
Rorty, Richard, 8–10

St Cyran (Jean Duvergier de Hauranne), 16, 18, 138 n. 54
Sartre, Jean-Paul, 122–3 n. 34
science, 26, 28
self-consciousness, 45, 118–22; *see also* reflection
sensation, 50–1, 56, 60–4, 65, 82–3, 123–4, 178
  and perception, 66, 123–6
sense data theory, 60, 68, 73, 76, 85, 125
skepticism, 7–8, 10, 19, 28, 36–7, 65–6, 74, 90, 131–6, 138
soul, immortality of, 30; *see also* mind
Spinoza, Benedictus de, 1, 5, 15
Suarez, Francisco, 143, 148–9, 151–6, 158 n. 27, 160–1
substance, 40–1, 43

and modifications, 40–4
substantial forms, 7, 32, 36
synthesis, 39–40

thought, *see* mind
transubstantiation, 7, 19, 23–5, 29,
    31–4

universals, 141–2, 150, 161; *see also*
    essences

vacuum, 49–50
Vasquez, Gabriel, 148–9

Wells, Norman, 164–5
Wilson, Margaret, 162–4

Yolton, John, 10